THE IDEA OF THE MODERN
in Literature and the Arts

OTHER BOOKS BY IRVING HOWE

A World More Attractive
Sherwood Anderson: A Critical Biography
William Faulkner: A Critical Study
Politics and the Novel
Thomas Hardy

THE IDEA OF
THE MODERN
in Literature and the Arts

Edited with an Introduction and Commentary by
IRVING HOWE

HORIZON PRESS   NEW YORK

The editor and publisher wish to thank all those who
have contributed to this volume. Acknowledgments for
individual selections will be found on the first page of
each selection.

Library of Congress Catalog Card No. 68-54188
ISBN 0-8180-1183-1
Printed in the United States of America

CONTENTS

Part Two

TWO MANIFESTOES

Part Three

A FEW MODERNIST MOVEMENTS

Part Four

SOME MAJOR FIGURES

THE IDEA OF THE MODERN
in Literature and the Arts

INTRODUCTION

The Idea of the Modern

IRVING HOWE

One of the most difficult but interesting problems in the study of literature concerns the use of historical categories such as "The Age of Milton" or "The Romantic Period." We fall much too easily into the habit of reifying our concepts, that is, of assuming that "The Age of Milton" and "The Romantic Period" are not merely conveniences of discourse but actual historical objects existing autonomously, out there. By way of reaction and hygiene a brilliant iconoclast appears to show us, as Professor A. O. Lovejoy has, that these historical categories are helplessly imprecise and that the unified style or sensibility to which they presumably refer are shot through with contradictions. In his famous essay, "On the Discrimination of Romanticisms," Lovejoy writes, "The word 'romantic' has come to mean so many things that, by itself, it means nothing. It has ceased to perform the function of a verbal sign." Professor Lovejoy then proceeds to exhibit the bewildering variety of ideas and sentiments that have become attached to the term "Romantic," thereby persuading us, at the very least, to caution and modesty in our use of such terms.

Yet it is not quite established that his demolition is a decisive one, or that his prescription—we should, he says, cease talking about Romanticism and instead block out a series of sharply differentiated Romanticisms—succeeds in overcoming the difficulties that prompted his inquiry. For there remains the crucial question: Why, historically, did this term accumulate such a rich horde of associations? Has this been merely the result of linguistic imprecision? And is there perhaps some underlying unity of attitudes by

11

means of which the great variety of Romanticisms can be linked with one another? For if there is not, then Lovejoy's approach seems open to the charge that he merely fractures the difficulty he began with, and that the literary trends he designates as Romanticisms might each better be given separate labels.

Historical complexities and confusions are seldom to be overcome by linguistic policing. A multitude of Romanticisms—or Romanticisms renamed—might prove analytically more troublesome than one. And there is the further danger that at the end of the road lies a radical nominalism, by means of which historical and thematic categories are dissolved and literary history, if any remains, consists of a mere shuffle from one isolated writer to another.

So, in compiling this anthology about literary modernism and here offering some views of my own, I choose to risk the very dangers against which Professor Lovejoy warns. I will be discussing a literary movement or period that I call "Modernism," while knowing full well that the term is elusive and protean, and its definition hopelessly complicated. That descriptive elements I attribute to this movement clash with one another, I acknowledge in advance. That it is hard to say whether a given writer, or a strand in the work of a writer, comes under the rubric of modernism, I also grant. Yet there is value in these difficulties: they point to the fascinating complexities of our subject.

Nor will I try to provide a neatly shaped synthesis of what modernism may be, for I neither have such an idea in mind nor believe it would be useful if I did. What follows are pieces and patches, a series of notes, with the ideas of many other writers—especially those included in this anthology—cheerfully drawn upon. Since modernism is a matter close to us in time, perhaps still alive in our own time, the important thing is not to be "definitive," which by the very nature of things is unlikely, but to keep ideas in motion, the subject alive.

I

In the past hundred years we have had a special kind of literature. We call it modern and distinguish it from the merely contemporary; for where the contemporary refers to time, the modern refers to sensibility and style, and where the contemporary is a term of neutral reference, the modern is a term of critical placement and judgment. Modernist literature seems now to be coming to an end, though we can by no means be certain and there are critics who would argue that, given the nature of our society, the modern period cannot come to an end.

The kind of literature called modern is almost always difficult to comprehend: that is a sign of its modernity. To the established guardians of culture, the modern writer seems wilfully inaccessible. He works with unfamiliar forms; he chooses subjects that disturb the audience and threaten its most cherished sentiments; he provokes traditionalist critics to such epithets as "unwholesome," "coterie," and "decadent."

The modern must be defined in terms of what it is not: the embodiment of a tacit polemic, an inclusive negative. Modern writers find that they begin to work at a moment when the culture is marked by a prevalent style of perception and feeling; and their modernity consists in a revolt against this prevalent style, an unyielding rage against the official order. But modernism does not establish a prevalent style of its own; or if it does, it denies itself, thereby ceasing to be modern. This presents it with a dilemma which in principle may be beyond solution but in practice leads to formal inventiveness and resourceful dialectic— *the dilemma that modernism must always struggle but never quite triumph, and then, after a time, must struggle in order not to triumph.*

Modernism need never come to an end, or at least we do not really know, as yet, how it can or will reach its end. The history of previous literary periods is relevant but probably not decisive here, since modernism, despite the precursors one can find in the past, is, I think, a novelty in the development of Western culture. What we do know, however, is that modernism can fall upon days of exhaustion, when it appears to be marking time and waiting for new avenues of release.

At certain points in the development of a culture, usually points of dismay and restlessness, writers find themselves affronting their audience, and not from decision or whim but from some deep moral and psychological necessity. Such writers may not even be aware that they are challenging crucial assumptions of their day, yet their impact is revolutionary; and once this is recognized by sympathetic critics and a coterie audience, the *avant garde* has begun to emerge as a self-conscious and combative group. Paul Goodman writes:

> ... there are these works that are indignantly rejected, and called not genuine art, but insult, outrage, *blague, fumiste,* wilfully incomprehensible. . . . And what is puzzling is not that they are isolated pieces, but some artists persistently produce such pieces and there are schools of such "not genuine" artists. What are they doing? In this case, the feeling of the audience is sound—it is always sound—there *is* insult, wilful incomprehensibility, experiment; and yet the judgment of the audience is wrong—it is often wrong—for this is a genuine art.

Why does this clash arise? Because the modern writer can no longer accept the claims of the world. If he tries to acquiesce in the norms of the audience, he finds himself depressed and outraged. The usual morality seems counterfeit; taste, a genteel indulgence; tradition, a wearisome fetter. It becomes a condition of being a writer that he rebel, not merely and sometimes not at all against received opinions, but against the received ways of doing the writer's work.

A modernist culture soon learns to respect, even to cherish, signs of its division. It sees doubt as a form of health. It hunts for ethical norms through underground journeys, experiments with sensation, and a mocking suspension of accredited values. Upon the passport of the Wisdom of The Ages, it stamps in bold red letters: *Not Transferable.* It cultivates, in Thomas Mann's phrase, "a sympathy for the abyss." It strips man of his systems of belief and his ideal claims, and then proposes the one uniquely modern style of salvation: a salvation by, of, and for the self. In modernist culture, the object perceived seems always on the verge of being swallowed up by the perceiving agent, and the act of perception in danger of being exalted to the substance of reality. *I see, therefore I am.*

Subjectivity becomes the typical condition of the modernist outlook. In its early stages, when it does not trouble to disguise its filial dependence on the romantic poets, modernism declares itself as an inflation of the self, a transcendental and orgiastic aggrandizement of matter and event in behalf of personal vitality. In the middle stages, the self begins to recoil from externality and devotes itself, almost as if it were the world's body, to a minute examination of its own inner dynamics: freedom, compulsion, caprice. In the late stages, there occurs an emptying-out of the self, a revulsion from the wearisomeness of individuality and psychological gain. (Three writers as exemplars of these stages: Whitman, Virginia Woolf, Beckett.) Modernism thereby keeps approaching—sometimes even penetrating —the limits of solipsism, the view expressed by the German poet Gottfried Benn when he writes that "there is no outer reality, there is only human consciousness, constantly building, modifying, rebuilding new worlds out of its own creativity."

Behind this extreme subjectivity lurks an equally extreme sense of historical impasse, the assumption that something about the experience of our ages is unique, a catastrophe without precedent. The German novelist Herman Hesse speaks about "a whole generation caught . . . between two ages, two modes of life, with the consequence that it loses all power to understand itself and has no standards, no security, no simple acquiescence." Above all, no simple acquiescence.

Whether all of this is true matters not nearly so much as the fact that modernist writers, artists, and composers —Joyce, Kafka, Picasso, Schoenberg—have apparently worked on the tacit assumption that it is true. The modernist sensibility posits a blockage, if not an end, to history: an apocalyptic *cul de sac* in which both teleological ends and secular progress are called into question, perhaps become obsolete. Man is mired—you can take your choice —in the mass, in the machine, in the city, in his loss of faith, in the hopelessness of a life without anterior intention or terminal value. By this late date, these disasters seem in our imaginations to have merged into one.

"On or about December 1910 human nature changed." Through this vivid hyperbole, Virginia Woolf meant to suggest that there is a frightening discontinuity between the traditional past and the shaken present; that the line of history has been bent, perhaps broken. Modernist literature goes on the tacit assumption that human nature has indeed changed, probably a few decades before the date given by Mrs. Woolf; or, as Stephen Spender remarks, that the circumstances under which we live, forever being transformed by nature, have been so radically altered that people feel human nature to have changed and thereby behave as though it has. Commenting on this notion,

Spender makes a keen distinction between the "Voltairean I" of earlier writers and the "I" of the moderns:

> The "Voltairean I" of Shaw, Wells and others acts upon events. The "modern I" of Rimbaud, Joyce, Proust, Eliot's *Prufrock* is acted upon by events. . . . The faith of the Voltairean egoists is that they will direct the powers of the surrounding world from evil into better courses through the exercise of the superior social or cultural intelligence of the creative genius, the writer-prophet. The faith of the moderns is that by allowing their sensibility to be acted upon by the modern experience as suffering, they will produce, partly as the result of unconscious processes, and partly through the exercise of critical consciousness, the idioms and forms of new art.

The consequences are extreme: a break-up of the traditional unity and continuity of Western culture, so that the decorums of its past no longer count for very much in determining its present, and a loosening of those ties that, in one or another way, had bound it to the institutions of society over the centuries. Not their enemies but art and literature themselves assault the *gemütlichkeit* of autonomy, the classical balances and resolutions of the past. Culture now goes to war against itself, partly in order to salvage its purpose, and the result is that it can no longer present itself with a Goethian serenity and wholeness. At one extreme, there is a violent disparagement of culture (the late Rimbaud), and at the other, a quasi-religion of culture (the late Joyce).

In much modernist literature, one finds a bitter impatience with the whole apparatus of cognition and the limiting assumption of rationality. The mind comes to be seen as an enemy of vital human powers. Culture becomes disenchanted with itself, sick over its endless refinements. There is a hunger to break past the bourgeois proprieties and self-containment of culture, toward a form of absolute personal speech, a literature deprived of ceremony and stripped to revelation. In the work of Thomas Mann, both what is rejected and what is desired are put forward with a high, ironic consciousness: the abandoned ceremony and the corrosive revelation.

But if a major impulse in modernist literature is a choking nausea before the idea of culture, there is another in which the writer takes upon himself the enormous ambition not to remake the world (by now seen as hopelessly recalcitrant and alien) but to reinvent the terms of reality. I have already quoted Benn's remark that "there is only human consciousness . . . rebuilding new worlds out of its own creativity." In a similar vein, the painter Klee once said that his wish was "not to reflect the visible, but to *make* visible." And Baudelaire wrote, "The whole visible universe is but an array of images and signs to which the imagination gives a place and relative value. . . ." At first glance, this sentence reads like something an English romantic poet or even a good American transcendentalist might have said; but in the context of Baudelaire's experience as a poet—that experience which led him to say that "every man who refuses to accept the conditions of life sells his soul"—it comes to seem the report of a desire to create, or perhaps re-create, the very grounds of being, through a permanent revolution of sensibility and style, by means of which art could raise itself to the level of white or (more likely) black magic. Rationalistic psychoanalysts might regard this ambition as a substitute gratification of the most desperate kind, a grandiose mask for inner weakness; but for the great figures of literary modernism it is the very essence of their task.

We approach here another dilemma of modernism, which may also in principle be beyond solution but in practice lead to great inventiveness—that, as the Marxist critic Georg Lukacs has charged, *modernism despairs of human history, abandons the idea of a linear historical development, falls back upon notions of a universal* condition humaine *or a rhythm of eternal recurrence, yet within its own realm is committed to ceaseless change, turmoil and recreation.* The more history comes to be seen as static (in the Marxist idiom: a locomotive stalled in an inescapable present), the more art must take on a relentless dynamism.

It is quite as if Hegel's "cunning of reason," so long a motor-force of progress in history, were now expelled from its exalted place and locked into the exile of culture. E. H. Gombrich speaks of philosophies of historical progress as containing "a strong Aristotelian ingredient insofar as they look upon progress as an evolution of inherent potentialities which will follow a predictable course and must reach a predictable summit." Modernist versions of literature do assign to themselves "an evolution of inherent potentialities": there is always the hope for still another breakthrough, always the necessary and prepared-for dialectical leap into still another innovation, always an immanent if by no means gradual progress in the life of a form. But these do not follow "a predictable course," nor can they reach "a predictable summit"—since the very idea of "predictable," or the very goal of "summit," violates the modernist faith in surprise, its belief in sensibility and style. And if history is indeed stalled in the sluggishness of the mass and the imperiousness of the machine, then culture must all the more serve as the agent of a life-enhancing turmoil.

The figure chosen to embody and advance this turmoil, remarks Gombrich, is the Genius, an early individualistic precursor of the *avant-garde* creative hero. If there is then "a conflict between a genius and his public," declares Hegel in a sentence which thousands of critics, writers and publicists will echo through the years, "it must be the public that is to blame . . . the only obligation the artist can have is to follow truth and his genius." Close to romantic theory at this point, modernism soon ceases to believe in the availability of "truth" or the disclosures of "genius." The dynamism to which it then commits itself —and here it breaks sharply from the romantics—becomes not merely an absolute without end but sometimes an absolute without discernible ends.

It is a dynamism of asking and learning not to reply. The past was devoted to answers; the modern period confines itself to questions. And after a certain point, the essence of modernism reveals itself in the persuasion that the true question, the one alone worth asking, cannot and need not be answered; it need only be asked over and over again, forever in new ways. It is as if the very idea of a question were redefined: no longer an interrogation but now a mode of axiomatic value. We represent ourselves, we establish our authenticity, by the questions we allow to torment us. "All of Dostoevsky's heroes question themselves as to the meaning of life," writes Albert Camus. "In this they are modern: they do not fear ridicule. What distinguishes modern sensibility from classical sensibility is that the latter thrives on moral problems and the former on metaphysical problems." A modernist culture is committed to the view that the human lot is inescapably problematic. Problems, to be sure, have been noticed at all times, but in a modernist culture the problematic as a style of existence and inquiry becomes imperious: men learn to find comfort in their wounds. Nietzsche says: "Truth has never yet hung on the arm of an absolute." The problematic is adhered to, not merely because we live in a time of uncertainty when traditional beliefs and absolute standards, having long disintegrated, give way to the makeshifts of relativism—that is by now an old, old story. The problematic is adhered to because it comes to be considered good, proper, and even beautiful that men should live in discomfort. Again Nietzsche:

> Objection, evasion, joyous distrust, and love of irony are signs of health; everything absolute belongs to pathology.

One consequence of this devotion to the problematic, not always a happy consequence, is that in modernist literature there is a turn from truth to sincerity, from the search for objective law to a desire for authentic response. The first involves an effort to apprehend the nature of the universe, and can lead to metaphysics, suicide, revolution, and God; the second involves an effort to discover our demons within, and makes no claim upon the world other than the right to publicize the aggressions of candor. Sincerity becomes the last-ditch defense for men without belief, and in its name absolutes can be toppled, morality dispersed, and intellectual systems dissolved. But a special kind of sincerity: where for the romantics it was often taken to be a rapid motion into truth, breaking past the cumbersomeness of intellect, now for the modernists it becomes a virtue in itself, regardless of whether it can lead to truth or whether truth can be found. Sincerity of feeling and exact faithfulness of language—which often means a language of fragments, violence, and exasperation —becomes a ruling passion. In the terrible freedom it allows the modernist writer, sincerity shatters the hypocrisies of bourgeois order; in the lawlessness of its abandonment, it can become a force of darkness and brutality.

Disdainful of certainties, disengaged from the eternal or any of its surrogates, fixated upon the minute particulars of subjective experience, the modernist writer regards settled assumptions as a mask of death and literature as an agent of metaphysical revolt. Restlessness becomes the sign of sentience, anxiety the premise of responsibility, peace the flag of surrender—and the typewriter the Promethean rock. Nowhere is this mode of sensibility expressed with greater energy than in an essay by the Russian novelist of the 1920's, Eugene Zamyatin. "On Literature, Revolution and Entropy", is a decisive manifesto of the modernist outlook: *[handwritten annotation]*

Revolution is everywhere and in all things: it is infinite, there is no final revolution, no end to the sequence of integers. Social revolution is only one in the infinite sequence of integers. The law of revolution is not a social law, it is immeasurably greater, it is a cosmic, universal law.

Red, fiery, death-dealing is the law of revolution; but that death is the birth of a new life, of a new star. And cold, blue as ice, as the icy interplanetary infinities is the law of entropy. The flame turns from fiery red to an even, warm pink, no longer death-dealing but comfort-producing; the sun ages and becomes a planet suitable for highways, shops, beds, prostitutes, prisons: that is a law. And in order to make the planet young again, we must set it afire, we must thrust it off the smooth highway of evolution: that is a law.

Explosions are not comfortable things. That is why the exploders, the heretics, are quite rightly annihilated by fire, by axes, and by words. Heretics are harmful to everybody today, to every evolution, to the difficult, slow, useful, so very useful, constructive process of coral reef building; imprudently and foolishly they leap into today from tomorrow. They are romantics. It was right and proper that in 1797 Babeuf had his head cut off; he had leaped into 1797, skipping one hundred and fifty years. It is equally right and proper that heretical literature that is damaging to dogma, should also have its head cut off: such literature is harmful.

But harmful literature is more useful than useful literature: because it is anti-entropic, militates against calcification, sclerosis, encrustedness, moss, peace. It is utopian and ridiculous. Like Babeuf, in 1797, it is right one hundred and fifty years later. . . .

The old, slow, soporific descriptions are no more. The order of the day is laconicism—but every word must be supercharged, high-voltage. Into one second must be compressed what formerly went into a sixty-second mixture. Syntax becomes elliptical, volatile; complicated pyramids of periods are dismantled and broken down into the single stones of independent clauses. In swift movement the canonical, the habitual eludes the eye: hence the unusual, often strange symbolism and choice of words. The image is sharp, synthetic, it contains only the one basic trait which one has time to seize upon from a moving automobile . . . A new form is not intelligible to all; for many it is difficult.

Maybe. The habitual, the banal is of course simpler, pleasanter, more comfortable. Euclid's world is very simple and Einstein's world is very difficult; nevertheless it is now impossible to return to Euclid's. No revolution, no heresy is comfortable and easy. Because it is a leap, it is a rupture of the smooth evolutionary curve, and a rupture is a wound, a pain. But it is a necessary wound: most people suffer from hereditary sleeping sickness, and those who are sick with this ailment must not be allowed to sleep, or they will go to their last sleep, the sleep of death.

Zamyatin's rhetoric is unmistakably that of modernism, and to follow the thrust of his language is to notice that he provides tacit answers to major questions: To what extent can modernism be seen as a phenomenon arising autonomously, as the outcome of an inner logic, from the development of earlier, especially romantic literature? And to what extent can it be located in terms of a need or drive toward formal experimentation?

Zamyatin suggests, rightly I think, that the seeds of modernism lie deep within the Romantic movement, but that revolutionary events in the outer world must occur before those seeds will sprout. The Romantic poets break loose from the classical-Christian tradition, but they do not surrender the wish to discover in the universe a network of spiritual meaning which, however precariously, can enclose their selves. They anticipate the preoccupation with psychic inwardness, by means of which the self is transformed into a cosmic center and mover, as this will later become characteristic of certain modernist writers; but they still seek to relate this preoccupation to transcendent values, if not sources, in the external world. For them the universe is still alert, still the active transmitter of spiritual signs.

Northrop Frye remarks that "the sense of identity with a larger power of creative energy meets us everywhere in Romantic culture," and Marius Bewley writes still more pointedly that "the desire to merge oneself with what is greater than onself—to take one's place in a divine or transcendental continuum of some kind—is indeed the central fact for most of the Romantics." Now it seems to me impossible that anyone should use language of this sort in describing the work of Joyce or Kafka, Baudelaire or Brecht. For the modernist writer the universe is a speechless presence, neither hospitable nor hostile; and after a time he does not agonize, as did nineteenth-century writers like Hardy, over the dispossession of man in the cosmic scheme. He takes that dispossession for granted and turns his anxieties inward, toward the dispossession of meaning from inner life. Whatever spiritual signs he hears come from within his own imaginative resources and are accepted pragmatically as psychic events. Romanticism is, among other things, an effort to maintain a transcendent perspective precisely as or because the transcendent objects of worship are being withdrawn; modernism follows upon the breakdown of this effort. To be sure, a writer like Yeats tries in his famous "system" to take his "place in a divine or transcendental continuum of some kind," but the attempt remains eccentric, willful and by no means organically related to his poetry. In his great lyrics Yeats shares in the premises and aftereffects of modernism.

To the second question posed in Zamyatin's manifesto he gives an answer that again seems correct. Formal experiment may frequently be a consequence or corollary of modernism, but its presence is not a sufficient condition for seeing a writer or a work as modernist. This view of the matter suggests that the crucial factor in the style of a literary movement or period is some sort of inspiriting "vision," a new way of looking upon the world and man's existence; and while such a "vision" will no doubt lead to radical innovations in form and language, there is by no means a direct or invariable correlation. In certain works of literature such as Thomas Mann's stories, formal experiment is virtually absent yet the spirit of modernism is extremely powerful, as a force of both liberation and mischief. Correspondingly, there are works in which the outer mannerisms and traits of the modern are faithfully echoed or mimicked but the animating spirit has disappeared; is that not a useful shorthand for describing much of the "advanced" writing of the years after the Second World War? A writer imbued with the modern spirit will be predisposed toward experiment, if only because he needs to make visibly dramatic his break from tradition; yet it is an error—and an error indulging the modernist desire to exempt itself from historical inquiry—to suppose that where one sees the tokens of experiment there must also be the vision of the modern. True modern

II

At this point my essay will have to suffer from what

Henry James called "a misplaced middle." For I should now speak at some length about the intellectual sources of modernism, especially those major figures in the nineteenth century who initiated the "psychology of exposure" —that corrosion of appearance to break into reality—by means of which old certainties were dislodged and new ones discouraged. I should speak about Frazer and his proclamation of archetypal rhythms in human life, above all the rhythm of the birth and rebirth of the gods, and the role of myth as a means for reestablishing ties with primal sources of experience in a world deadened by "functional rationality." I should speak about Marx, who unmasked —they were all unmaskers, the great figures of the nineteenth century—the fetichism of a commodity-producing society that "resolves personal worth into exchange value" and in which the worker's deed "becomes an alien power . . . forcing him to develop some specialized dexterity at the cost of a world of productive impulses." I should speak about Freud, who focuses upon the irremediable conflict between nature and culture, from which there followed the notorious "discomforts of civilization," the damage done the life of instinct. I should speak, above all, about Nietzsche, a writer whose gnomic and paradoxical style embodies the very qualities of modernist sensibility. But there is no space, and perhaps by now these are familiar matters. Let me therefore hasten to a few topics concerning the formal or literary attributes of modernism, in some instances merely listing and in others providing a bit of illustrative detail.

1) The Rise of the Avant-Garde as a Special Caste.

Forming a kind of permanent if unacknowledged and disorganized opposition, the modernist writers and artists constitute a special caste within or at the margin of society, an *avant-garde* marked by aggressive defensiveness, extreme self-consciousness, prophetic inclination and the stigmata of alienation. "Bohemia," writes Flaubert, "is my fatherland," Bohemia both as an enclave of protection within a hostile society and as a place from which to launch guerrilla raids upon the bourgeois establishment, frequently upsetting but never quite threatening its security. The *avant-garde* abandons the useful fiction of "the common reader;" it demands instead the devotions of a cult. The *avant-garde* abandons the usual pieties toward received esthetic assumptions; "no good poetry," writes Ezra Pound in what is almost a caricature of modernist dogma, "is ever written in a manner twenty years old." The *avant-garde* scorns notions of "responsibility" toward the audience; it raises the question of whether the audience exists—of whether it should exist. The *avant-garde* proclaims its faith in the self-sufficiency, the necessary irresponsibility, and thereby the ultimate salvation of art.

As a device of exposition I write in the present tense; but it seems greatly open to doubt whether by now, a few decades after the Second World War, there can still be located in the West a coherent and self-assured *avant-garde*. Perhaps in some of the arts, but probably not in literature. Only in the Communist countries is there beyond question a combative and beleaguered *avant-garde*, for there as a rule the state persecutes or seriously inconveniences modern writers and artists, so that it forces them into a self-protective withdrawal, sometimes an "internal emigration."

In the war between modernist culture and bourgeois society, something has happened recently that no spokesman for the *avant-garde* quite anticipated. Bracing enmity has given way to wet embraces, the middle class has discovered that the fiercest attacks upon its values can be transposed into pleasing entertainments, and the *avant-garde* writer or artist must confront the one challenge for which he has not been prepared: the challenge of success. Contemporary society is endlessly assimilative, even if it tames and vulgarizes what it has learned, sometimes foolishly, to praise. The *avant-garde* is thereby no longer allowed the integrity of opposition or the coziness of sectarianism; it must either watch helplessly its gradual absorption into the surrounding culture or try to preserve its distinctiveness by continually raising the ante of sensation and shock—itself a course leading perversely to its growing popularity with the bourgeois audience. There remains, to be sure, the option for the serious writer that he go his own way regardless of fashion or cult.

 Still another reason should be noticed for the recent break-up of the *avant-garde*. It is difficult to sustain the stance of a small principled minority in opposition to established values and modes of composition, for it requires the most remarkable kind of heroism, the heroism of patience. Among the modernist heroes in literature only James Joyce, I would say, was able to live by that heroism to the very end. For other writers, more activist in temper or less firm in character, there was always the temptation to veer off into one or another prophetic stance, often connected with an authoritarian politics. Apart from its intrinsic disasters, this temptation meant that the writer would sooner or later abandon the confinements of the *avant-garde* and try, however delusionally, to reenter the arena of history. Yeats and Pound on the right, Brecht, Malraux, and Gide on the left: all succumbed to the glamour of ideology or party machines, invariably with painful results. Fruitful as the *avant-garde* intransigence was for literature itself and inescapable as it may have been historically, it did not encourage a rich play of human feelings. On the contrary, in every important literature except the Yiddish, the modernist impulse was accompanied by a revulsion against traditional modes of nineteenth-century liberalism and by a repugnance for the commonplace materials of ordinary life (again with the exception of Joyce). Imperiousness of mind and impatience with flesh were attitudes shared by Yeats and Malraux, Eliot and Brecht. Disgust with urban trivialities and contempt for *l'homme moyen sensual* streak through many modernist poems and novels.

That modernist literature apprehended with an unrivaled power the collapse of traditional liberalism, its lapse into a formalism ignoring both the possibilities of human grandeur and the needs of human survival, is not to be questioned. But especially in Europe, where democracy has never been the common premise of political life to the extent that it has in the United States, this awareness of the liberal failure frequently led to authoritarian adventures: the haughty authoritarianism of Yeats, with his fantasies of the proud peasant, and the arrogant presumptuousness of Malraux, with his visions of the heroic revolutionist. It is by no means possible to pass an unambiguous judgment on the literary consequences, since major writing can be released through distasteful doctrine. But once such writers turned to daily politics and tried to connect themselves with insurgent movements, they were well on their way to abandoning the *avant-garde* position. And in retrospect even those of us committed, however uneasily, to the need for "commitment" will probably have to conclude that it would have been much better for both literature and society if the modernist masters had kept themselves free from politics. Only Joyce, the greatest and most humane of them all, remained pure in his devotion to a kind of literary monasticism; and Beckett, the most gifted and faithful of his disciples, has remained pure in that devotion to this very day.

2) The Problem of Belief Becomes Exacerbated, Sometimes to the Point of Dismissal.

At a time when there are a number of competing world outlooks, each radically in conflict with the other, there arise severe difficulties in trying to relate the tacit but controlling assumptions of the writer to those of the reader. The bonds of premise between the two are broken, and must now become a matter of inquiry, effort, conflict. We read "To Posterity," a poem by the German Communist writer Bertolt Brecht, in which he offers an incomparable evocation of the travail of Europe in the period between wars—"we changed our country more often than our shoes"—yet simultaneously weaves in a tacit justification for his support of the tyrannical Stalinist dictatorship. How are we to respond to this? We may say that the doctrine is irrelevant, as many critics do say, and that would lead us to the impossible position that the thought or commanding idea of a poem need not be considered in forming a judgment of its value. Or we may say that the doctrine, being obnoxious, destroys our pleasure in the poem, as some critics do say, and that would lead us to the impossible position that our judgment of the work is determined by our agreement or disagreement with the author's ideology.

The problem appears with great force in the early phases of the modernist period and is then reflected in the criticism of T. S. Eliot and I. A. Richards; but later there arises a new impulse to dissolve the whole problem and see literature as ahistorical, a structure beyond opinion or belief, a performance. Weariness sets in, and not merely with this or the other belief, but with the whole idea of belief. Through the brilliance of its straining, the modern begins to exhaust itself. This topic is so complex and requires such detailed attention, I can do no more than note it here and move on toward

3) *A Central Direction in Modernist Literature is Toward the Self-Sufficiency of the Work.*

The crucial instance is that of symbolist poetry. Symbolism moves toward an art severed from common life and experience—a goal perhaps unrealizable but remarkably valuable as a "limit" of striving and motion. The Symbolists, as Marcel Raymond remarks, "share with the Romantics a reliance upon the epiphany, the moment of intense revelation; but they differ sharply about its status in nature and its relation to art. Wordsworth's spiritual life is founded on moments of intense illumination, and his poetry describes these and relates them to the whole experience of an ordered lifetime." For the Symbolist poet, the archetypal figure in modernism, there is no question, however, of *describing* such an experience; for him the moment of illumination occurs only through the action of the poem, only through its thrust as a particular form. Nor is there any question of relating it to the experience of a lifetime, for it is unique, transient, available only in the matter— perhaps more important, only in the moment—of the poem. The poet does not transmit as much as he engages in a revelation. And thereby the Symbolist poet tends to become a *magus*, calling his own reality into existence and making poetry into what Baudelaire called "suggestive magic."

Mallarmé, the Symbolist master, and Defoe, the craftsman of verisimilitude, stand at opposite poles of the esthetic spectrum yet share a desire to undo the premises of traditional art. Neither can bear the idea of the literary work as something distinct from yet dependent upon the external world. Defoe wishes to collapse his representation into the world, so that the reader will feel that the story of Moll Flanders *is* reality; Mallarmé wishes to purge his revelation of the contingent, so that the moment of union with his poem becomes the world. Both are enemies of Aristotle.

Stretched to its theoretic limit, symbolism proposes to disintegrate the traditional duality between the world and its representation. It finds intolerable the connection between art and the flaws of experience; it finds intolerable the commonly accepted distance between subject and act of representation; it wishes to destroy the very program of representation, either as objective *mimesis* or subjective expression. It is equally distant from realism and expressionism, faithfulness to the dimensions of the external and faithfulness to the distortions of the eye. Symbolism proposes to make the poem not merely autonomous but hermetic, and not merely hermetic but sometimes impenetrable. Freed from the dross of matter and time, poetry may then regain the aura of the mysterious. Passionately monistic, symbolism wishes finally that the symbol cease being symbolic and that it become an act or object without "reference," sufficient in its own right. Like other extreme versions of modernism, symbolism rebels against the preposition "about" in statements which begin "art is about . . ." It yearns to shake off the burden of meaning, the alloy of idea, the coarseness of opinion; it hopes for sacrament without religion. To fill up the spaces of boredom, it would metamorphose itself into the purity of magic— magic that, at its purest, is religion without costs.

In his brilliant book *From Baudelaire to Surrealism,* Marcel Raymond writes about the Symbolist vision:

> This state of happiness, "perfect and complete," ineffable as such, is also ephemeral. When it is gone, man is left with an even more acute awareness of his limitations and of the precariousness of his life. He will not rest until he has again forced the gates of Paradise, or if this is impossible, until he has profited from these revelations. . . . The soul engages in a kind of game, but aspires to an activity that is more elevated than any game—aspires to recreate its lost happiness by means of the *word.* And the function of these images, whose elements are borrowed from the dust of sensation, is not to describe external objects, but to prolong or revive the original ecstacy. "In this state of illusion," says Novalis, "it is less the subject who perceives the object than conversely, the objects which come to perceive themselves in the subject". . . . Words are no longer signs; they participate in the objects, in the psychic realities they evoke.

If, for a moment, the poet is here a kind of god, or surrogate god, he finds that after six days of creation he cannot rest on the seventh: his work has crumbled into "the dust of sensation" and he must start again, shuffling the materials of omnipotence and helplessness, forced to recognize once again the world he had hoped to transcend— perhaps had even managed to transcend—through the power of the word.

Here the crucial instance is Rimbaud, breaking with the

conception of language as a way of conveying rational thought, returning to its most primitive quality as a means of arousing emotions, incantatory, magical and automatistic. Rimbaud praised Baudelaire in terms of his own artistic ends: "To inspect the invisible and hear things unheard [is] entirely different from gathering up again the spirit of dead things. . . ."

In sum, the Symbolists hoped:

a) to create an autotelic realm of experience in their poetry, with a minimum of references back or correspondence to the external world, and with an effort to establish the effect of formal coherence through an epiphany of impression;

b) to abandon for the most part logical structures and to create a revelation of insight as a substitute for orderly and formal resolutions;

c) to depend heavily on the association of images, sometimes on kinesthesia and dissonance of images;

d) and thereby to make the writing of the poem itself into the dominant matter of the poem.

4) The Idea of Esthetic Order Is Abandoned or Radically Modified.

To condemn modernist literature for a failure to conform to traditional criteria of unity, order, and coherence is to miss the point, since, to begin with, it either rejects these criteria implicitly or proposes radical new ways of embodying them. When the distinguished critic Yvor Winters attacks the "fallacy of imitative form" (e.g., literary works dealing with the chaos of modern life themselves take on the appearance and sometimes the substance of chaos), he is in effect attacking modernist writing as such, since much of it cannot dispense with this "fallacy." In its assumption that the sense of the real has been lost in conventional realism, modern writing yields to an imperative of distortion. A "law" could be advanced here: *modernist literature replaces the traditional criteria of esthetic unity with the new criterion of esthetic expressiveness, or perhaps more accurately, it downgrades the value of esthetic unity in behalf of even a jagged and fragmented expressiveness.*

The expectation of formal unity implies an intellectual and emotional, indeed a philosophic composure; it assumes that the artist stands above his material, controlling it and aware of an impending resolution; it assumes that the artist has answers to his questions or that answers can be had. But for the modern writer none of these assumptions holds, or at least none of them can simply be taken for granted. He presents dilemmas; he cannot and soon does not wish to resolve them; he offers his *struggle* with them as the substance of his testimony; and whatever unity his work possesses, often not very much, comes from the emotional rhythm, the thrust toward completion, of that struggle. After Kafka it becomes hard to believe not only in answers but even in endings.

Or as Graham Hough shrewdly remarks about Eliot's *Wasteland:*

> . . . we became satisfied with a level of coherence that we should never have found sufficient in any earlier poem. The unity of emotional effect withdrew attention from the logical discontinuity, the extraordinary rhetorical diversity. A poem about frustration, aridity, fear and the perversions of life—these signs were to be read by anyone. They were read, and in combination with the modern urban imagery they instigated the critics who said that the poem expressed "the disillusionment of a generation." For this, some years later, they were sternly reproved by the author; but they were no doubt expressing, in their way, the only sense they had of a unity of purpose in the poem.

5) Nature Ceases to Be a Central Subject and Setting of Literature.

Beginning partly with Wordsworth, nature is transformed from an organic setting into a summoned or remembered *idea.* Nature ceases to be natural. We remark upon the river Liffey, or the Mississippi woods, or the big two-hearted river, or the Abruzzi countryside, but for the most part as a token of deprivation and sometimes as a mere willed sign of nostalgia. They are elsewhere, not our home.

6) Perversity—Which Is to Say: Surprise, Excitement, Shock, Terror Affront—Becomes a Dominant Motif.

I borrow from G. S. Frazer a charming contrast between a traditional poet

Love to Love calleth,

Love unto Love replieth—
From the ends of the earth, drawn by invisible bands,
Over the dawning and darkening lands
Love cometh to Love.
To the heart by courage and might
Escaped from hell,
From the torment of raging fire,
From the signs of the drowning main,
From the shipwreck of fear and pain
From the terror of night.

and a modernist poet

>   I hate and love
>   You ask, how can that be?
>   I do not know, but know it tortures me.

The traditional poet is Robert Bridges, who lived as far back as the early twentieth century; the modern poet, our twin, is Catullus.

The modernist writer strives for sensations, in the serious sense of the term; his epigone, in the frivolous sense. The modernist writer thinks of subject matter not as something to be rehearsed or recaptured but to be conquered and enlarged. He has little use for wisdom; or if he does, he conceives of it not as something to be dug out of the mines of tradition, but to be won for himself through an exercise in self-penetration, sometimes self-disintegration. He becomes entranced with depths—whichever you choose: the depths of the city, or the self, or the underground, or the slums, or the extremes of sensation induced by sex, liquor, drugs; or the shadowed half-people crawling through the interstices of society: lumpens, criminals, hipsters; or the drives at the base of consciousness. Only Joyce, among the modernist writers, negotiates the full journey into and through these depths while yet emerging into the commonplace streets of the city and its ongoing commonplace life—which is, I think, one reason he is the greatest of the modernist writers, as also perhaps the one who points a way beyond the liberation of modernism.

The traditional values of decorum, both in the general ethical sense and the strictly literary sense, are overturned. Everything must now be explored to its outer and inner limits; but more, there are to be no limits. And then, since learning seems often to be followed by ignorance, there come the demi-prophets who scorn the very thought of limits; so that they drive themselves into the corner of

wishing always to go beyond while refusing to acknowledge a line beyond which to go.

7) *Primitivism Becomes a Major Terminus of Modernist Writing.*

A plenitude of sophistication narrowing into decadence
—this means that primitivism will soon follow. The search
for meaning through extreme states of being reveals a
yearning for the primal, for surely man cannot have been
bored even at the moment of his creation! I have already
spoken of the disgust with culture, the rage against cultivation that is so important a part of modernism: the turning
in upon one's primary characteristics, the hatred of one's
gifts, the contempt for intelligence, which cuts through the
work of men so different as Rimbaud, Dostoevsky, and
Hart Crane. For the modern sensibility is always haunted
by the problem of succession: what, after such turnings
and distentions of sensibility, can come next? One of the
seemingly hopeful possibilities is a primitivism bringing a
vision of new manliness, health, blood consciousness, a relief from enervating rationality. A central text is Lawrence's story "The Woman Who Rode Away"—that realistic fable, at once so impressive and ridiculous—in which a
white woman seeks out an Indian tribe to surrender her
"quivering nervous consciousness" to its stricken sun god
and thereby "accomplish the sacrifice and achieve the
power."

But within the ambience of modernism there is another,
more ambiguous and perhaps sinister kind of primitivism:
the kind that draws us not with the prospect of health but
of decay, the primitive as atavistic, an abandonment of
civilization and thereby, perhaps, its discontents. The central fiction expressing this theme is Conrad's *Heart of
Darkness* in which Marlow, the narrator and raisonneur,
does not hesitate to acknowledge that the pull of the jungle for Kurtz and also, more ambiguously, for himself is
not that it seems to him (to quote Lionel Trilling) "noble
and charming, or even free but . . . base and sordid—and
for *that* reason compelling: he himself feels quite overtly
its dreadful attraction." In this version of primitivism,
which is perhaps inseparable from the *ennui* of decadence,
the overwhelming desire is to shake off the burdens of social restraint, the disabling and wearisome moralities of

civilized inhibition. The Greek poet Cavafy has written a brilliant poem in which the inhabitants of a modern city wait for a threatened invasion by barbarians and then, at the end, suffer the exasperating disappointment that the barbarians may, after all, not come. The people of the city will have to continue living as in the past, and who can bear it?

> What does this sudden uneasiness mean,
> and this confusion? (How grave the faces have become!)
> Why are the streets and squares rapidly emptying,
> and why is everyone going back
> home so lost in thought?

> Because it is night and the barbarians have not come,
> and some men have arrived from the frontiers
> and they say that there are no barbarians any longer
> and now, what will become of us without barbarians?
> These people were a kind of solution.

8) In the Novel There Appears a Whole New Sense of Character, Structure and the Role of the Protagonist or Hero. *Existential Condition*

The problematic nature of experience tends to replace the experience of human nature as the dominant subject of the modern novel. Abandoning the assumption of a life that is knowable, the novelist turns to the problem of establishing a bridgehead into knowability as the precondition for portraying any life at all. His task becomes not so much depiction as the hypothesizing of a set of *as if* terms, by means of which he may lend a temporary validation to his material.

Characters in a novel can no longer be assumed, as in the past, to be fixed and synthetic entities, with a set of traits available through notations of conduct and reports of psychic condition. The famous remark of D. H. Lawrence—that he had lost interest in creating the "old stable ego of character," but wished to posit "another ego, according to whose action the individual is unrecognizable, and passes through, as it were, allotropic states which it needs a deeper sense than any we've been used to exercise, to discover are states of the same radically unchanged element"—this is not merely a statement of what he would try to do in *The Rainbow* and *Women in Love;* it also reflects a general intention among modern novelists. Character, for modernists like Joyce, Mrs. Woolf, and Faulkner, is regarded not as a coherent, definable, and well-structured entity, but as a psychic battlefield, or an insoluble puzzle, or the occasion for a flow of perceptions and sensations. This tendency to dissolve character into a stream of atomized experiences, a kind of novelistic *pointillism,* gives way, perhaps through extreme reaction, to an opposite tendency (yet one equally opposed to traditional concepts of novelistic character) in which character is severed from psychology and confined to a sequence of severely objective events.

Still more striking are the enormous changes which the modern novel brings about in its treatment of the hero, and for a moment I shall here abandon my telegraphic approach and stop for a few bits of detail.

The modern world has lost the belief in a collective destiny. Hence, the hero finds it hard to be certain that he possesses—or that anyone can possess—the kind of powers that might transform human existence.

Men no longer feel themselves bound in a sacred and often enough, in a temporal kinship. Hence, the hero finds it hard to believe in himself as a *chosen* figure acting in behalf of a divine commandment or national will.

Since the beginnings of the bourgeois era, a central problem for reflective men has been the relation of the individual to the collectivity. In modern fiction, this problem often appears as a clash between a figure of consciousness who embodies the potential of the human and a society moving in an impersonal rhythm that is hostile or, what is perhaps worse, indifferent to that potential. One likes to feel, by way of contrast, that in certain kinds of ancient or traditional heroes there was a union of value and power, a sense of the good and the capacity to act it out. But in modern literature, value and power are taken to be radically dissociated. In Hemingway's novels, the price of honor is often a refusal of the world. In Malraux's novels, the necessity for action is crossed by a conviction of its absurdity. In Silone's novels, the condition of humaneness is a readiness to act. Between the apprehension and the deed falls a shadow of uncertainty.

D. H. Lawrence, not only a great novelist but himself a major hero of modern literature, embodies this duality. At one point he says, "Insofar as I am I, and only I am I, and

I am only I, insofar as I am inevitably and eternally alone, it is my last blessedness to know it, and to accept it, and to live with this as the core of my self-knowledge." It is the self-knowledge of the Lawrentian hero, strong in pride, sick in strength. But there is another D. H. Lawrence: "What ails me is the absolute frustration of my primeval societal instinct. . . . I think societal instinct much deeper than sex instinct—and societal repression much more devastating. . . . I am weary even of my individuality, and simply nauseated by other people's." It is the yearning of the Lawrentian hero, eager for disciples, driven to repel those who approach him.

This is a conflict that, in our time, cannot be resolved. The Lawrentian hero remains a man divided between the absolutism of his individuality and the frustration of his societal instinct. *nyt munk are mulmet in p-s*

Let me push ahead a bit further and list several traits of "the modern hero," though not in the delusion that any fictional character fulfills all or even most of them:

—The modern hero is a man who believes in the necessity of action; he wishes, in the words of Malraux, to put "a scar on the map." Yet the moral impulsions that lead him to believe in action, also render him unfit for action. He becomes dubious about the value of inflicting scars and is not sure he can even locate the map.

—He knows that traditionally the hero is required to act out the part of bravery, but he discovers that his predicament requires courage. Bravery signifies a mode of action, courage a mode of being. And since he finds it difficult to reconcile the needs of action with those of being, he must learn that to summon courage he will have to abandon bravery. The sense of the burden he must carry brings him close to the situation described by William James: "Heroism is always on a precipitous edge, and only keeps alive by running. Every moment is an escape."

—He knows that the hero can act with full powers only if he commands, for his followers and himself, an implicit belief in the meaningfulness of the human scheme. But the more he commits himself to the gestures of heroism, the more he is persuaded of the absurdity of existence. Gods do not speak to him, prophets do not buoy him, nor doctrines assuage him.

—The classical hero moved in a world charged with a

sense of purpose. In the early bourgeois era, the belief in purpose gave way to a belief in progress. This the hero managed to survive, if only because he often saw through the joke of progress. But now his problem is to live in a world that has moved beyond the idea of progress; and that is hard.

—The modern hero often begins with the expectation of changing the world. But after a time his central question becomes: can I change myself? He asks, in the words of Herman Hesse's Demian, "I wanted only to try to live in obedience to the promptings which came from my true self. Why was that so very difficult?"

—If the modern hero decides the world is beyond changing, he may try, as in the novels of Hemingway, to create an hermetic world of his own in which an unhappy few live by a self-willed code that makes possible—they tell themselves—struggle, renewal, and honorable defeat.

—Still, the modern hero often continues to believe in the quest, and sometimes in the grail too; only he is no longer persuaded that a quest is necessarily undertaken through public action and he is unsure as to where the grail can be found. If he happens to be an American named Jay Gatsby, he may even look for it on the shores of Long Island. There is reason to believe that this is a mistake.

—The modern hero moves from the heroic deed to the heroism of consciousness, a heroism often available only in defeat. He comes as a conqueror and stays as a pilgrim. And in consciousness he seeks those moral ends which the hero is traditionally said to have found through the deed. He learns, in the words of Kyo Gisors in Malraux's *Man's Fate,* that "a man resembles his suffering."

—The modern hero discovers that he cannot be a hero. Yet only through his readiness to face the consequences of this discovery can he salvage a portion of the heroic.

9) And Last: Nihilism Becomes the Central Preoccupation, the Inner Demon, at the Heart of Modern Literature.

In its multiplicity and brilliant confusion, its commitment to an esthetic of endless renewal—in its improvisation of "the tradition of the new," a paradox envisaging the limit of *limitlessness*—modernism is endlessly open to portraiture and analysis. For just as some of its greatest works strain toward a form freed from beginning or end, so modernism strains toward a life without fixity or conclusion. If, nevertheless, there is in literary modernism a dominant preoccupation that the writer must either subdue or by which he will surely be destroyed, it is the specter of nihilism.

Nihilism is a term not only wide-ranging in reference but heavily charged with historical emotion. It signifies at least some of the following:

A specific doctrine, positivistic in stress, of an all-embracing rebellion against traditional authority that appeared in mid-nineteenth century Russia;

A consciously affirmed and accepted loss of belief in transcendent imperatives and secular values as guides to moral conduct, together with a feeling that there is no meaning resident—or, at least, further resident—in human existence;

A loss of those tacit impulsions toward an active and striving existence that we do not even know to be at work in our consciousness until we have become aware of their decline.

In Western literature, nihilism is first and most powerfully foreshadowed by Dostoevsky: there is nothing to believe in but the senses and the senses soon exhaust themselves, God is impossible but all is impossible without Him. Dostoevsky is maliciously witty, maliciously inventive in his perception of the faces of nihilism. He sees it, first, as a social disorder without boundary or shame: Pyotr Verhovensky in an orgy of undoing, mocking the very idea of purpose, transforming the ethic of modernist experiment into an appeal for collective suicide, seizing upon the most exalted words in order to hollow them out through burlesque. "If there's no God, how can I be a captain then," asks an old army officer in *The Possessed,* and in the derision that follows one fancies that Dostoevsky joins in half-contempt, half-enchantment. Nihilism appears in moral guise through the figures of Kirillov and Ivan Karamazov, the first a man of purity and the second of seriousness; that both are good men saves them not at all, for emptiness, says Dostoevsky, lodges most comfortably in the hearts of the disinterested. And in Stavrogin, that "subtle serpent" stricken with metaphysical despair and haunted by "the demon of irony," nihilism achieves an ultimate of representation: nothingness in flesh, flesh that would be nothing. "We are all nihilists," says Dostoevsky in the very course of his struggle to make himself into something else. His great achievement is to sense, as Nietzsche will later state, the intrinsic connection between nihilism as doctrine and nihilism as experience of loss. Just as Jane Austen saw how trivial lapses in conduct can lead to moral disaster, so Dostoevsky insisted that casual concessions to boredom can drive men straight into the void.

Flaubert, though not concerned with the problem abstractly, writes: "Life is so horrible that one can only bear it by avoiding it. And that can be done by living in the world of Art." The idea of art as a sanctuary from the emptying-out of life is intrinsic to modernism: it is an idea strong in Nietzsche, for whom the death of God is neither novelty nor scandal but simply a given fact. The resulting disvaluation of values and the sense of bleakness which follows, Nietzsche calls nihilism. He sees it as connected with the assertion that God exists, which robs the world of ultimate significance, and with the assertion that God does not exist, which robs everything of significance.

> The destruction of the moral interpretation of the world, which has no sanction any more after it has attempted to flee into some beyond, ends in nihilism. "All is senseless. . . ." Since Copernicus man rolls from the center into "X". . . . What does nihilism mean? That the highest values disvalue themselves. The goal is lacking; the answer is lacking to our "Why?"

Fundamentally, then, nihilism comes to imply a loss of connection with the sources of life, so that both in experience and literature it is always related to, while analytically distinguishable from, the blight of boredom.

Recognizing all this, Dostoevsky tries to frighten the atheist both within himself and within his contemporaries by saying that once God is denied, everything—everything terrible—has become possible. Nietzsche gives the opposite answer, declaring that from the moment man believes neither in God nor immortality, "He becomes responsible for everything alive, for everything that, born of suffering, is condemned to suffer from life." And thus for Nietzsche, as later for the existentialists, a confrontation of the nihilist void becomes the major premise of human recovery.

With remarkable powers of invention and variation, this

theme makes its way through all of modernist literature. In Kafka's work, negation and faith stand forever balanced on the tip of a question-mark: there are no answers, there are no endings, and whether justice can be found at the trial or truth in the castle we can never know for certain. The angel with which Kafka wrestles heroically and without let-up is the angel of nothingness. Proust constructs a social world marvellously thick and rich in texture yet a shadow too, which a mere wind blows away; and the only hope we have that some meaning may be salvaged is through the power of art, that thin cloak between men and the beyond which neverthless carries "the true last judgment."

This very power of art is seen by Mann as a demon of nihilism trailing both himself and his surrogate figures from novel to novel, as a portent of disease in "Death in Venice," as a creator-destroyer in *Doctor Faustus* who disintegrates everything through parody. Brecht leers at the familiar strumpet of city nihilism, vomits with disgust when she approaches too closely, and then kidnaps her for a marriage with the authoritarian idea: the result endears him to the contemporary world. But it is Joyce who engages in the most profound modern exploration of nihilism, for he sees it everywhere, in the newspaper office and the church, on the street and in bed, through exaltation and routine. Exposing his characters to every version of nausea and self-disgust, bringing Stephen Dedalus to his outcry of *"Nothung"* in the brothel, Joyce emerges, as William Troy remarks, with "an energetic and still uncorrupted affirmation of life that is implicit in every movement of his writing." As for those who follow these masters, they seem to have relaxed in the death-struggle with the shapeless demon and some, among the more fashionable of the moment, even strike a pleasant truce with him. But the power of example remains a great one, and if a writer like Norman Mailer does not choose to wrestle with the angel Kafka encountered, there are moments when he is prepared to challenge it to a bit of amiable hand-wrestling.

Nihilism lies at the center of all that we mean by modernist literature, both as subject and symptom, a demon overcome and a demon victorious. For the terror which haunts the modern mind is that of a meaningless and eternal death. The death of the gods would not trouble us if

nonsense, self-pity

we, in discovering that they have died, did not have to die alongside them. Heroically the modern sensibility struggles with its passion for eternal renewal, even as it keeps searching for ways to secure its own end.

But no, it will not die, neither heroically nor quietly, in struggle or triumph. It will live on, beyond age, through vulgar reincarnation and parodic mimesis. The lean youth has grown heavy; he chokes and gasps with the approval of the world he had dismissed; he cannot find for himself the pure air of neglect. Not the hostility of those who came before but the patronage of those who come later—that is the torment of modernism.

How, come to think of it, do great cultural movements reach their end? It is a problem our literary historians have not sufficiently examined, perhaps because beginnings are more glamorous, and a problem that is now especially difficult because there has never, I think, been a cultural period in Western history quite like the one we call modern. But signs of a denouement begin to appear. A lonely gifted survivor, Beckett, remains to remind us of what modernism once was. Meanwhile, the decor of yesterday is appropriated and slicked up; the noise of revolt, magnified in a frolic of emptiness; and what little remains of modernism, denied so much as the dignity of opposition.

How enviable death must be to those who no longer have reason to live yet are unable to make themselves die! Modernism will not come to an end; its war chants will be repeated through the decades. For what seems to await it is a more painful and certainly less dignified conclusion than that of previous cultural movements: what awaits it is publicity and sensation, the kind of savage parody which may indeed be the only fate worse than death.

Part One

GENERAL CONSIDERATIONS

This first group of essays consists mainly of efforts at general description of literary modernism. Stephen Spender, Lionel Trilling, Ortega y Gassett and William Phillips provide analyses of modernism, both as a distinctively literary phenomenon and as a reflection of recent historical developments. There follow two short items by David Jones, the Anglo-Welsh poet and author of In Parenthesis, together with a lengthy review by Harold Rosenberg of the book in which these items appear. All together, these comprise a vivid example of the inner stresses and strains which are at work within modernism. Next come two essays by Paul Goodman and Richard Chase that discuss the distinctive role of the avant-garde as the special carrier of modernism, and finally an essay by Randall Jarrell that sees modernism as a movement that has come, or is coming, to an end.

Moderns and Contemporaries

BY STEPHEN SPENDER

There is art which is modern, different from several movements grouped approximately under the heading 'modernism'. Modern art is that in which the artist reflects awareness of an unprecedented modern situation in its form and idiom. The quality which is called modern shows in the realized sensibility of style and form more than in the subject matter. Thus, early in the scientific and industrial era, the age of Progress, I would not call Tennyson, Ruskin, Carlyle moderns because although they were aware of the effects of science, and most contemporary in their interest, they remained within the tradition of rationalism, unshaken in the powers of what Lawrence called the 'conscious ego'. They had the Voltairean 'I', the confidence that they stood outside a world of injustices and irrationality which they judged clearly with their powers of reason and imagination. They regarded themselves as in a line of writer-prophets. Their sensibility was not the product of the times that they deplored.

They did not feel that they had been conditioned in their own natures by the values of a materialist society, and that they had somehow to reflect and respond to the effects of such conditioning in their art: perhaps by allowing unconscious forces to erupt through its surfaces; or perhaps by the cultivation of an extreme critical awareness, as it were an uninterrupted stream of communication with the values of the past, in what they wrote. The Voltairean individualists, most of them influenced by socialist ideas, and believers in progress, regarded contemporary society from a point of view stemming from the French Revolution. They judged the world in which they lived by the most up-to-date developments of materialist thinking.

What I call the Voltairean 'I' participates in, belongs to,

From *The Struggle of the Modern* by Stephen Spender. Reprinted by permission of the University of California Press.

the history of progress. When it criticizes, satirizes, attacks, it does so in order to influence, to direct, to oppose, to activate existing forces. The Voltairean 'I' of Shaw, Wells, and the others, acts upon events. The modern 'I' of Rimbaud, Joyce, Proust, Eliot's *Prufrock* is acted upon by them. The Voltairean 'I' has the characteristics—rationalism, progressive politics, etc.—of the world the writer attempts to influence, whereas the modern 'I' through receptiveness, suffering, passivity, transforms the world to which it is exposed. The faith of the Voltairean egoists is that they will direct the powers of the surrounding world from evil into better courses through the exercise of the superior social or cultural intelligence of the creative genius, the writer prophet. The faith of the moderns is that by allowing their sensibility to be acted upon by the modern experience as suffering, they will produce, partly as the result of unconscious processes, and partly through the exercise of critical consciousness, the idioms and forms of new art. The modern is the realized consciousness of suffering, sensibility and awareness of the past.

The Voltairean egoists are contemporaries without being, from an aesthetic or literary point of view, moderns. What they write is rationalist, sociological, political and responsible. The writing of the moderns is the art of observers conscious of the action of the conditions observed upon their sensibility. Their critical awareness includes ironic self-criticism. *No I am not Prince Hamlet nor was meant to be,* thinks Prufrock, who in his doubting self-awareness certainly reflects the sensibility of early Eliot. But Prufrock's contemporaries—Shaw, Wells, Bennett—had not the least doubt about themselves. In a world of confusion they were clear-sighted social prophets.

The attitude of the latterday Voltairean egoists is amusingly demonstrated by a now almost forgotten episode of the late 1920's. I remember it, because when I was a boy it fascinated me.

The firm of Harrods invited H. G. Wells, Arnold Bennett, and Bernard Shaw to write articles as publicity, dealing with such aspects of Harrods as might appeal to them. Harrods of course took the honest dealer's risk of offering them a free hand to be appreciative or critical, as they chose. All three refused, but in letters of sufficient length to fill up a whole page of advertising taken by Harrods in several newspapers. All the parties concerned seemed to have had their cake and eaten it. Remembering the episode, I wrote recently to Harrods and asked for copies of the published texts, with which they have kindly provided me. It seems to me that the reason why the memory of them has remained in my mind is because the replies reveal the fundamental attitudes of writers in a radical rationalist tradition, with a developed sense of responsibility towards their public, better than considered declarations of faith might do.

Shaw, after animadverting on 'puffery', argues that for him to give his signed statement in support of a commercial house would be like his paying critics to approve his plays. Theatre critics

> write in a judicial capacity. But so do all authors whose work is of sufficient weight and depth to have a formative effect on the public mind. For such an author to accept payment from a commercial enterprise for using his influence to induce the public to buy its wares would be to sin against the Holy Ghost. . . . By all means let our commercial houses engage skilled but nameless scribes . . . to write their advertisements as such. But a writer who has been concentrated by Fame to the service of the public, and has thus become prophet as well as author, must take wages in no other service.

Arnold Bennett admits that he has no objection to the proposal:

> I see no possible reason against my acceptance, except one. The reason is that public opinion is not yet ripe to approve the employment of responsible imaginative writers to whom it has granted a reputation, in any scheme of publicity for a commercial concern. Personally I differ from public opinion in this matter; but the opinion exists and I will not flout it. In flouting it I should certainly lose caste, and I do not intend to lose caste by creating a precedent which could result, for me, in a dangerous notoriety. The time must inevitably come, sooner or later, when the precedent will be created, and after it is established people will wonder why it should ever have met with opposition.

The attitude of Bennett is not, like that of Shaw and Wells, that of the prophet, but more like that of the reluctant public servant. One recalls that such poetry as there undoubtedly is in his novels is of the department store—the shop windows alight at dusk, stuffed with merchandise displayed like tropical fish in their illuminated tanks:

As a writer I have always been keenly interested in the very impressive phenomenon of the big departmental store, regarded either as a picturesque spectacle, or as a living organism, or as a social portent.

H. G. Wells declares:

I have to rout about in my mind, to discover the hidden almost instinctive reason

for refusal. Of course, when found, it turns out to be that

rightly or wrongly, the writer takes himself more seriously than that. In his heart he classes himself not with the artists but with the teachers and prophets.

He adds that apart from this objection the

project is most attractive. I can imagine nothing more amusing and exciting than to study your marvellous organization closely and explain its working. Some day I shall do something of the sort and come to you for particulars. But you will pay me nothing for that. I shall do it because it will interest me and because I think it will interest my readers. Facts you may give me with both hands, but not money. . . . I have already sketched the appearance of your type of business in *Clissold* and of something distantly akin in *Tono Bungay*.

I think these unguarded self-revelations are interesting, not because of something innocently disingenuous about refusals which are really disguised acceptances, but because they show how wholeheartedly Shaw, Wells and Bennett accept responsibility to the world of public interests and materialist values even if they opposed the economic system as such. In fairness one should add that the principles of Wells and Shaw were not the same as those of Harrods—and perhaps it was only politeness that prevented their saying so here—but they were those of business (if publicly owned), just the same. All of them plead a sense of responsibility for the writer which is nevertheless not that of the artist—it is, responsibility to be a social prophet. It is interesting to recall that in the famous epistolary controversy with Henry James, after the publication of his novel *Boon*, containing a parody of James' later manner, Wells describes himself as a 'journalist' rather than an artist. To Henry James—the 'journalist'; but to Harrods 'teacher, priest, or prophet'.

What would have been the answers of James Joyce, D. H. Lawrence, T. S. Eliot or Virginia Woolf if they had received the proposal from Harrods? At least one of them might have been more tempted than were Wells, Shaw and Bennett. But I can't feel the temptation would have been of the same kind. They would not have thought that their business—producing literary consumer goods—was after all a branch of Harrods—the book department; that their success, like that of the other departments in a store, was judged by their capacity to sell their particular literary article. They would not have described themselves as 'prophets'— at least not in any religion known to Harrods. They would have regarded advertising as the most questionable activity of commerce. James Joyce might have taken the offer as a joke or treated it as an exercise and therefore have gone in for it. To guess what he might have replied would make an amusing literary competition.

It may have been a virtue in Bennett, Wells and Shaw that they could take Harrods' offer 'on the level'; and it may have been a failing in the moderns that they would have treated it sniggeringly if they did not repudiate it disgustedly. I have winkled this odd episode from my memory. Perhaps it throws light on why a younger English generation of writers such as Kingsley Amis and John Wain, reacting against the modern movement, prefers Arnold Bennett to Virginia Woolf. The candid response of Bennett might appeal to them.

The episode draws attention to the division between what I call 'contemporary' and 'modern'. Shaw, Wells and Bennett thought of themselves as prophets of a materialist society. The way in which the kind of life they describe in their works is up to date, is the way in which Harrods is enterprising. Wells and Bennett indeed go out of their way —as we have seen—to insist that they have described just such a 'living organism' and 'sociological portent' in novels which were by no means social satire. If Joyce had boasted that there was an apparition of Harrods in *Ulysses* the irony would have been apparent. The appeal of Harrods is rejected by Shaw, Wells and Bennett on account of a responsibility towards the same public with the same interests as Harrods. But the 'moderns', Joyce, Lawrence, Eliot, Woolf, would, as literary artists, feel an entirely different kind of responsibility. They would feel responsible to a past which had been degraded by commerce, a past of realer values betrayed by advertising. They would feel that their responsibility towards themselves was as artists, and not as money-makers producing a consumers' product.

It makes no difference to my argument that Eliot was at one time a bank clerk, that Joyce regarded himself as a good business man, and even as a socialist, that Lawrence was only too glad to sell articles to the popular press. These things only emphasize that the life and feeling out of which they wrote was different from that in which they made choices when voting in an election, or fighting in a war, or supporting themselves and their families.

The contemporary belongs to the modern world, represents it in his work, and accepts the historic forces moving through it, its values of science and progress. By this I do not mean that he is uncritical of the world in which he finds himself. On the contrary, he is quite likely to be a revolutionary. For the social scene is one of conflicts, and in reflecting its events and values the contemporary will be taking sides in these conflicts but doing so on terms—of whichever side—laid down by society. The contemporary is a partisan in the sense of seeing and supporting partial attitudes. However, in a world torn by passionate conflicts he cannot have a contemporary attitude which sees modern life as a whole. The modern tends to see life as a whole and hence in modern conditions to condemn it as a whole. When writers became engaged in conflicts—as some did, for example, during the 'thirties when they supported the cause of anti-Fascism which seemed that of freedom and humanity, and as some do today when they represent the interests of an emergent working class—they tend to be 'contemporary' rather than 'modern'.

The contemporary is involved in conflicts, but fundamentally he accepts the forces and the values of today which are fighting one another, with the same weapons of power, ideology and utilitarian philosophy, for different goals. Thus the socialist Wells accepts the same values of distributing consumer goods as the department store, but he thinks that the store should be owned by the government, and that goods distributed should be different. And when he says that he is a prophet he means that he looks forward to the distribution through a socialist society of better consumer goods among a population of enlightened utilitarians, through the directed efforts of scientists. The extent to which Wells himself has lost interest in the past tradition reflects that to which the world made by science has outdistanced the past.

The modern is acutely conscious of the contemporary scene, but he does not accept its values. To the modern, it seems that a world of unprecedented phenomena has today cut us off from the life of the past, and in doing so from traditional consciousness. At the same time it is of no use trying to get back into the past by ignoring the present. If we consider ourselves as belonging not just to our own particular movement in time but also to the past, then we must also be fully aware of our predicament which is that of past consciousness living in the present.

The modern is the past become conscious at certain points, which are ourselves living in the present. Hence we find that the modern in his work is occupied with trying to bridge a gulf within his own awareness, of past from present. With his sensibility he is committed to the present; with his intellect he is committed to criticizing that present by applying to it his realization of the past. The great fusions of present and past are works such as Joyce's *Ulysses* or Picasso's *Guernica*. In *Ulysses* an attempted realization of the whole of contemporary life at a particular time and place is brought into collision with the Homeric epic interpreted into the terms of that present. In *Guernica,* by a process the opposite of this, the terror of a modern air raid is translated into the imagery of classical Greek or Mithraic tragedy—the sacrificial bull, the sword, the flaming torch.

The Modern as Vision of the Whole

BY STEPHEN SPENDER

The movements of modern literature and art—the 'isms'
—are programmes of techniques for expressing this whole
view of the past-future confrontation. There are different
types of programmes which might be analysed as establishing the following categories:

1. *Realization* through new art of the modern experience.
2. The invention through art of a *pattern of hope,* in-
fluencing society.
3. The idea of an art which will fuse past with present
into the modern symbolism of *a shared life.*
4. The *alternate life of art.*
5. *Distortion.*
6. The *revolutionary concept of tradition.*

1. *Realization* is the primary gesture of modernism, the
determination to invent a new style in order to express the
deeply felt change in the modern world. Industrial towns,
machines, revolutions, scientific thinking, are felt to have
altered the texture of living. Everyday language and taste
reflect these changes, even though the image they mirror is
ugly. It is only art that remains archaic, forcing its ideas
into forms and manners that are outmoded. Therefore artists have to learn the idiom of changed speech, vision and
hearing, and then mould the modern experience into
forms either revolutionized or modified.

The outstanding characteristic of realization is, then, the
great attention paid to inventing an idiom which responds
to the tone of voice of contemporaries, the changed vision
of a world of machines and speed: the rhythms of an altered contemporary tempo, the new voice of a humanity

From *The Struggle of the Modern* by Stephen Spender. Reprinted
by permission of the University of California Press.

at times when the old social hierarchies are breaking down.

The street speaks the idiom and the idiom, in the mind of the artist, invents the form. Eliot and Joyce in their early work are realizers of the modern idiom in their poetry and their poetic prose. In music Alban Berg's *Wozzeck* is a classic example of the realization of the 1920's in Germany as idiom. In his Blue Period, Picasso had supremely this quality of realization, as did Eliot in the *Preludes:*

> I am moved by fancies that are curled
> Around these images, and cling;
> The notion of some infinitely gentle
> Infinitely suffering thing.

The human element is often reduced to pathos, clownishness, in *Wozzeck,* Blue Period Picasso, the early Eliot, *Petroushka.* In Apollinaire as in some of the German Expressionists, this clownishness acquires a quality of touching and nobly absurd heroism, a gay despair.

2. By *the pattern of hope,* I mean—and this certainly will seem an unfashionable view today—the idea that modern art might transform the contemporary environment, and hence, by pacifying and ennobling its inhabitants, revolutionize the world (there is, surely, a pun on this idea in the programme of Eugene Jolas in the magazine *Transition*—'the revolution of the word').

The word *hope* has to be understood seriously, as Malraux still intended it when he entitled his Spanish civil war novel *Espoir.* Early in the century, hope was based on the international inter-arts community of the alliance between the ballet, architecture, furniture design, painting, music and poetry, all of them participating in the movement to revolutionize taste, and at the same time make it an operative acting and criticizing force in modern life. The way in which art might revolutionize the environment and hence, by implication, people living in it, is explored in many of the manifestos of poets and painters early in the century. The famous *Der Blaue Reiter* (1914), the anthology of the group of painters which was founded in Munich in 1909, is prefaced with remarks of which these are characteristic:

> 'Everything which comes into being, on earth can only have its beginning.' This sentence by Daeubler might stand

written over all our inventing and all our aims. A fulfil-
ment will be attained, some time, in a new world, in another existence (*dasein*). On earth we are only able to state
the theme. This first volume is the prelude to a new theme.
. . . We wander with our passionate wishes through the art
of this time and through the present age.

This is touching, innocent, mysteriously exciting. The
same dream of transforming the world—but this time the
world of actuality in which we live—is expressed by
Wyndham Lewis, a decade later, in *The Tyro:*

> Art, however, the greatest art, even, has it in its power to
> influence everybody. Actually the shapes of the objects
> (houses, cars, dresses and so forth) by which they are sur-
> rounded have a very profound subconscious effect on peo-
> ple. A man might be unacquainted with the very existence
> of a certain movement in art, and yet his life would be
> modified directly if the street he walked down took a cer-
> tain shape, at the dictates of an architect under the spell of
> that movement, whatever it were. Its forms and colours
> would have a tonic or a debilitating effect on him, an emo-
> tional value. Just as he is affected by the changes of the
> atmosphere, without taking the least interest in the cyclonic
> machinery that controls it, so he would be directly affected
> by any change in his physical milieu.
>   A man goes to choose a house. He is attracted by it or
> not, often, not for sentimental or practical reasons, but for
> some reason that he does not seek to explain, and that yet
> is of sufficient force to prevent him from, or decide him on
> taking it. This is usually an example of the functioning of
> the aesthetic sense (however underdeveloped it may be in
> him) of which we are talking. The painting, sculpture and
> general design of today, such as can be included in the
> movement we support, aims at nothing short of a physical
> reconstructing and recording of the visible part of the
> world.

The basic reason for hope is that art might re-connect
the life, which has been driven inwards into the isolated
being of the artist, with the external world, by accomplish-
ing a revolution in the lives of people converted to
share the visions of modern creation. In being victimized,
oppressed, and in having dreams, the artist already meets
half-way the insulted and the oppressed who fight for
change, although their aspirations may be far removed
from his visions. But it is important to him that his visions
are nevertheless closer to the poor and the powerless than
to the rich and those who enjoy power. Hence the current
of revolutionary feeling which runs alike through dadaist,

expressionist and surrealist manifestos. Each group claims to be the true revolutionaries, and that the life-force which it represents would join with the force of the social revolution. If only the revolutionaries were not too philistine to realize that modern art represents the democracy of the unconscious forces which should be equated with economic democracy! Hence the surrealists were later to insist that they were communists. Some of them—Aragon, Tristan Tzara—even, as surrealists, joined the communist party, later to renounce surrealism as bourgeois.

3. Art which will transform reality into *shared inner life,* is the converse of (2) which would transform inner vision into outer social change. It is the idea that the images of the materialist modern world can be 'interpreted', made to become symbols of inner life where they are reconciled with the older things symbolized by words like 'jug', 'mountain', 'star', 'cross'. This process was the infinitely patient research of experience of Rilke. It finds its completest realization in the *Duino Elegies,* where the Angels are set up as almost machine-like figures over the human landscape in which there is the fair, the world of values, that are money. The angels are perpetually occupied in transforming the world of outward materialism back into inner tragic values.

The connection of poetry here with iconographic modern painting is evident. One of the *Duino Elegies* is inspired by Picasso's *Les Saltimbanques,* in which Rilke sees the method of interpretation of the performers in the fairground who are at once traditional and contemporary.

4. *The alternate life of art.* By this I mean something different from (2), the hope that art might become the agency for inspiring a transformed society, and (3) the use of art to interpret the external materialism into the language of inner life. The alternate life is when it is intended that the processes of art are brought close to borderline ecstatic or sexual experiences. I am thinking here of the exaltation of violence, sexual relations, madness, drugs, through art which is regarded by the artists as a transition towards the actual experience of these states. Lawrence surely often regarded his writing not as an end but as a means of inducing in the reader a state of feeling which would release in him the 'dark forces' or 'phallic consciousness', or the approach to the mystic-physical sexual union which were

more important to him than that he should create literature.

The tendency here is to regard writing as hallucinatory: that is to say as a literary technique for inducing non-literary sensations. The poet, supposedly, has a peculiar insight into life-sensations which he upholds as more real than the externals which are everyday reality. The surrealists used poetry as a technique for inducing states of mind supposedly super-real. It might be said that surrealist writing is itself the super-reality, but if this were true, it would only be in the way that incantation may itself be what is invoked: a strangeness of feeling induced by the language that lies beyond the threshold of the words.

However much one disapproves of non-literary aims in literature, nevertheless it is easy to understand the temptation today for modern artists to use art as a modern kind of magic. Two definitions of surrealism, by André Breton, which I quote from David Gascoyne's *Surrealism,* are relevant:

'SURREALISM, n. Pure psychic automatism, by which it is intended to express, verbally, in writing, or by other means, the real process of thought. Thought's dictation, in the absence of all control exercised by the real reason and outside all aesthetic or moral preoccupations.'
'ENCYCL. *Philos.* Surrealism rests in the belief in the superior reality of certain forms of association neglected heretofore; in the omnipotence of the dream and in the disinterested play of thought. It tends definitely to do away with all other psychic mechanisms and to substitute itself for them in the solution of the principal problem of life.'

Just as futurism is the expression of an impulse to repudiate the whole of the past which is common to several movements called by different names, so surrealism has features in common with quite other movements. All the 'alternate life of art' movements attempt to discover through art, or to use art to discover, spiritual, sensual, or esoteric forces, which restore the balance of inner life against industrialized societies.

The tendency to seek such a compensation of life through art, and of art through life, was already present with Byron and Keats. Sensuality tinged with despair and anticipation of death produced a mood in which Keats regarded the taste of a peach or rose, with its further suggestion of a drug, as lines of poetry. Keats was tasting, I suggest, at these moments the sensation of his own being as a poet. Today at a later stage of individual despair there is a meeting ground in drugs, violence, sexual relations, hallucination, madness, between poets and non-poets who live the life of poetry regarded as experienced sensation. Not the poets who are influenced by Dylan Thomas, but the hangers-on who imitate his life, think they ARE Dylan Thomas. The 'dark forces' released through sexual passion or through 'phallic consciousness', the mystical-physical sexual union, surely suggest in Lawrence a meeting in which the art-sensation is transformed into the life-sensation. The reader is recommended to have sex in the way which will identify for him the sensation described in the words. Significantly, Lawrence disapproved of all sex which is not experienced exactly in the way that he describes, or prescribes it. And the purpose of this is not, of course, pornographic. It is to assert the proximate reality and force of experienced sensation against the abstract supra-personal forces of machinery and social organization.

Here, the confusion of art-experience with life-experience seems dangerous. The example of movements like that of the Beatniks in America shows the degradation of life, through art and of art through life, which follows from the substitution of what is supposed to be the life of the artist for the discipline required to create art.

5. *Distortion* is much more obviously an element in modern visual art than in literature. One has only to call to mind Picasso's women's faces with features pulled about, displaced, rearranged, of the bulges and holes in Henry Moore's sculpture, and most of all, of the paintings of Francis Bacon, who in an earlier age might have been described as the Master of the Distortions, to realize this. And in fact I owe most of what follows on this subject to remarks made to me by Francis Bacon and Henry Moore.

For Francis Bacon, distortion is an essential development of his art, and perhaps of all modern art, and in it several distinct aims coincide. In the first place, modern distortion is the last phase in interpreting, selecting and changing the image at the end of the line of the tradition. It is the new twist given to the game of art, the something which the modern artist can do with the material he handles, to the nature he sees, which has not been done before.

But arising from this, secondly, distortion is a way of expressing the felt truth of the relationship of the subjective artist to the objective reality in this time. Consider for instance the implications of a statement: 'A portrait is always also a self-portrait.' This means that the painter regards the image of the model he sees as fused with an image of himself which he carries round in his mind, and which, for the sake of describing the truth of his own limitations, he has to project into the portrait. The fusion here is, to the spectator, evidently distorting. But one must add to this account that this way of looking at things, of regarding the artist's self-image as the prime factor of his consciousness which affects his vision of everything, and which cannot be evaded, is a result of our time. Moreover, if the artist is thus a prisoner of the moment, the subject is also. One might say that the element of distortion is the factor of the relationship of subjective self to objective reality multiplied by the present moment in time.

I remarked to Henry Moore one day that I was particularly struck by his 'three quarters figure' 1961, a distorted figure with a lumpy grotesquely shaped torso and a head half bird-beak, half hippopotamus. He said he was glad I liked it because a good many people had not seen the point of it, and it was one he liked himself. The next time we met I could not resist asking him what the point he had in mind was. He answered that what he was trying to do was pull the human body about as much as possible, distending it here, pushing it in there, and putting on to it a non-human head, but nevertheless retaining its recognizability as a human figure.

Thinking this over, and having the experience of the 'three quarters figure' much in mind, I began to notice, in this my middle age, that what Moore was doing to this figure, distending it here, pushing it in there, time was palpably doing to my own body! It seemed to me then that the 'three quarters figure' was full of dark references to the sculpture which is of time upon flesh, the subjective experience of growing old, whereas the beaked or trunked head referred perhaps to the depersonalizing objective forces of the time in which we live. These last sentences are my interpretation, not Henry Moore's.

It may seem from what I have written above that distortion is a factor in painting and sculpture but not in writing. On reflection I do not think this is so. I think that the

interior monologue, as it is used in *Ulysses,* for example, is
a technique of distortion, employed very much in the
manner of Picasso or Francis Bacon. The character of
Bloom is created for the reader by Bloom's thoughts.
These thoughts, which are represented to us as the result
of the action of events in the environment upon Bloom's
sensibility, are distorted by his sensibility. Moreover the
context of Bloom's environment is distorted by the forcing
against it of the Homeric parallel of the Odyssey. Thus
not only is Bloom's vision distorted but the world he sees
is also one of distortion.

In later Yeats the imagery that most suggests the present, although it may be derived from the past, is of some
inhuman distorted half-bird half-beast:

> Here at right of the entrance this bronze head,
> Human, superhuman, a bird's round eye,
> Everything else withered and mummy-dead.

Obviously the scene here is a museum, but the horrific
force of the grotesque head is that it is seen through—invented by, one might say—contemporary eyes. Yeats in
putting the Egyptian statue's head into his poem is doing
what Moore does when his inhuman superhuman heads of
human bodies recall some shadowy night of past statuary
and architecture.

6. By the *revolutionary concept of tradition,* I mean the
introduction, into certain works, of critically selected traditions. Often such use of tradition seems outrageous to
those who regard themselves as traditionalists, but who are
better described as academics or conventionalists. A famous example of the transformation, distortion and even
perversion of a tradition into modern expression that
seemed to contemporaries its opposite, was Baudelaire's
Fleurs du Mal. The traditionally Catholic consciousness of
Baudelaire realizes itself in the pursuit of evil. Grace is
discovered in damnation, and the only part of the faith
that does not seem to have undergone a terrible transmutation is the doctrine of Original Sin. The process by
which the little flowers of St. Francis become in the late
nineteenth century the flowers of evil is, as it were, sometimes reversible. Intensity of corruption or debauchery can
be taken as a sign of grace. Claudel was converted to Catholicism by reading the poems of Rimbaud, *poète maudit*

par excellence, and one can imagine readers being converted to religion by Dylan Thomas' poetry.

The idea of tradition as an explosive force, an unknown
quantity almost, an apocalyptic mystery, something sought
out from the past and chosen by the modern artist, perhaps
in a spirit of grotesque mimicry, something disturbing and
shocking, belongs to the early phase of modernism in poetry and fiction. In painting it still retains the enormous
eclecticism of Malraux's *Musée Imaginaire,* the whole of
visual art contained within the walls of the contemporary
skull, and in one timeless moment.

On the Modern Element in Modern Literature

BY LIONEL TRILLING

The title I have given to this discourse makes reference
to a lecture which Matthew Arnold delivered a little over
a century ago. I cannot expect a quick and general recognition of the allusion, for this particular one of Arnold's
lectures is not widely known. "On the Modern Element in
Literature" has a signal importance in its author's career
—it was Arnold's first lecture as Professor of Poetry at
Oxford, and it inaugurated not only his professorship but
his career in criticism. The lecture as it was delivered in
1857 was a great success, but Arnold was not pleased with
it; he never wanted it to be part of the canon of his work,
he never put it into any of the volumes of critical essays
he brought out in his lifetime. Yet he did not entirely dis-
own it; after the passage of a decade he published it in
Macmillan's Magazine, explaining that he did so because
it made a certain point about the nature of Hellenism
which at that time needed to be made. He apologized for
the inadequacy of the piece in a prefatory note, speaking
of its deficiencies in content, but more emphatically of its
wrongness of tone. He said that it was composed in a style
which he had since learned to dislike, what he called the
style of the "doctor" rather than in the style which he
called that of the "explorer." In describing the rejected
style as that of the doctor, Arnold very likely had in mind
the Scriptural injunction which he liked to quote, "Be ye
not called Rabbi," that is to say, be ye not called doctor
—be ye not one who claims to have the doctrine.

At this distance of time from him, we incline to think
of Arnold as the doctor *par excellence,* as the man above
all others writing in English who fixed the critical doctrine
and handed it down. But he thought of himself in quite

the opposite way, as a spirit *ondoyant et divers,* flexible and various, as a mind peculiarly individual and personal, asking the question which, as he said, Goethe had taught modern Europe to ask: "But is it true? Is it true for *me?*" In his own sense of himself as a critic, he was the explorer, with all that the word may suggest of freedom, curiosity, risk.

I shall presently recur to Arnold's lecture in a substantive way, but I refer now to Arnold's remarks about its style in order to find sanction for the mode in which I shall deal with my subject. I have the intention of talking about a certain theme which appears frequently in modern literature—so frequently, indeed, and in so striking a manner, that it may be said to constitute one of the shaping and controlling ideas of our epoch. I can identify it by calling it the disenchantment of our culture with culture itself—it seems to me that the characteristic element of modern literature, or at least of the most highly developed modern literature, is the bitter line of hostility to civilization which runs through it. It happens that my present awareness of this theme is involved in a personal experience, and I am impelled to speak of the theme not abstractly but as it actually exists for me, with the husks of my experience clinging untidily to it. If Arnold is right, if the critic should be the explorer rather than the doctor, then the avowedly personal mode cannot be wholly unbecoming to him, it is not inappropriate to the critic's function to talk about his personal experience of an idea. And I shall go so far in doing this as to describe the actual circumstances in which the experience took place. These circumstances are pedagogic—they consist of some problems in teaching modern literature to undergraduates and my attempt to solve these problems. And perhaps I ought to admit at once that, as much as about modern literature itself, I am talking about the teaching of modern literature. I know that pedagogy is a depressing subject to all persons of sensibility, and yet I shall not apologize for speaking about it because the teaching of literature and especially modern literature constitutes one of the most salient and significant characteristics of the culture of our time. Indeed, if we are on the hunt for *the* modern element of modern literature, we might want to find it in the susceptibility of modern literature to being made into an academic subject.

Here, then, is my experience.

For some years I have taught the course in modern literature in Columbia College. I did not undertake the course without misgivings and I have never taught it with an undivided mind. My doubts do not refer to the value of the literature itself, only to the educational propriety of its being studied in college. These doubts persist in the face of my entire awareness that the relation of our collegiate education to modernity is no longer an open question. The unargued assumption of most curriculums is that the real subject of all study is the modern world; that the justification of all study is its immediate and presumably practical relevance to modernity; that the true purpose of all study is to lead the young person to be at home in, and in control of, the modern world. There is really no way of quarreling with this belief, nor with what follows upon it, the framing of curriculums of which the substance is chiefly contemporary or at least makes ultimate reference to what is contemporary.

It might be asked why anyone should *want* to quarrel with this assumption. To that question I can only return a defensive, eccentric, self-depreciatory answer. It is this: that to some of us, as we go on teaching, if we insist on thinking of our students as the creators of the intellectual life of the future, there comes a kind of despair. It does not come because our students fail to respond to ideas, rather because they respond to ideas with a happy vagueness, a delighted glibness, a joyous sense of power in the use of received or receivable generalizations, a grateful wonder at how easy it is to formulate and judge, at how little resistance language offers to their intentions. When that despair strikes us, we are tempted to give up the usual and accredited ways of evaluating education, and instead of prizing responsiveness and aptitude, we set store by some sign of personal character in our students, some token of individual will. We think of this as taking the form of resistance and imperviousness, of personal density or gravity, of some power of supposing that ideas are real, a power which will lead a young man to say, "But is this really true—is it true for me?" And to say this not in the modern way, not following the progressive educational prescription to "think for yourself," which means to think in the progressive pieties rather than in the conservative pieties (if any of the latter do still exist), but to say it from his sense of himself as a person rather than as a bundle of attitudes and responses which are all alert to please the teacher and the progressive community.

We can't do anything about the quality of personal being of our students, but we are led to think about the cultural analogue of a personal character that is grave, dense, and resistant—we are led to think about the past. Perhaps the protagonist of Thomas Mann's story, "Disorder and Early Sorrow" comes to mind, that sad Professor Cornelius with his intense and ambivalent sense of history. For Professor Cornelius, who is a historian, the past is dead, is death itself, but for that very reason it is the source of order, value, piety, and even love. If we think about education in the dark light of the despair I have described, we wonder if perhaps there is not to be found in the past that quiet place at which a young man might stand for a few years, at least a little beyond the competing attitudes and generalizations of the present, at least a little beyond the contemporary problems which he is told he can master only by means of attitudes and generalizations, that quiet place in which he can be silent, in which he can *know* something—in what year the Parthenon was begun, the order of battle at Trafalgar, how Linear B was deciphered: almost anything at all that has nothing to do with the talkative and attitudinizing present, anything at all rather than variations of the accepted formulations about *anxiety,* and *urban society,* and *alienation,* and *Gemeinschaft* and *Gesellschaft,* all the matter of the academic disciplines which are founded upon the modern self-consciousness and the modern self-pity. The modern self-pity is certainly not without its justification; but, if the grounds for our self-pity are ever to be overcome, we must sometimes wonder whether that task is likely to be accomplished by minds which are taught in youth to accept these sad conditions of ours as ineluctable, and as the only right objects of contemplation. And quite apart from any practical consequences, there is the simple aesthetic personal pleasure of having to do with young minds, and maturing minds, which are free of cant, which are, to quote an old poet, "fierce, moody, patient, venturous, modest, shy."

This line of argument I have called eccentric and maybe it ought to be called obscurantist and reactionary. Whatever it is called, it is not likely to impress a committee on the curriculum. It was, I think, more or less the line of argument of my department in Columbia College, when, up to a few years ago, it decided, whenever the question came up, not to carry its courses beyond the late nineteenth century. But our rationale could not stand against the representations which a group of students made to our dean and which he communicated to us. The students wanted a course in modern literature—very likely, in the way of students, they said that it was a scandal that no such course was being offered in the College. There was no argument that could stand up against this expressed desire: we could only capitulate, and then, with pretty good grace, muster the arguments that justified our doing so. Was not the twentieth century more than half over? Was it not nearly fifty years since James wrote "Portrait of a Lady"? George Meredith had not died until 1909, and even the oldest among us had read one of his novels in a college course—many American universities had been quick to bring into their purview the literature of the later nineteenth century, and even the early twentieth century; there was a strong supporting tradition for us. Had not Yeats been Matthew Arnold's contemporary for twenty-three years?

Our resistance to the idea of the course had never been based on an adverse judgment of the literature itself. We are a department not only of English but of comparative literature, and if the whole of modern literature is surveyed, it could be said—and we were willing to say it—that no literature of the past matched the literature of our time in power and magnificence. Then too, it is a difficult literature, and it is difficult not merely as defenders of modern poetry say that all literature is difficult. We nowadays believe that Keats is a very difficult poet, but his earlier readers did not. We now see the depths and subtleties of Dickens, but his contemporary readers found him as simply available as a plate of oysters on the half shell. Modern literature, however, shows its difficulties, at first blush; they are literal as well as doctrinal difficulties, and they are to be dealt with by young men brought up with a lax secondary education and an abstract and generalized college education—if our students are to know their modern literary heritage, surely they need all the help that a teacher can give?

These made cogent reasons for our decision to establish, at long last, the course in modern literature. They also made a ground for our display of a certain mean-spirited, last-ditch vindictiveness. I recall that we said something like, "Very well, if they want the modern, let them have it —let them have it, as Henry James says, full in the face. We shall give the course, but we shall give it on the highest level, and if they think, as students do, that the modern is the facile, the easily comprehended, let them have their gay and easy time with Yeats and Eliot, with Joyce and Proust and Kafka, with Lawrence, Mann, and Gide."

Eventually the course fell to me to give. I approached it with an uneasiness which has not diminished with the passage of time—it has, I think, even increased. It arises, this uneasiness, from my personal relation with the works that form the substance of the course. Almost all of them have been involved with me for a long time—I invert the natural order not out of lack of modesty but taking the cue of W. H. Auden's remark that a real book reads us. I have been read by Eliot's poems and by *Ulysses* and by *Remembrance of Things Past* and by *The Castle* for a good many years now, since early youth. Some of these books at first rejected me; I bored them. But as I grew older and they knew me better, they came to have more sympathy with me and to understand my hidden meanings. Their nature is such that our relationship has been very intimate. No literature has ever been so shockingly personal as ours —it asks every question that is forbidden in polite society. It asks us if we are content with our marriages, with our family lives, with our professional lives, with our friends. It is all very well for me to describe my course in the college catalogue as "paying particular attention to the role of the writer as a critic of his culture"—this is sheer evasion: the questions asked by our literature are not about our culture but ourselves. It asks us if we are content with ourselves, if we are saved or damned—more than with anything else, our literature is concerned with salvation. No literature has even been so intensely spiritual as ours. I do not venture to call it religious, but certainly it has the special intensity of concern with the spiritual life which Hegel noted when he spoke of the great modern phenomenon of the secularization of spirituality.

I do not know how other teachers deal with this extravagant personal force of modern literature, but for me it makes difficulty. Nowadays the teaching of literature inclines to a considerable technicality, but when the teacher has said all that can be said about formal matters, about verse-patterns, metrics, prose conventions, irony, tension, etc., he must confront the necessity of bearing personal testimony. He must use whatever authority he may possess to say whether or not a work is true; and if not, why not; and if so, why so. He can do this only at considerable cost to his privacy. How does one say that Lawrence is right in his great rage against the modern emotions, against the modern sense of life and ways of being, unless one speaks from the intimacies of one's own feelings, and one's own sense of life, and one's own wished-for way of being? How, except with the implication of personal judgment, does one say to students that Gide is perfectly accurate in his representation of the awful boredom and slow corruption of respectable life? Then probably one rushes in to say that this doesn't of itself justify homosexuality and the desertion of one's dying wife, certainly not. But then again, having paid one's *devoirs* to morality, how does one rescue from morality Gide's essential point about the supreme rights of the individual person, and without making it merely historical and totally academic?

My first response to the necessity of dealing with matters of this kind was resentment of the personal discomfort it caused me. These are subjects we usually deal with either quite unconsciously or in the privacy of our own conscious minds, and if we now and then disclose our thoughts about them, it is to friends of equal age and especial closeness. Or if we touch upon them publicly, we do so in the relative abstractness and anonymity of print. To stand up in one's own person and to speak of them in one's own voice to an audience which each year grows younger as one grows older—that is not easy, and probably it is not decent.

And then, leaving aside the personal considerations, or taking them merely as an indication of something wrong with the situation, can we not say that, when modern literature is brought into the classroom, the subject being taught is betrayed by the pedagogy of the subject? We have to ask ourselves whether in our day too much does not come within the purview of the academy. More and more, as the universities liberalize themselves, and turn their beneficent imperialistic gaze upon what is called Life Itself, the feeling grows among our educated classes that little can be experienced unless it is validated by some established intellectual discipline, with the result that experi-

ence loses much of its personal immediacy for us and becomes part of an accredited societal activity. This is not
entirely true and I don't want to play the boring academic
game of pretending that it *is* entirely true, that the university mind wilts and withers whatever it touches. I must believe, and I do believe, that the university study of art is
capable of confronting the power of a work of art fully
and courageously. I even believe that it can discover and
disclose power where it has not been felt before. But the
university study of art achieves this and chiefly with works
of art of an older period. Time has the effect of seeming to
quiet the work of art, domesticating it and making it into a
classic, which is often another way of saying that it is an
object of merely habitual regard. University study of the
right sort can reverse this process and restore to the old
work its freshness and force—can, indeed, disclose un-
guessed-at power. But with the works of art of our own
present age, university study tends to accelerate the process
by which the radical and subversive work becomes the classic work, and university study does this in the degree that it
is vivacious and responsive and what is called non-aca-
demic. In one of his poems Yeats mocks the literary scholars, "the bald heads forgetful of their sins," "the old,
learned, respectable bald heads," who edit the poems of the
fierce and passionate young men.

> Lord, what would they say
> Did their Catullus walk this way?

Yeats, of course, is thinking of his own future fate, and no
doubt there is all the radical and comical discrepancy that
he sees between the poet's passions and the scholars'
close-eyed concentration on the text. Yet for my part,
when I think of Catullus, I am moved to praise the tact of
all those old heads, from Heinsius and Bentley to Munro
and Postgate, who worked on Codex G and Codex O and
drew conclusions from them about the lost Codex V—for
doing only this and for not trying to realize and demonstrate the true intensity and the true quality and the true
cultural meaning of Catullus's passion and managing to
bring it somehow into eventual accord with their respectability and baldness. Nowadays we who deal with books in
universities live in fear that the World—which we imagine
to be a vital, palpitating, passionate, reality-loving World

—will think of us as old, respectable, and bald, and we see
to it that in our dealings with Yeats—to take him as the
example—his wild cry of rage and sexuality is heard by
our students and quite thoroughly understood by them as
—what is it that we eventually call it?—a significant expression of our culture. The exasperation of Lawrence and
the subversiveness of Gide, by the time we have dealt with
them boldly and straightforwardly, are notable instances of
the *alienation of modern man as exemplified by the artist.*
"Compare Yeats, Gide, Lawrence, and Eliot in the use
which they make of the theme of sexuality to criticize the
deficiencies of modern culture. Support your statement by
specific references to the work of each author." Time: one
hour. And the distressing thing about our examination
questions is that they are not ridiculous, they make perfectly good sense—such good sense that the young person who
answers them can never again know the force, the terror,
of what has been communicated to him by the works he is
being examined on.

Very likely it was with the thought of saving myself
from the necessity of speaking personally and my students
from the betrayal of the full harsh meaning of a great literature that I first taught my course in as *literary* a way as
possible. A couple of decades ago the discovery was made
that a literary work is a structure of words: this doesn't
seem a surprising thing to have learned except in its polemical tendency, which is to urge us to minimize the
amount of attention we give to the poet's social and
personal will, to what he wants to happen outside the
poem as a result of the poem; it urges us to fix our minds
on what is going on inside the poem. For me this polemical tendency has been of the greatest usefulness, for it has
corrected my inclination to pay attention chiefly to what
the poet *wants.* For two or three years I directed my
efforts toward dealing with the matter of the course chiefly
as structures of words, in a formal way with due attention
paid to the literal difficulty which marked so many of the
works. But it went against the grain. It went against my
personal grain. It went against the grain of the classroom
situation, for formal analysis is best carried on by ques-
tion-and-answer, which needs small groups, and the regis-
tration for the course in modern literature in any college is
sure to be large. And it went against the grain of the authors themselves—structures of words they may indeed

have created, but these structures were not pyramids or triumphal arches, they were manifestly contrived not to be static and commemorative but mobile and aggressive, and one does not describe a quinquireme or a howitzer or a tank without estimating how much *damage* it can do.

Eventually I had to decide that there was only one way to give the course, which was to give it without strategies and without conscious caution. It was not honorable, neither to the students nor to the authors, to conceal or disguise my relation to the literature, my commitment to it, my fear of it, my ambivalence toward it. The literature had to be dealt with in the terms it announced for itself. As for the students, I have never given assent to the modern saw about "teaching students, not subjects"—I have always thought it right to teach subjects, believing that if one gives his first loyalty to the subject, the student is best instructed. So I resolved to give the course with no considerations in mind except my own interests. And since my own interests lead me to see literary situations as cultural situations, and cultural situations as great elaborate fights about moral issues, and moral issues as having something to do with gratuitously chosen images of personal being, and images of personal being as having something to do with literary style, I felt free to begin with what for me was a first concern, the animus of the author, the objects of his will, the things he wants or wants to have happen.

I went so far in my cultural and non-literary method as to decide that I would begin the course with a statement of certain themes or issues that might especially engage our attention. I even went so far in non-literariness as to think that my purposes would best be served if I could contrive a "background" for the works we would read—I wanted to propose a history for the themes or issues that I hoped to discover. I did not intend that this history should be either very extensive or very precise. I wanted merely a *sense* of a history, some general intuition of a past. And because there is as yet no adequate general work of history of the culture of the last two hundred years, I asked myself what books of the age just preceding ours had most influenced our literature, or, since I was far less concerned with showing influence than with discerning a tendency, what older books might seem to fall into a line the direction of which pointed to our own literature and thus might serve as a prolegomenon to the course.

It was virtually inevitable that the first work that should have sprung to mind was Sir James Frazer's *The Golden Bough*, not, of course, the whole of it, but certain chapters, those that deal with Osiris, Attis, and Adonis. Anyone who thinks about modern literature in a systematic way takes for granted the great part played in it by myth, and especially by those examples of myth which tell about gods dying and being reborn—the imagination of death and rebirth, reiterated in the ancient world in innummerable variations that are yet always the same, captivated the literary mind at the very moment when, as all accounts of the modern age agree, the most massive and compelling of all the stories of resurrection had lost much of its hold upon the world.

Perhaps no book has had so decisive an effect upon modern literature as Frazer's. It was beautifully to my purpose that it had first been published ten years before the twentieth century began. Yet forty-three years later, in 1933, Frazer delivered a lecture, very eloquent, in which he bade the world be of good hope in the face of the threat to the human mind that was being offered by the Nazi power. He was still alive in 1941. Yet he had been born in 1854, three years before Matthew Arnold gave the lecture "On the Modern Element in Literature." Here, surely, was history, here was the past I wanted, beautifully connected with our present. Frazer was wholly a man of the nineteenth century, and the more so because the eighteenth century was so congenial to him—the lecture of 1933 in which he predicted the Nazi defeat had as its subject Condorcet's *Progress of the Human Mind;* when he took time from his anthropological studies to deal with literature, he prepared editions of Addison's essays and Cowper's letters. He had the old lost belief in the virtue and power of rationality. He loved and counted on order, decorum, and good sense. This great historian of the primitive imagination was in the dominant intellectual tradition of the West that, since the days of the pre-Socratics, has condemned the ways of thought that we call primitive.

In short, Frazer—at least in his first or conscious intention—was a perfect representative of what Matthew Arnold meant by a modern age. And perhaps nothing could make clearer how the conditions of life and literature have changed in a hundred years than to note the difference between the way in which Arnold defines the modern element in literature and the way in which we must define it.

If we speak of modernity, we should have it in mind that the terms' of the endowment of the Poetry Chair at Oxford required that the Professor lecture on the ancient literatures and that he speak in Latin. This will suggest that Arnold's making the idea of modernity the subject of his inaugural was not without its subversiveness. Arnold met the requirement of dealing with the classic writers— his lecture is about the modern element in the ancient literatures. But he asked for permission to lecture, in English, not because he was unable to speak in Latin but because he wished to be understood by more than scholars. Permission was granted by the University, with what reluctance I do not know, or with what sad sense that another bastion of the past had fallen, and in an English which was perhaps doctoral but certainly lucid, Arnold undertook to define what he called the modern element.

Arnold used the word modern in a wholly honorific sense. So much so, indeed, that he seems to dismiss all temporal idea from the word and makes it signify certain timeless intellectual and civil virtues. A society, he said, is a modern society when it maintains a condition of repose, confidence, free activity of the mind, and the tolerance of divergent views. A society is modern when it affords sufficient material well-being for the conveniences of life and the development of taste. And, finally, a society is modern when its members are intellectually mature, by which Arnold means that they are willing to judge by reason, to observe facts in a critical spirit, and to search for the law of things. By this definition Periclean Athens is for Arnold a modern age, Elizabethan England is not; Thucydides is a modern historian, Sir Walter Raleigh is not.

I shall not go into further details of Arnold's definition or description of the modern.* I have said enough, I think, to suggest what Arnold was up to, what he wanted to see realized as the desideratum of his own society, what ideal

---

* I leave out of my summary account the two supreme virtues that Arnold ascribes to the most successful examples of a "modern" literature. One is the power of effecting an "intellectual deliverance," by which Arnold means leading men to comprehend the "vast multitude of facts" which make up "a copious and complex present, and behind it a copious and complex past." The other is "adequacy," the ability to represent the complex high human development of a modern age "in its completest and most harmonious" aspect, doing so with "the charm of that noble serenity which always accompanies true insight."

he wanted the works of intellect and imagination of his
own time to advance. And at what a distance his ideal of
the modern puts him from our present sense of modernity,
from our modern literature! To anyone conditioned by our
modern literature Arnold's ideal of order, convenience, decorum, and rationality might well seem to reduce itself to
the small advantages and excessive limitations of the middle-class life of a few prosperous nations of the nineteenth
century. Arnold's historic sense presented to his mind the
long, bitter, bloody past of Europe, and he seized passionately upon the hope of true civilization at last achieved.
But the historic sense of our literature has in mind a long
excess of civilization to which it ascribes the bitterness and
blood of both the past and of the present and of which it
conceives the peaceful aspects to be mainly contemptible
—its order achieved at the cost of extravagant personal
repression, either that of coercion or that of acquiescence;
its repose otiose; its tolerance either flaccid or capricious;
its material comfort corrupt and corrupting; its taste a
manifestation either of timidity or of pride; its rationality
attained only at the price of energy and passion.

For the understanding of this radical change of opinion
nothing is more illuminating than to be aware of the dou-
bleness of mind of the author of *The Golden Bough*. I
have said that Frazer in his conscious mind and in his first
intention exemplifies all that Arnold means by the modern.
He often speaks quite harshly of the irrationality and the
orgiastic excesses of the primitive religions he describes,
and even Christianity comes under his criticism both because it stands in the way of rational thought and because
it can draw men away from intelligent participation in the
life of society. But Frazer had more than one intention,
and he had an unconscious as well as a conscious mind. If
he deplores the primitive imagination, he does not fail to
show it as also wonderful and beautiful. It is the rare
reader of *The Golden Bough* who finds the ancient beliefs
and rituals wholly alien to him. It is to be expected that
Frazer's adduction of the many pagan analogues to the
Christian mythos will be thought by Christian readers to
have an adverse effect on faith, it was undoubtedly Frazer's purpose that it should, yet many readers will feel that
Frazer makes all faith and ritual indigenous to humanity,
virtually biological; they feel, as DeQuincey put it, that
not to be at least a *little* superstitious is to lack generosity

of mind. Scientific though his purpose was, Frazer had the effect of validating and even of seeming to propose to modern times those old modes of experiencing the world which, beginning with the Romanticists, modern men have sought to revive in order to escape from positivism and common sense.

The direction of the imagination upon great and mysterious objects of worship is not the only means men use to liberate themselves from the bondage of quotidian fact, and although Frazer can scarcely be held accountable for the ever-growing modern attraction to the extreme mental states, to rapture, ecstasy, and transcendence, which are achieved by drugs, trance, music and dance, orgy, and derangement of personality, yet he did provide a bridge to the understanding and acceptance of these states, he proposed to us the idea that the desire for them and the use of them for heuristic purposes is a common and acceptable manifestation of human nature.

This one element of Frazer's masterpiece could scarcely fail to suggest the next of my prolegomenal works. It is worth remarking that its author is in his own way as great a classical scholar as Frazer himself—Nietzsche was the Professor of Classical Philology at the University of Basel when, at the age of 27, he published his essay, *The Birth of Tragedy*. After the appearance of this stunningly brilliant account of Greek civilization, of which Socrates is not the hero but the villain, what can possibly be left to us of that rational and ordered Greece, that modern, that eighteenth-century, Athens that Arnold so entirely relied on as the standard for judging all civilizations? Professor Kaufmann is right when he warns us against supposing that Nietzsche exalts Dionysus over Apollo and tells us that Nietzsche "emphasizes the Dionysiac only because he feels that the Apollonian genius of the Greeks cannot be fully understood apart from it." But no one reading Nietzsche's essay for the first time is likely to heed this warning. What will reach him before due caution intervenes, before he becomes aware of the portentous dialectic between Dionysus and Apollo, is the excitement of his sudden liberation from Aristotle, the joy that he takes in his willingness to believe the author's statement that, "art rather than ethics constitutes the essential metaphysical activity of man," that tragedy has its source in the Dionysiac rapture, "whose closest analogy is furnished by physical intoxication," and that this rapture, in which "the individual forgets himself completely," was in itself no metaphysical state but an orgiastic display of lust and cruelty, "of sexual promiscuity overriding every form of tribal law." This sadistic and masochistic frenzy, Nietzsche is at pains to insist, needs the taming hand of Apollo before it can become tragedy, but it is the primal stuff of the great art, and to the modern experience of tragedy this explanation of it seems far more pertinent than Aristotle's, with its eagerness to forget its origin in its achievement of a noble *apatheia*.

Of supreme importance in itself, Nietzsche's essay had for me the added pedagogic advantage of allowing me to establish an historical line back to William Blake. Nothing is more characteristic of modern literature than its discovery and canonization of the primal, non-ethical energies, and the historical point could be made the better by remarking the correspondence of thought of two men of different nations and separated from each other by a good many decades, for Nietzsche's Dionysus and Blake's Hell are much the same thing.

Whether or not Joseph Conrad read either Blake or Nietzsche I do not know, but his *Heart of Darkness* follows in their line. This very great work has never lacked for the admiration it deserves, and it has been given a kind of canonical place in the legend of modern literature by Eliot's having it so clearly in mind when he wrote *The Waste Land* and his having taken from it the epigraph to "The Hollow Men." But no one, to my knowledge, has ever confronted in an explicit way its strange and terrible message of ambivalence toward the life of civilization. Consider that its protagonist Kurtz is a progressive and a liberal and that he is the highly respected representative of a society which undertakes to represent itself as benign, although in fact it is vicious. Consider too that he is a practitioner of several arts, a painter, a writer, a musician, and into the bargain a political orator. He is at once the most idealistic and the most practically successful of all the agents of the Belgian exploitation of the Congo. Everybody knows what truth about him Marlow discovers—that Kurtz's success is the result of a terrible ascendancy he has gained over the natives of his distant station, an ascendancy which is derived from his presumed magical or divine powers, that he has exercised his rule with the extreme of

cruelty, that he has given himself to unnamable acts of
lust. This is the world of the darker pages of *The Golden
Bough*. It is one of the great points of Conrad's story that
Marlow speaks of the primitive life of the jungle not as
being noble or charming or even free but as being base
and sordid—and for *that* reason compelling: he himself
feels quite overtly its dreadful attraction. It is to this devil-
ish baseness that Kurtz has yielded himself, and yet Marlow, although he does indeed treat him with hostile irony,
does not find it possible to suppose that Kurtz is anything
but a hero of the spirit. For me it is still ambiguous whether Kurtz's famous deathbed cry, "The horror! The horror!" refers to the approach of death or to his experience
of savage life. Whichever it is, to Marlow the fact that
Kurtz could utter this cry at the point of death, while
Marlow himself, when death threatens him, can know it
only as a weary greyness, marks the difference between the
ordinary man and a hero of the spirit. Is this not the essence of the modern belief about the nature of the artist,
the man who goes down into that hell which is the historical beginning of the human soul, a beginning not outgrown but established in humanity as we know it now,
preferring the reality of this hell to the bland lies of the
civilization that has overlaid it?

This idea is proposed again in the somewhat less powerful but still very moving work with which I followed
Heart of Darkness, Thomas Mann's *Death in Venice*. I
wanted this story not so much for its account of an extrav-
agantly Apollonian personality surrendering to forces that,
in his Apollonian character, he thought shameful—although this was certainly to my purpose—but rather for
Aschenbach's fevered dreams of the erotic past, and in
particular that dream of the goat-orgy which Mann, being
the kind of writer he is, having the kind of relation to
Nietzsche he had, might well have written to serve as an
illustration of what *The Birth of Tragedy* means by religious frenzy, the more so, of course, because Mann
chooses that particular orgiastic ritual, the killing and eating of the goat, from which tragedy is traditionally said to
have been derived. A notable element of this story in
which the birth of tragedy plays an important part is that
the degradation and downfall of the protagonist is not represented as tragic in the usual sense of the word—that is,
it is not represented as a great deplorable event. It is a

commonplace of modern literary thought that the tragic mode is not available even to the gravest and noblest of our writers. I am not sure that this is the deprivation that some people think it to be and a mark of our spiritual inferiority. But if we ask why it has come about, one reason may be that we have learned to think our way back through tragedy to the primal stuff out of which tragedy arose. If we consider the primitive forbidden ways of conduct which traditionally in tragedy lead to punishment by death, we think of them as being the path to reality and truth, to an ultimate self-realization. We have always wondered if tragedy itself may not have been saying just this in a deeply hidden way, drawing us to think of the hero's sin and death as somehow conferring justification, even salvation of a sort—no doubt this is what Nietzsche had in mind when he said that "tragedy denies ethics." What tragedy once seemed to hint, our literature now is willing to say quite explicitly. If Mann's Aschenbach dies at the height of his intellectual and artistic powers, at the behest of a passion that his ethical reason condemns, we do not take this to be a defeat, rather a kind of terrible rebirth: at his latter end the artist knows a reality that he had until now refused to admit to consciousness.

This being so, how fortunate that the Anchor edition of *The Birth of Tragedy* should include Nietzsche's *The Genealogy of Morals*. For here, among many other ideas most pertinent to the *mystique* of modern literature, was the view of society which is consonant with the belief that art and not ethics constitutes the essential metaphysical activity of man and with the validation and ratification of the primitive energies. Nietzsche's theory of the social order dismisses all ethical impulse from its origins—the basis of society is to be found in the rationalization of cruelty: as simple as that. Nietzsche has no ultimate Utopian intention in saying this, no hope of revising the essence of the social order, although he does believe that its pain can be mitigated. He represents cruelty as a social necessity, for only by its exercise could men ever have been induced to develop a continuity of will: nothing else than cruelty could have created in mankind that memory of intention which makes society possible. The method of cynicism which Nietzsche pursued—let us be clear that it is a method and not an attitude—goes so far as to describe punishment in terms of the pleasure derived from the exercise of cruelty: "Compensation," he says, "consists in a legal warrant entitling one man to exercise his cruelty on another." There follows that most remarkable passage in which Nietzsche describes the process whereby the individual turns the cruelty of punishment against himself and creates the bad conscience and the consciousness of guilt which manifests itself as a pervasive anxiety. Nietzsche's complexity of mind is beyond all comparison, for in this book which is dedicated to the liberation of the conscience, Nietzsche makes his defense of the bad conscience as a decisive force in the interests of culture. It is much the same line of argument that he takes when, having attacked the Jewish morality and the priestly existence in the name of the health of the spirit, he reminds us that only by his sickness does man become interesting.

From *The Genealogy of Morals* to Freud's *Civilization and Its Discontents* is but a step, and some might think that, for pedagogic purposes, the step is so small as to make the second book supererogatory. But although Freud's view of society and culture has indeed a very close affinity to Nietzsche's, Freud does add certain considerations which are essential to our sense of the modern disposition.

For one thing, he puts to us the question of whether or not we want to *accept* civilization. It is not the first time that the paradox of civilization has been present to the mind of civilized people, the sense that civilization makes men behave worse and suffer more than does some less developed state of human existence. But hitherto all such ideas were formulated in a moralizing way—civilization was represented as being "corrupt," a divagation from a state of innocence. Freud had no illusions about a primitive innocence, he conceived no practicable alternative to civilization. In consequence there was a unique force to the question he asked: whether we wished to accept civilization, with all its contradictions, with all its pains—pains, for "discontents" does not accurately describe what Freud has in mind. He had his own answer to the question—his tragic, or stoic, sense of life dictated it: we do well to accept it, although we also do well to cast a cold eye on the fate that makes it our better part to accept it. Like Nietzsche, Freud thought that life was justified by our heroic response to its challenge.

But the question Freud posed has not been set aside or

closed up by the answer that he himself gave to it. His answer, like Nietzsche's, is essentially in the line of traditional humanism—we can see this in the sternness with which he charges women not to interfere with men in the discharge of their cultural duty, not to claim men for love and the family to the detriment of their free activity in the world. But just here lies the matter of Freud's question that the world more and more believes Freud himself did not answer. The pain that civilization inflicts is that of the instinctual renunciation that civilization demands, and it would seem that fewer and fewer people wish to say with Freud that the loss of instinctual gratification, emotional freedom, or love, are compensated for either by the security of civilized life or the stern pleasures of the moral masculine character. The possibility of options different from the one that Freud made is proposed theoretically by two recent books, Herbert Marcuse's *Eros and Civilization* and Norman O. Brown's *Life Against Death.*

With Freud's essay I brought to a close my list of prolegomenal books for the first term of the course. I shall not do much more than mention the books with which I introduced the second term, but I should like to do at least that. I began with *Rameau's Nephew,* thinking that the peculiar moral authority which Diderot assigns to the envious, untalented unregenerate protagonist was peculiarly relevant to the line taken by the ethical explorations of modern literature. Nothing is more characteristic of the literature of our time than the replacement of the hero by what has come to be called the anti-hero, in whose indifference to or hatred of ethical nobility there is presumed to lie a special authenticity. Diderot is quite overt about this—he himself in his public character is the deuteroganist, the "honest consciousness," as Hegel calls him, and he takes delight in the discomfiture of the decent, dull person he is by the Nephew's nihilistic mind.

It seemed to me too that there was particular usefulness in the circumstance that this anti-hero should avow so openly his *envy,* which de Tocqueville has called the ruling emotion of democracy, and that, although he envied anyone at all who had access to the creature-comforts and the social status which he lacked, what chiefly animated him was envy of men of genius. Ours is the first cultural epoch in which many men aspire to high achievement in the arts and, in their frustration, form a dispossessed class which cuts across the conventional class lines, making a proletariat of the spirit.

Although *Rameau's Nephew* was not published until fairly late in the century, it was known in manuscript by Goethe and Hegel; it suited the temper and won the admiration of Marx and Freud for reasons that are obvious. And there is ground for supposing that it was known to Dostoevsky, whose *Notes from Underground* is a restatement of the essential idea of Diderot's dialogue in terms both more extreme and less genial. The Nephew is still on the defensive—he is naughtily telling secrets about the nature of man and society. But Dostoevsky's underground man shouts aloud his envy and hatred and carries the ark of his self-hatred and alienation into a remorseless battle with what he calls "the good and the beautiful," mounting an attack upon every belief not merely of bourgeois society but of the whole humanist tradition. The inclusion of *Notes from Underground* among my prolegomenal books constituted something of a pedagogic risk, for if I wished to emphasize the subversive tendency of modern literature, here was a work which made all subsequent subversion seem like affirmation, so radical and so brilliant was its negation of our pieties and assumptions.

I hesitated in compunction before following *Notes from Underground* with Tolstoy's *Deah of Ivan Ilytch*, which so ruthlessly and with such dreadful force destroys the citadel of the commonplace life in which we all believe we can take refuge from ourselves and our fate. But I did assign it and then two of Pirandello's plays which, in the atmosphere of the sordidness of the commonplace life, undermine all the certitudes of the commonplace, commonsense mind.

From time to time I have raised with myself the question of whether my choice of these prolegomenal works was not extravagant, quite excessively tendentious. I have never been able to believe that it is. And if these works do indeed serve to indicate in an accurate way the nature of modern literature, a teacher might find it worth asking how his students respond to the strong dose.

One response I have already described—the readiness of the students to engage in the process that we might call the socialization of the anti-social, or the acculturation of the anti-cultural, or the legitimization of the subversive. When the term-essays come in, it is plain to me that almost none of the students have been taken aback by what they have read: they have wholly contained the attack. The chief exceptions are the few who simply do not comprehend, although they may be awed by, the categories of our discourse. In their papers, like poor hunted creatures in a Kafka story, they take refuge first in misunderstood large phrases, then in bad grammar, then in general incoherence. After my pedagogical exasperation has run its course, I find that I am sometimes moved to give them a queer respect, as if they had stood up and said what in fact they don't have the wit to stand up and say: "Why do you harry us? Leave us alone. We are not Modern Man. We are the Old People. Ours is the Old Faith. We serve the little Old Gods, the gods of the copybook maxims, the small, dark, somewhat powerful deities of lawyers, doctors, engineers, accountants. With them is neither sensibility nor *angst*. With them is no disgust—it is they, indeed, who make ready the way for 'the good and the beautiful' about which low-minded doubts have been raised in this course, that 'good and beautiful' which we do not possess and don't want to possess but which we know justifies our lives. Leave us alone and let us worship our gods in the way they approve, in peace and unawareness." Crass, but —to use that interesting modern word which we have learned from the curators of museums—authentic. The rest, the minds that give me the A papers and the B papers and even the C+ papers, move through the terrors and mysteries of modern literature like so many Parsifals, asking no questions at the behest of wonder and fear. Or like so many seminarists who have been systematically instructed in the constitution of Hell and the ways to damnation. Or like so many *readers,* entertained by moral horror stories. I asked them to look into the Abyss, and, both dutifully and gladly, they have looked into the Abyss, and the Abyss has greeted them with the grave courtesy of all objects of serious study, saying: "Interesting, am I not? And *exciting,* if you consider how deep I am and what dread beasts lie at my bottom. Have it well in mind that a knowledge of me contributes materially to your being whole, or well-rounded, men."

In my distress over the outrage I have conspired to perpetrate upon a great literature, I wonder if perhaps I have not been reading these papers too literally. After all, a term-essay is not a diary of the soul, it is not an occa-

sion for telling the truth. What my students might reveal
of their true feelings to a younger teacher they will not reveal to me; they will give me what they conceive to be the
proper response to the official version of terror I have
given them. I bring to mind their faces, which are not necessarily the faces of the authors of these unperturbed papers, nor are they, not yet, the faces of fathers of families,
or of theater-goers, or of buyers of modern paintings: not
yet. I must think it possible that in ways and to a degree
which they keep secret they have responded directly and
personally to what they have read.

And if they have? And if they have, am I the more content?

What form would I want their response to take? It is a
teacher's question that I am asking, not a critic's. We have
decided in recent years to think of the critic and the teacher of literature as one and the same, and no doubt it is
both possible and useful to do so. But there are some
points at which the functions of the two do not coincide,
or can be made to coincide only with great difficulty. Of
criticism we have been told, by Arnold, that "it must be
apt to study and praise elements that for fulness of spiritual perfection are wanted, even though they belong to a
power which in the practical sphere may be maleficent."
But teaching, or at least undergraduate teaching, is not
given the same licensed mandate—cannot be given it because the teacher's audience, which stands before his very
eyes, as the critic's audience does not, asks questions about
"the practical sphere," as the critic's audience does not.
For instance, on the very day that I write this, when I had
said to my class all I could think of to say about *The
Magic Mountain* and invited questions and comments, one
student asked, "How would you generalize the idea of the
educative value of illness, so that it would be applicable
not only to a particular individual, Hans Castorp, but to
young people at large?" It makes us smile, but it was
asked in all seriousness, and it is serious in its substance,
and it had to be answered seriously, in part by the reflection that this idea, like so many ideas encountered in the
books of the course had to be thought of as having reference only to the private life; that it touched the public life
only in some indirect or tangential way; that it really
ought to be encountered in solitude, even in secrecy, since
to talk about it in public and in our academic setting was

to seem to propose for it a public practicality and thus to distort its meaning. To this another student replied; he said that, despite the public ritual of the classroom, each student inevitably experienced the books in privacy and found their meaning in reference to his own life. True enough, but the teacher sees the several privacies coming together to make a group, and they propose—no doubt the more because they come together every Monday, Wednesday, and Friday at a particular hour—the idea of a community, that is to say, "the practical sphere."

This being so, the teacher cannot escape the awareness of certain circumstances which the critic, who writes for an ideal, uncircumstanced reader, has no need to take into account. The teacher considers, for example, the social situation of his students—they are not of patrician origin, they do not come from homes in which stubbornness, pride, and conscious habit prevail, nor are they born into a culture marked by these traits, a culture in which other interesting and valuable things compete with and resist ideas; they come, mostly, from "good homes" in which authority and valuation are weak or at least not very salient and bold, so that ideas have for them, at their present stage of development, a peculiar power and preciousness. And in this connection the teacher will have in mind the peculiar prestige that our culture, in its upper reaches, gives to art, and to the ideas that art proposes—the agreement, ever growing in assertiveness, that art yields more truth than any other intellectual activity. In this culture what a shock it is to encounter Santayana's acerb skepticism about art, or Keats's remark, which the critics and scholars never take notice of, presumably because they suppose it to be an aberration, "This is the very thing in which consists poetry; and if so it is not so fine a thing as philosophy—For the same reason that an eagle is not so fine a thing as a truth." For many students no ideas that they will encounter in any college discipline will equal in force and sanction the ideas conveyed to them by modern literature.

The author of *The Magic Mountain* once said that all his work could be understood as an effort to free himself from the middle class, and this, of course, will serve to describe the chief intention of all modern literature. And the means of freedom which Mann prescribes (the characteristic irony notwithstanding) is the means of freedom which in effect all of modern literature prescribes. It is, in the words of Clavdia Chauchat, *"se perdre et même . . . se laisser dépérir,"* and thus to name the means is to make plain that the end is not merely freedom from the middle class but freedom from society itself. I venture to say that the idea of losing oneself up to the point of self-destruction, of surrendering oneself to experience without regard to self-interest or conventional morality, of escaping wholly from the societal bonds, is an "element" somewhere in the mind of every modern person who dares to think of what Arnold in his unaffected Victorian way called "the fulness of spiritual perfection." But the teacher who undertakes to present modern literature to his students may not allow that idea to remain in the *somewhere* of his mind; he must take it from the place where it exists habitual and unrealized and put it in the conscious forefront of his thought. And if he is committed to an admiration of modern literature, he must also be committed to this chief idea of modern literature. I press the logic of the situation not in order to question the legitimacy of the commitment, or even the propriety of expressing the commitment in the college classroom (although it does seem odd!) but to confront those of us who do teach modern literature with the striking actuality of our enterprise.

The Dehumanization of Art

BY JOSÉ ORTEGA Y GASSET

1. *Artistic Art*

If the new art is not accessible to every man this implies that its impulses are not of a generically human kind. It is an art not for men in general but for a special class of men who may not be better but who evidently are different.

One point must be clarified before we go on. What is it the majority of people call aesthetic pleasure? What happens in their minds when they "like" a work of art; for instance, a theatrical performance? The answer is easy. A man likes a play when he has become interested in the human destinies presented to him, when the love and hatred, the joys and sorrows of the personages so move his heart that he participates in it all as though it were happening in real life. And he calls a work "good" if it succeeds in creating the illusion necessary to make the imaginary personages appear like living persons. In poetry he seeks the passion and pain of the man behind the poet. Paintings attract him if he finds on them figures of men or women whom it would be interesting to meet. A landscape is pronounced "pretty" if the country it represents deserves for its loveliness or its grandeur to be visited on a trip.

It thus appears that to the majority of people aesthetic pleasure means a state of mind which is essentially indistinguishable from their ordinary behavior. It differs merely in accidental qualities, being perhaps less utilitarian, more intense, and free from painful consequences. But the object towards which their attention and, consequently, all their other mental activities are directed is the same as in daily life: people and passions. By art they understand a means through which they are brought in contact with interesting human affairs. Artistic forms proper—figments, fantasy— are tolerated only if they do not interfere with the perception of human forms and fates. As soon as purely aesthetic elements predominate and the story of John and Mary grows elusive, most people feel out of their depth and are at a loss what to make of the scene, the book, or the painting. As they have never practiced any other attitude but the practical one in which a man's feelings are aroused and he is emotionally involved, a work that does not invite sentimental intervention leaves them without a cue.

Now, this is a point which has to be made perfectly clear. Not only is grieving and rejoicing at such human destinies as a work of art presents or narrates a very different thing from true artistic pleasure, but preoccupation with the human content of the work is in principle incompatible with aesthetic enjoyment proper.

Good

We have here a very simple optical problem. To see a thing we must adjust our visual apparatus in a certain way. If the adjustment is inadequate the thing is seen indistinctly or not at all. Take a garden seen through a window. Looking at the garden we adjust our eyes in such a way that the ray of vision travels through the pane without delay and rests on the shrubs and flowers. Since we are focusing on the garden and our ray of vision is directed toward it, we do not see the window but look clear through it. The purer the glass, the less we see it. But we can also deliberately disregard the garden and, withdrawing the ray of vision, detain it at the window. We then lose sight of the garden; what we still behold of it is a confused mass of color which appears pasted to the pane. Hence to see the garden and to see the windowpane are two incompatible operations which exclude one another because they require different adjustments.

Similarly a work of art vanishes from sight for a beholder who seeks in it nothing but the moving fate of John and Mary or Tristan and Isolde and adjusts his vision to this. Tristan's sorrows are sorrows and can evoke compassion only in so far as they are taken as real. But an object of art is artistic only in so far as it is not real. In order to enjoy Titian's portrait of Charles the Fifth on horseback we must forget that this is Charles the Fifth in person and see instead a portrait—that is, an image, a fiction. The portrayed person and his portrait are two entirely different things; we are interested in either one or the other. In the first case we "live" with Charles the Fifth, in the second we look at an object of art.

But not many people are capable of adjusting their perceptive apparatus to the pane and the transparency that is the work of art. Instead they look right through it and revel in the human reality with which the work deals. When they are invited to let go of this prey and to direct their attention to the work of art itself they will say that they cannot see such a thing, which indeed they cannot, because it is all artistic transparency and without substance.

During the nineteenth century artists proceeded in all too impure a fashion. They reduced the strictly aesthetic elements to a minimum and let the work consist almost entirely in a fiction of human realities. In this sense all normal art of the last century must be called realistic. Beethoven and Wagner were realistic, and so was Chateaubriand as well as Zola. Seen from the vantage-point of our day Romanticism and Naturalism draw closer together and reveal their common realistic root.

Works of this kind are only partially works of art, or artistic objects. Their enjoyment does not depend upon our power to focus on transparencies and images, a power characteristic of the artistic sensibility; all they require is human sensibility and willingness to sympathize with our neighbor's joys and worries. No wonder that nineteenth century art has been so popular; it is made for the masses inasmuch as it is not art but an extract from life. Let us remember that in epochs with two different types of art, one for minorities and one for the majority, the latter has always been realistic.[1]

I will not now discuss whether pure art is possible. Perhaps it is not; but as the reasons that make me inclined to think so are somewhat long and difficult the subject better be dropped. Besides, it is not of major importance for the matter in hand. Even though pure art may be impossible there doubtless can prevail a tendency toward a purification of art. Such a tendency would effect a progressive elimination of the human, all too human, elements pre-

[1] For instance in the Middle Ages. In accordance with the division of society in the two strata of noblemen and commoners, there existed an aristocratic art which was "conventional" and "idealistic," and a popular art which was realistic and satirical.

dominant in romantic and naturalistic production. And in
this process a point can be reached in which the human
content has grown so thin that it is negligible. We then
have an art which can be comprehended only by people
possessed of the peculiar gift of artistic sensibility—an art
for artists and not for the masses, for "quality" and not
for hoi polloi.

That is why modern art divides the public into two classes, those who understand it and those who do not understand it—that is to say, those who are artists and those
who are not. The new art is an artistic art.

I do not propose to extol the new way in art or to condemn the old. My purpose is to characterize them as the
zoologist characterizes two contrasting species. The new
art is a world-wide fact. For about twenty years now the
most alert young people of two successive generations—in
Berlin, Paris, London, New York, Rome, Madrid—have
found themselves faced with the undeniable fact that they
have no use for traditional art; moreover, that they detest
it. With these young people one can do one of two things:
shoot them, or try to understand them. As soon as one decides in favor of the latter it appears that they are endowed with a perfectly clear, coherent, and rational sense
of art. Far from being a whim, their way of feeling represents the inevitable and fruitful result of all previous artistic achievement. Whimsical, arbitrary, and consequently
unprofitable it would be to set oneself against the new
style and obstinately remain shut up in old forms that are
exhausted and the worse for wear. In art, as in morals,
what ought to be done does not depend on our personal
judgment; we have to accept the imperative imposed by
the time. Obedience to the order of the day is the most
hopeful choice open to the individual. Even so he may
achieve nothing; but he is much more likely to fail if he
insists on composing another Wagnerian opera, another
naturalistic novel.

In art repetition is nothing. Each historical style can en-
gender a certain number of different forms within a generic type. But there always comes a day when the magnificent mine is worked out. Such, for instance, has been the
fate of the romantico-naturalistic novel and theater. It is a
naïve error to believe that the present infecundity of these
two genres is due to lack of talent. What happens is that
the possible combinations within these literary forms are

exhausted. It must be deemed fortunate that this situation coincides with the emergence of a new artistic sensibility capable of detecting other untouched veins.

When we analyze the new style we find that it contains certain closely connected tendencies. It tends (1) to dehumanize art, (2) to avoid living forms, (3) to see to it that the work of art is nothing but a work of art, (4) to consider art as play and nothing else, (5) to be essentially ironical, (6) to beware of sham and hence to aspire to scrupulous realization, (7) to regard art as a thing of no transcending consequence.

In the following I shall say a few words about each of these features of modern art. . . .

2. *First Installment of the Dehumanization of Art*

With amazing swiftness modern art has split up into a multitude of divergent differences. Nothing is easier than to stress the differences. But such an emphasis on the distinguishing and specific features would be pointless without a previous account of the common fund that in a varying and sometimes contradictory manner asserts itself throughout modern art. Did not Aristotle already observe that things differ in what they have in common? Because all bodies are colored we notice that they are differently colored. Species are nothing if not modifications of a genus, and we cannot understand them unless we realize that they draw, in their several ways, upon a common patrimony.

I am little interested in special directions of modern art and, but for a few exceptions, even less in special works. Nor do I, for that matter, expect anybody to be particularly interested in my valuation of the new artistic produce. Writers who have nothing to convey but their praise or dispraise of works of art had better abstain from writing. They are unfit for this arduous task.

The important thing is that there unquestionably exists in the world a new artistic sensibility.[2] Over against the multiplicity of special directions and individual works, the new sensibility represents the generic fact and the source, as it were, from which the former spring. This sensibility

---

[2] This new sensibility is a gift not only of the artist proper but also of his audience. When I said above that the new art is an art for artists I understood by "artists" not only those who produce this art but also those who are capable of perceiving purely artistic values.

it is worth while to define. And when we seek to ascertain the most general and most characteristic feature of modern artistic production we come upon the tendency to dehumanize art. After what we have said above, this formula now acquires a tolerably precise meaning.

Let us compare a painting in the new style with one of, say, 1860. The simplest procedure will be to begin by setting against one another the objects they represent: a man perhaps, a house, or a mountain. It then appears that the artist of 1860 wanted nothing so much as to give to the objects in his picture the same looks and airs they possess outside it when they occur as parts of the "lived" or "human" reality. Apart from this he may have been animated by other more intricate aesthetic ambitions, but what interests us is that his first concern was with securing this likeness. Man, house, mountain are at once recognized, they are our good old friends; whereas on a modern painting we are at a loss to recognize them. It might be supposed that the modern painter has failed to achieve resemblance. But then some pictures of the 1860's are "poorly" painted, too, and the objects in them differ considerably from the corresponding objects outside them. And yet, whatever the differences, the very blunders of the traditional artist point toward the "human" object; they are downfalls on the way toward it and somehow equivalent to the orienting words "This is a cock" with which Cervantes lets the painter Orbanejo enlighten his public. In modern paintings the opposite happens. It is not that the painter is bungling and fails to render the natural (natural = human) thing because he deviates from it, but that these deviations point in a direction opposite to that which would lead to reality.

Far from going more or less clumsily toward reality, the artist is seen going against it. He is brazenly set on deforming reality, shattering its human aspect, dehumanizing it. With the things represented on traditional paintings we could have imaginary intercourse. Many a young Englishman has fallen in love with Gioconda. With the objects of modern pictures no intercourse is possible. By divesting them of their aspect of "lived" reality the artist has blown up the bridges and burned the ships that could have taken us back to our daily world. He leaves us locked up in an abstruse universe, surrounded by objects with which human dealings are inconceivable, and thus compels us to improvise other forms of intercourse completely distinct from our ordinary ways with things. We must invent unheard-of-gestures to fit those singular figures. This new way of life which presupposes the annulment of spontaneous life is precisely what we call understanding and enjoyment of art. Not that this life lacks sentiments and passions, but those sentiments and passions evidently belong to a flora other than that which covers the hills and dales of primary and human life. What those ultra-objects[3] evoke in our inner artist are secondary passions, specifically aesthetic sentiments.

It may be said that, to achieve this result, it would be simpler to dismiss human forms—man, house, mountain—altogether and to construct entirely original figures. But, in the first place, this is not feasible.[4] Even in the most abstract ornamental line a stubborn reminiscence lurks of certain "natural" forms. Secondly—and this is the crucial point—the art of which we speak is inhuman not only because it contains no things human, but also because it is an explicit act of dehumanization. In his escape from the human world the young artist cares less for the *"terminus ad quem,"* the startling fauna at which he arrives, than for the *"terminus a quo,"* the human aspect which he destroys. The question is not to paint something altogether different from a man, a house, a mountain, but to paint a man who resembles a man as little as possible; a house that preserves of a house exactly what is needed to reveal the metamorphosis; a cone miraculously emerging—as the snake from his slough—from what used to be a mountain. For the modern artist, aesthetic pleasure derives from such a triumph over human matter. That is why he has to drive home the victory by presenting in each case the strangled victim.

It may be thought a simple affair to fight shy of reality, but it is by no means easy. There is no difficulty in painting or saying things which make no sense whatever, which are unintelligible and therefore nothing. One only needs to

[3] "Ultraism" is one of the most appropriate names that have been coined to denote the new sensibility.

[4] An attempt has been made in this extreme sense—in certain works by Picasso—but it has failed signally.

assemble unconnected words or to draw random lines. [5]
But to construct something that is not a copy of "nature"
and yet possesses substance of its own is a feat which presupposes nothing less than genius.

"Reality" constantly waylays the artist to prevent his
flight. Much cunning is needed to effect the sublime escape. A reversed Odysseus, he must free himself from his
daily Penelope and sail through reefs and rocks to Circe's
Faery. When, for a moment, he succeeds in escaping the
perpetual ambush, let us not grudge him a gesture of arrogant triumph, a St. George gesture with the dragon pros-
trate at his feet. . . .

3. Inversion

In establishing itself in its own right, the metaphor assumes a more or less leading part in the poetical pursuit.
This implies that the aesthetic intention has veered round
and now points in the opposite direction. Before, reality
was overlaid with metaphors by way of ornament; now the
tendency is to eliminate the extrapoetical, or real, prop
and to "realize" the metaphor, to make it the res poetica.
This inversion of the aesthetic process is not restricted to
the use made of metaphors. It obtains in all artistic means
and orders, to the point of determining—in the form of a
tendency[6]—the physiognomy of all contemporary art.

The relation between our mind and things consists in
that we think the things, that we form ideas about them.
We possess of reality, strictly speaking, nothing but the
ideas we have succeeded in forming about it. These ideas
are like a belvedere from which we behold the world.
Each new idea, as Goethe put it, is like a newly developed
organ. By means of ideas we see the world, but in a natural attitude of the mind we do not see the ideas—the
same as the eye in seeing does not see itself. In other
words, thinking is the endeavor to capture reality by

---

5 This was done by the Dadaistic hoax. It is interesting to note again
(see the above footnote) that the very vagaries and abortive experiments of the new art derive with a certain cogency from its organic
principle, thereby giving ample proof that modern art is a unified
and meaningful movement.

6 It would be tedious to warn at the foot of each page that each of
the features here pointed out as essential to modern art must be
understood as existing in the form of a predominant propensity,
not of an absolute property.

means of ideas; the spontaneous movement of the mind
goes from concepts to the world.
But an absolute distance always separates the idea from
the thing. The real thing always overflows the concept that
is supposed to hold it. An object is more and other than
what is implied in the idea of it. The idea remains a bare
pattern, a sort of scaffold with which we try to get at reality. Yet a tendency resident in human nature prompts us to
assume that reality is what we think of it and thus to con-
found reality and idea by taking in good faith the latter
for the thing itself. Our yearning for reality leads us to an
ingenuous idealization of reality. Such is the innate predisposition of man.

If we now invert the natural direction of this process; if,
turning our back on alleged reality, we take the ideas for
what they are—mere subjective patterns—and make them
live as such, lean and angular, but pure and transparent; in
short, if we deliberately propose to "realize" our ideas—
then we have dehumanized and, as it were, derealized
them. For ideas are really unreal. To regard them as reality is an idealization, a candid falsification. On the other
hand, making them live in their very unreality is—let us
express it this way—realizing the unreal as such. In this
way we do not move from the mind to the world. On the
contrary, we give three-dimensional being to mere patterns, we objectify the subjective, we "worldify" the immanent.

A traditional painter painting a portrait claims to have
got hold of the real person when, in truth and at best, he
has set down on the canvas a schematic selection, arbitrarily decided on by his mind, from the innumerable traits
that make a living person. What if the painter changed his
mind and decided to paint not the real person but his own
idea, his pattern, of the person? Indeed, in that case the
portrait would be the truth and nothing but the truth, and
failure would no longer be inevitable. In foregoing to em-
ulate reality the painting becomes what it authentically is:
an image, an unreality.

Expressionism, cubism, etc., are—in varying degree—
attempts at executing this decision. From painting things,
the painter has turned to painting ideas. He shuts his eyes
to the outer world and concentrates upon the subjective
images in his own mind.

Notwithstanding its crudeness and the hopeless vulgarity

of its subject, Pirandello's drama *Six Characters in Search of an Author* is, from the point of view of an aesthetic theory of the drama, perhaps one of the most interesting recent plays. It supplies an excellent example of this inversion of the artistic attitude which I am trying to describe. The traditional playwright expects us to take his personages for persons and their gestures for the indications of a "human" drama. Whereas here our interest is aroused by some personages as such—that is, as ideas or pure patterns.

Pirandello's drama is, I dare say, the first "drama of ideas" proper. All the others that bore this name were not dramas of ideas, but dramas among pseudo persons symbolizing ideas. In Pirandello's work, the sad lot of each of the six personages is a mere pretext and remains shadowy. Instead, we witness the real drama of some ideas as such, some subjective phantoms gesticulating in an author's mind. The artist's intent to dehumanize is unmistakable, and conclusive proof is given of the possibility of executing it. At the same time, this work provides a model instance for the difficulty of the average public to accommodate their vision to such an inverted perspective. They are looking for the human drama which the artist insists on presenting in an offhand, elusive, mocking manner putting in its place—that is, in the first place—the theatrical fiction itself. Average theater-goers resent that he will not deceive them, and refuse to be amused by that delightful fraud of art—all the more exquisite the more frankly it reveals its fraudulent nature.

4. Iconoclasm

It is not an exaggeration to assert that modern paintings and sculptures betray a real loathing of living forms or forms of living beings. The phenomenon becomes particularly clear if the art of these last years is compared with that sublime hour when painting and sculpture emerge from Gothic discipline as from a nightmare and bring forth the abundant, world-wide harvest of the Renaissance. Brush and chisel delight in rendering the exuberant forms of the model-man, animal, or plant. All bodies are welcome, if only life with its dynamic power is felt to throb in them. And from paintings and sculptures organic form flowers over into ornament. It is the epoch of the cornucopias whose torrential fecundity threatens to flood all space with round, ripe fruits.

Why is it that the round and soft forms of living bodies are repulsive to the present-day artist? Why does he replace them with geometric patterns? For with all the blunders and all the sleights of hand of cubism, the fact remains that for some time we have been well pleased with a language of pure Euclidean patterns.

The pheonomenon becomes more complex when we remember that crazes of this kind have periodically recurred in history. Even in the evolution of prehistoric art we observe that artistic sensibility begins with seeking the living form and then drops it, as though affrighted and nauseated, and resorts to abstract signs, the last residues of cosmic or animal forms. The serpent is stylized into the meander, the sun into the swastica. At times, this disgust at living forms flares up and produces public conflicts. The revolt against the images of Oriental Christianism, the Semitic law forbidding representation of animals—an attitude opposite to the instinct of those people who decorated the cave of Altamira—doubtless originate not only in a religious feeling but also in an aesthetic sensibility whose subsequent influence on Byzantine art is clearly discernible.

A thorough investigation of such eruptions of iconoclasm in religion and art would be of high interest. Modern art is obviously actuated by one of these curious iconoclastic urges. It might have chosen for its motto the commandment of Porphyrius which, in its Manichaean adaptation, was so violently opposed by St. Augustine: *Omne corpus fugiendum est*—where *corpus,* to be sure, must be understood as "living body." A curious contrast indeed with Greek culture which at its height was so deeply in love with living forms.

5. *Negative Influence of the Past*

This essay, as I have said before, confines itself to delineating the new art by means of some of its distinguishing features. However, it is prompted by a curiosity of wider scope which these pages do not venture to satisfy but only wish to arouse in the reader; whereupon we shall leave him to his own meditations.

Elsewhere [7] I have pointed out that it is in art and pure science, precisely because they are the freest activities and least dependent on social conditions, that the first signs of any changes of collective sensibility become noticeable. A fundamental revision of man's attitude toward life is apt to find its first expression in artistic creation and scientific theory. The fine texture of both these matters renders them susceptible to the slightest breeze of the spiritual trade-winds. As in the country, opening the window of a morning, we examine the smoke rising from the chimney-stacks in order to determine the wind that will rule the day, thus we can, with a similar meteorologic purpose, study the art and science of the young generation.

The first step has been to describe the new phenomenon. Only now that this is done can we proceed to ask of which new general style of life modern art is the symptom and the harbinger. The answer requires an analysis of the causes that have effected this strange about-face in art. Why this desire to dehumanize? Why this disgust at living forms? Like all historical phenomena this too will have grown from a multitude of entangled roots which only a fine flair is capable of detecting. An investigation of this kind would be too serious a task to be attacked here. However, what other causes may exist, there is one which, though perhaps not decisive, is certainly very clear.

We can hardly put too much stress on the influence which at all times the past of art exerts on the future of art. In the mind of the artist a sort of chemical reaction is set going by the clash between his individual sensibility and already existing art. He does not find himself all alone with the world before him; in his relations with the world there always intervenes, like an interpreter, the artistic tradition. What will the reaction of creative originality upon the beauty of previous works be like? It may be positive or negative. Either the artist is in conformity with the past and regards it as his heritage which he feels called upon to perfect; or he discovers that he has a spontaneous indefinable aversion against established and generally acclaimed art. And as in the first case he will be pleased to settle down in the customary forms and repeat some of their sacred patterns, thus he will, in the second, not only deviate

[7] Cf. The author's book *The Modern Theme* (The C. W. Daniel Company, London: 1931), p. 26.

from established tradition but be equally pleased to give to his work an explicit note of protest against the time-honored norms.

The latter is apt to be overlooked when one speaks of the influence of the past on the present. That a work of a certain period may be modeled after works of another previous period has always been easily recognized. But to notice the negative influence of the past and to realize that a new style has not infrequently grown out of a conscious and relished antagonism to traditional styles seems to require somewhat of an effort.

As it is, the development of art from Romanticism to this day cannot be understood unless this negative mood of mocking aggressiveness is taken into account as a factor of aesthetic pleasure. Baudelaire praises the black Venus precisely because the classical is white. From then on the successive styles contain an ever increasing dose of derision and disparagement until in our day the new art consists almost exclusively of protests against the old. The reason is not far to seek. When an art looks back on many centuries of continuous evolution without major hiatuses or historical catastrophes its products keep on accumulating, and the weight of tradition increasingly encumbers the inspiration of the hour. Or to put it differently, an ever growing mass of traditional styles hampers the direct and original communication between the nascent artist and the world around him. In this case one of two things may happen. Either tradition stifles all creative power—as in Egypt, Byzantium, and the Orient in general—or the effect of the past on the present changes its sign and a long epoch appears in which the new art, step by step, breaks free of the old which threatened to smother it. The latter is typical of Europe whose futuristic instinct, predominant throughout its history, stands in marked contrast to the irremediable traditionalism of the Orient.

A good deal of what I have called dehumanization and disgust for living forms is inspired by just such an aversion against the traditional interpretation of realities. The vigor of the assault stands in inverse proportion to the distance. Keenest contempt is felt for nineteenth century procedures although they contain already a noticeable dose of opposition to older styles. On the other hand, the new sensibility exhibits a somewhat suspicious enthusiasm for art that is most remote in time and space, for prehistoric or savage primitivism. In point of fact, what attracts the modern artist in those primordial works is not so much their artistic quality as their candor; that is, the absence of tradition.

If we now briefly consider the question: What type of life reveals itself in this attack on past art? we come upon a strange and stirring fact. To assail all previous art, what else can it mean than to turn against art itself? For what is art, concretely speaking, if not such art as has been made up to now?

Should that enthusiasm for pure art be but a mask which conceals surfeit with art and hatred of it? But, how can such a thing come about? Hatred of art is unlikely to develop as an isolated phenomenon; it goes hand in hand with hatred of science, hatred of state, hatred, in sum, of civilization as a whole. Is it conceivable that modern Western man bears a rankling grudge against his own historical essence? Does he feel something akin to the *odium professionis* of medieval monks—that aversion, after long years of monastic discipline, against the very rules that had shaped their lives? [8]

This is the moment prudently to lay down one's pen and let a flock of questions take off on their winged course.

[8] It would be interesting to analyze the psychological mechanisms through which yesterday's art negatively affects the art of today. One is obvious: ennui. Mere repetition of a style has a blunting and tiring effect. In his *Principles of Art History; the Problem of the Development of Style in Later Art* (London: Bell, 1932) Heinrich Wölfflin mentions the power of boredom which has ever again mobilized art and compelled it to invent new forms. And the same applies to literature, only more so. Cicero still said *"latine loqui"* for "speaking Latin"; but in the fifth century Apollinaris Sidonius resorted to *"latialiter insusurrare."* For too many centuries the same had been said with the same words.

Artistic Truth and Warped Vision

BY WILLIAM PHILLIPS

Almost from the beginning, our culture has had a double image of the creative man: he was believed to be obsessed, perhaps even mad, yet at the same time he was thought to have some extraordinary gift of insight, some great wisdom not shared by ordinary people. This apparent contradiction has never been resolved; sometimes it was the normality of the artist that was emphasized, while at other times his prophetic powers were stressed, though usually the question was solved by ignoring it. With the development of psychoanalysis, the problem has taken on a new cast. At first, it was simply assumed that art is in some manner connected with neurosis, though there was disagreement about whether art expresses neurosis or the catharsis of the neurosis. More recently, however, the trend has been mostly the other way, to dissociate the work of art from the neurosis of the author, and to regard it as a "normal" achievement, a triumph of health over sickness.

This more wholesome view of the creative process is often put forward in the language of psychoanalysis, but it also obviously reflects the need for personal tranquillity and social adjustment that dominates the mood of the present. For one thing, the discovery that neurosis is curable, putting it within the domain of health and hygiene, was bound to make creative aberration less palatable. Even more important, the association of psychological disorder with the estrangement of the modern artist—as in the cult of the unique, from Rimbaud to Dylan Thomas—has made it difficult to distinguish the neurotic from the anarchic personality. Though it is still not clear whether the bohemian dedication to depravity simply releases neurosis, or is tied up with it, we think of the two as belonging together. Hence our feelings about the relation of neurosis and creativity are likely to be colored by our views on the social position of the artist; and in a period of respectability and cultural timidity it is not surprising that abnormality and unconventionality are often confused, and both frowned upon.

When we speak of the artist as "mad" or "neurotic" the terms do not simply refer to the state of his mental health; they give a mythic picture of the creative man: inspired, rebellious, dedicated, obsessive, and alienated, as well as neurotic; and they also suggest the evil and irrational underworld of experience dredged up by the modern writer. Thomas Mann's celebration, for example, of the role of disease in the making of art stems from a sense of the moral and psychological ambiguities in any work of art as well as in the life of the artist, and from Mann's belief that the artist has been chosen to enrich the imagination of the community though he is in some ways outside its pale. On the other hand, many recent demands for normality have questioned the need for anything against the grain, irresponsible, or offbeat in art. The fact is that the work of writers like Gide or Joyce represents a different kind of experience from that of the common run of fiction; and it is this experience, rather than the neurosis of the author, that is rejected in the name of normality, which is taken to be synonymous with whatever is conventional and popular.

Perhaps it is because philistinism has been associated with health, in our culture, that many of us prefer to make some connection, however loose, between art and neurosis, though there is still very little evidence of a scientific nature to support such a view. It is true that most advanced art, at least in our time, seems to have thrived in an atmosphere of abnormality, and that the lives of most creative figures read like case histories. But, as Lionel Trilling has pointed out in a remarkably cogent essay ("Art and Neurosis," PR, 1945), there is no reason to believe that neurosis itself is the creative force. There is also the question of the work: is it neurotic or not?—and if not, what does it mean to say that the artist is a neurotic? Even if neurosis is shown to have something to do with art, we still have to ask whether all neuroses are related to all art or whether only some kinds of art are traceable to certain neuroses, and whether the neurosis of the artist produces, conditions, or is transmuted or sublimated into art. To put the question in a more general way, what we need to know is how the neurosis of the artist, which is a form of disorder, can shape a work of art that has value and meaning for an entire civilization. Thus we are really questioning what was once assumed: that madness and wisdom may go hand in hand.

One reason we know so little about the relation of neurosis to art is that we know so little about art. It might have been expected that psychoanalysis would clarify some of these questions; and actually it has thrown some light on one side of the problem, by defining the neurotic mechanism and by giving an exact account of the neurosis of many writers, painters, and musicians. But, despite the vast number of studies on the subject by psychoanalysts, we still have no answer to some of the basic questions. Much of the writing on art by psychoanalysts combines bad taste— as when *Death of a Salesman* is treated as a classic—with some contrived, jargonized theory. The approach to painting and music, [1] based largely on a "literary" version of content, has been most primitive, and its value has been biographical rather than aesthetic. But even the best of psychoanalytic writing in this vein suffers from the lack of an accepted philosophy of art; hence it has had either to adopt or improvise one. Some analysts have taken art to be a form of communication, others a mode of expression, and the traditional definitions of meaning, form, content, and audience have all found their way into psychoanalytic writing. Most aesthetic systems in the past have been no better than the insight that went into their formulation, and when they simply are tacked on to some doctrine in another field, like psychoanalysis, the result is at best a tour de force. Even so brilliant an essay as Ernest Jones's famous study of *Hamlet*, which traces the Oedipal motives in the play, makes the assumption that works of art are great and lasting when, like *Hamlet*, they deal with primal conflicts. Such an assumption is, of course, too simple and schematic, and though Jones's piece does enlarge our under-

---

[1] Most of the examples I am using here are drawn from literature, because the formal content of painting and music has a much more complex and less obvious connection with psychological motives, and these media require special analysis. I do believe, however, that all of the arts, and creative thinking as well, have the same basic relation to neurosis.

standing of the play, it is not, in itself, a first-rate example of literary criticism or of aesthetics.

Freud's few attempts to explain the nature of art are not very impressive, though of course Freud himself—like most outstanding thinkers—was superior not only to his followers but often to his own theories. Perhaps the least impressive of Freud's observations was that it was the desire for fame, power, and the love of women that lay behind the creative will of the writer. Nor do I find a satisfactory explanation of the creative act in the analogies to day-dreaming and fantasy-building noted by Freud. As for the *origin* of the creative gift, Freud insisted on many occasions that psychoanalysis had no special explanation for this mysterious force, though the concept of sublimation would suggest that all the achievements of civilization come from the taming of the id. Freud's contribution to the problem of art lies mainly, I think, in the examples he set in his profound essays on such figures as Dostoevsky and Leonardo, where he made a number of interesting correlations between the neurotic pattern of these artists' lives and the content of their works, touching on the meaning of those correlations in a purely speculative and tentative manner.

Any total approach to art that sees the creative gift or process as a form of neurosis is bound to produce a lopsided and absurd theory. If art is considered as a form of sublimation, or a variety of dream or fantasy, or even as a therapeutic activity, then we have no criteria for judging it, nor any way of distinguishing it from other kinds of dream or fantasy, or therapy. And as for the many ingenious exercises, revealing art to be oral or anal, sadistic or masochistic, narcissistic, totemic, the best that can be said of them is that they apply equally well to a doodle, a Grandma Moses, or a Jackson Pollock, though, of course, they cover more of the doodle. Nor can we attribute the power or significance of a work of art to the neurosis of the author, for then we would have to assume that its meaning lay wholly in its psychological content, which corresponded not only to the neuroses of the author, but to those of the audience as well. Such a novel as *The Possessed* would have to be read merely as a story of the criminal mind, and we could not account for its stature as a political novel.

It seems meaningless to speak of *neurotic* art, except in referring to the exercises of mental patients, which might yield something neurotic—or psychotic[2]—but not art. On the other hand, it is equally meaningless to speak of a *healthy* art or of the creative act as a triumph of health over illness, since the term healthy can only be pejorative: it does not describe a specific form or content. If all we mean by a triumph of such health is that instead of collapsing a writer produced a poem or story, then this is only another way of saying that his neurosis did not completely paralyze him. To characterize, for example, Rilke's spurts of productivity, in between long fallow periods, as signs of health is simply to juggle the word so as to define writing as healthy. One might just as well call it neurotic, since the process of composition was obsessive and dreamlike. Certainly the creative act often resembles compulsive fits and states of hallucination, and all we gain by calling it healthy rather than neurotic is the reassurance of knowing that we are not reveling in disease.

In what sense, then, does neurosis have something to do with art? To begin with, there is the fact that many, if not most, writers, painters, and musicians in the modern period have been neurotic. It is true, of course, that people who are not creative may also be neurotic; hence the popular belief that the connection between art and neurosis has been much exaggerated. Perhaps the only way to settle this question in a seemingly scientific way would be to tabulate neuroses to determine whether creative people suffer more than others, and whether their neuroses are different in kind or degree. In a time when every conceivable question has become the subject of a poll, it is surprising that no statistical study of neurosis has ever been attempted. But even if such a study showed, as I suspect it would, that creative people are distinguished not by their neurosis but by their creations, it still might be true that neurosis, though not *sufficient* for the production of art, may be *necessary* for it. Recently a study of a German writer and thinker appeared under the title, *The Mind of a Genius.* Though it was obviously not its intent, what struck one

---

[2] I have been using mainly the more common and less extreme term "neurotic," but much of what I have been saying could apply to psychosis or psychotic tendencies.

most about the book was the fact that the subject's genius lay not in his achievement but in his personality and intellectual habits, which combined boldness and originality with eccentricity. Somewhere in his make-up was an essential flaw, perhaps in his intelligence, but he had what might be called a neurotic predisposition toward ideas.

Strictly speaking, a neurosis is an insoluble conflict within the unconscious that may lead to aberration in one's behavior or state of mind. In this technical sense, neurosis would be pertinent to art only if we thought of art itself as an aberration or sublimation. But using the term more loosely, in neurosis, as well as in psychosis, there is often a distortion of experience, so that certain human events and relations are given an undue—sometimes obsessive—emphasis. In someone who is not creative, a distorted view of reality is part of his illness and inability to adjust and may be of no intellectual interest: indeed, the paranoia of a trivial mind is incredibly boring. In someone like Kafka, however, the paranoid twist in both the life and the writing was coupled with a gift of a high order and a mind capable of original and striking observations. The same was true in D. H. Lawrence, whose sexual dreams would have had only a clinical interest without his intellectual powers.

Now much modern writing is centered in some obsessive theme or some biased image of human affairs, growing out of the fixations of the author. Take even so constructed a work as *The Waste Land:* its meanings would seem to be mainly cultural and religious; but what Eliot is concerned with, in our culture and religion as well as in our personal lives, is the breakdown of identity, and the image of breakdown is provided by the sexual ambiguity of Tiresias,[3] which I take to be the psychological core of the poem. The homosexual theme crops up constantly, usually in an explicit way, but I think it is also expressed symbolically in the perversion of feelings and the spiritual impotence running through *The Waste Land.* One would have to know more about Eliot's private preoccupations to speculate further about the effect of this neurosis on his entire vision, but I think it is reasonable to assume that this

---

[3] Despite Eliot's own note on the importance of Tiresias in the scheme of *The Waste Land,* most commentators have not given him more weight than any other element in the poem, perhaps because their methods precluded a psychological approach.

vision reflects the more personal elements in his writing.
This is not to say that *The Waste Land* is a neurotic
poem, any more than, say, *Gulliver's Travels* or even *The
Trial* are neurotic works, though Swift and Kafka were
known to be mentally disturbed to the point of partial
breakdown and inability to function in crucial areas of
their lives. What then does it mean to say that Swift's or
Kafka's writings contained some central distortion of experience traceable to the neuroses of the authors? The
answer, I think, is that their neurotic impressions of the
world coincided with impressions that were not neurotic
and served to organize and energize the latter. In the case
of Kafka, the paranoia, for example, that colored his personal and sexual relations became in his fiction a kind of
psychological focus for a world in which the characters
are the victims of organized ignorance and authority; and
the living Kafka's search for his psychic identity becomes
in his writing a search for a religious and metaphysical
identity. The work of neurotic writers can be characterized
as neurotic only by reducing its total meaning to its seemingly neurotic components—which, in turn, are assumed
to be identical with the neurosis of the author. Thus
Kafka's novels can be considered neurotic only if we interpret them, as some analysts and critics actually have done,
as fictionalized projections of Kafka's own derangements.

Now we come to another paradox: for the unique combination of neurotic experience with some apparently objective or plausible view of the world, such as we find in
writers like Kafka or Eliot, seems to be characteristic of
much modern literature. Indeed, it is this combination that
we designate as the *modern experience*, and this experience, though seemingly shared by a sufficient number of
readers and writers to make up a tradition, has at the
same time certain affinities with neurotic experience. Such
themes as loneliness, self-doubt, hypersensitivity, loss of
identity, estrangement from the community—all have their
counterparts among the common neuroses; and the two
modes of experience, normal and abnormal, often have
been joined in such a way that it becomes meaningless to
distinguish between them. How can we set Swift's neurotic
misanthropy apart from the powerful satire of his writings, which, ironically enough, are assigned to school children for didactic as well as literary reasons? If Gide's

homosexuality was a "sickness," what shall we call the moral implications of his concern with the truth of one's own being? Is *Death in Venice* a study of degeneration or a parable of a modern writer? In each case I suppose we would have to say the content was both normal and abnormal, but that is the same as saying it is neither; or perhaps, to put it more precisely, there has been in each case a conjunction of neurotic experience with experience that we assume to be normal—by which we apparently mean an experience shared by a sufficient number of cultivated people to make it seem objective, general, and typical.

If some such combination of the objective and neurotic is characteristic of modern writing, we can only speculate about the way the two have been brought together. It has been suggested at various times, particularly when our political morale has been low, that our civilization is neurotic; this would, of course, make it unnecessary to explain any single neurotic strain in our art or culture. I suspect that describing an entire culture as neurotic is nothing more than a juggling of terms to make all art—what about our philosophy and our science?—neurotic by definition. If our civilization is neurotic, then everything and everyone is neurotic, and we have no way of judging it or knowing whether a re-creation of it is distorted or not. The collectivization of neurosis transforms the neurotic artist into a psychological conformist.

One simple explanation of the way neuroses legitimately find their way into any of the arts would be that the writer's world has been created mainly by his intelligence acting on what he has inherited from his culture, and that his neuroses are then brought into play as he personalizes his experience. Another might be that only writers endowed with certain kinds of neuroses, along with their imaginative gifts, can thrive, in the Darwinian sense, at any given time. Someone like Hemingway, who has put his adolescent ideas to literary use, might not have been so successful in a classical period that put a premium on intellectual order and maturity. Or, perhaps, a process of natural selection takes place even earlier, before creation begins, and only certain kinds of neurotics are able to make the break with the community necessary to enter the unstable world of the arts. Surely, there must be some significance in the large number of homosexuals peopling the intellectual and artistic professions, especially the dance and the theater, today. We know that the faculty we call talent is not sufficient to produce "art": thousands of people have enough verbal and narrative skill to write and even to find a market. Our idea of art embraces, in addition to control of the medium, a profound and arresting sense of the world, and it is conceivable that this power, though mainly intellectual, is enhanced by a disposition, which we would call neurotic, to reject conventional attitudes.

The question remains as to how a view of the world that has been warped, if only partially, by neurosis can be said to be truthful, objective, or morally stimulating. The question is bound up with many philosophical considerations, including the very nature of art and truth, that are themselves in dispute. But this much can be said: the idea that art is the dispenser of moral and philosophical truths is only a myth, though a prevailing one in our culture. Like most other myths, this one has great suggestive power, linking art to other pursuits that enlarge our vision and understanding, but it cannot be applied literally without falling into didacticism.

From the time of Plato and Aristotle there has been an almost constant pressure, from many different sources, to enlist the arts in the service of some higher aim or some larger truth. Rarely and only for short spells was it permissible for a novel, say, or a painting to steer clear of the claims of morality, politics, or religion; usually it was considered frivolous and irresponsible to think of the arts in their own terms. At first there was the messianism of Christianity, then the Protestant ethic, and more recently the growth of utilitarian ideals, the development of a social conscience, and the confusion of art with education in the spread of middle and high culture—all these forces have conspired to get us to believe that art is supposed to make us better and wiser. There may be some ambiguity about whether art is by nature concerned with truth and morality or whether that is its ideal purpose toward which it must strive at all times. In either case the effect is the same: art has become an easy prey in our culture to all kinds of theories and causes that claim to have discovered some medical, moral, or historical truth.

Now part of the difficulty obviously comes from the fact that none of the arts is self-contained. Despite the efforts of many formalist critics to define a work of art as the sum of its textual or plastic qualities and to judge it mostly in technical terms, the fact is that art has always absorbed the moods and currents of the civilization that produced it. And though I do not want to go into aesthetics at this point, I think it can be said that we regard a work of art as good or bad because of the way its formal qualities are combined with what we roughly call its vision, or its values, or its range of consciousness. But this is not at all the same thing as saying that literature, to take the art most filled with *content,* has a moral purpose, a position which has been quite fashionable ever since the idea of political responsibility was abandoned; or that it reflects or asserts something known as "truth," a point of view that has lately been gaining ground. Of course the notion of truth is an old naturalist slogan, but all it meant in that context was to promote the kind of fiction that represented the texture of average, daily plebeian existence, and insofar as naturalism contained any idea of truth or reality, it was that life is grimy and frustrated and full of social injustice. This was simply a literary movement riding the tail of a social movement.

The more recent turn toward the concept of truth in art is something else; it is actually a turn against the idea of alienation, dissidence, and rebellion. For it ignores the question of values and tends to minimize the attitudes of commitment to new forces and rebellion against old ones that lie behind fresh creative movements and the audiences that support them. It seems meaningless to insist that a work of art conveys some lasting human truth: what is the "universal" truth in Joyce's *Portrait of the Artist as a Young Man* or Picasso's *Three Musicians* or one of Schoenberg's compositions? (Incidentally, the word "truth" is often only a synonym for verisimilitude or for insight into human behavior.) Aside from the mastery of the medium, we have, in modern art at least, not a permanent truth but different accents or points of view that at best are true only for a small number of people and perhaps only for a limited span. In our time many innovations have been carried out by an avant-garde concerned not with the truth but with some new, irreverent, often shocking stand against prevailing moods and opinions. And perhaps the decline of the avant-garde has something to do with the high regard these days, not only for the notion of truth, but also for that of normality and respectability of the arts.

Just as other periods sometimes regarded the imagination as a wild, demonic force, we now like to think of it as quite tame and orderly; and we tend to associate abnormality with literary postures and false ideas. But let us not be fooled into thinking these views are objective or that they help clarify the relations between art, truth, and morality. They are merely symptoms of the times; and their literary meaning lies mainly in the fact that they serve to promote one creative strain rather than another. Thus in recent years there has been a growing tendency to tear down the more obviously neurotic and alienated writers, the extremists, like Kafka, Proust, Joyce, even Dostoevsky, and to elevate such figures as Dickens, George Eliot, and Trollope, who seemingly stand for a more orderly and "wholesome" kind of experience. No doubt the tension between these two traditions has played a large part in the literary life of the past century, and we have tended to associate greater abnormality with those whom Van Wyck Brooks once called "coterie" writers, largely because they symbolized a more radical break with existing norms. As Gide, who favored the wilder talents, put it: "There do exist geniuses, Victor Hugo for example, sane and whole. Their perfect spiritual poise precludes the possibility of any fresh problem. Rousseau without the leaven of madness, would, I am sure, be no better than an undigested Cicero. . . . The individual who is abnormal refuses to submit to laws already established." At the same time, we should note that the cleavage is not absolute. Someone like Mann, for example, was torn between the two traditions; and it is amusing to watch the efforts today to transform Whitman into a man of the main stream.

If, however, we investigate the life and work of the individual writer, the distinction between the normal and the abnormal in literature turns out to be largely programmatic rather than scientific. Henry James or T. S. Eliot, for example, who are usually assumed to be on the side of order and classicism, may be just as neurotic—in their work as well as in their private lives—as Joyce or Kafka; and as for the question of truth, I see no way of deciding which one of them is closer to the "truth" in his writing. The national and personal ambiguities in the work of James, which were bound up in some way with the ambi-

Not as
rebellion
but as false
or limited

guities of his own life, are just as true as, say, Joyce's rejection, in the name of the uncompromising artist, of "my home, my fatherland, or my church," which was also tied up with some neurotic need to dissociate himself from the conventional world.

The opposition between "truth" and "neurosis" is actually a clash of two myths, the myth of the artist as philosopher and moralist and the myth of the messianic madman. It is the traditional split, celebrated by Nietzsche, between the Apollonian and Dionysian view of art: between Apollo, the god of light, poetry, and prophecy, who stood for self-control, tranquillity, and radiance, and Dionysius, who represented frenzy, intoxication, and mystery, and brought art to the edge of barbarism and pathology. In our time, however, the distinction between the two is slowly disappearing, and—who knows?—maybe some day the neurotic artist will become a pillar of society. *They have : VG*

Past and Present

BY DAVID JONES

Sir,

Mr. —— —— in his appreciation of a book of mine touches upon the issue of 'past' and 'present' in relation to · the practice of the arts among ourselves and I wonder if you would allow me the following comment?

Mr. —— is in full agreement with a contention touched upon in my Preface that for a work to be valid it must in some way or other be conditioned by the present—it must have 'nowness'. But he argues that what I preach in my Preface I do not practise in my book. He bases this criticism on the content of the book and not upon the form. He says, in effect, that the book draws mainly on the last few millenniums *exclusive of the last few decades* and that this past is 'irrevocably past away'. There is no space here to discuss whether this is so or not; but supposing it to be so, what are we to infer? That, e.g., the Use of Bangor, the Cretan labyrinth and the Jurassic Dinosaurs are irrelevant for the contemporary artist and are thereby taboo for contemporary poetry? My own answer is in the negative, because in so far as he has access to it, by however attenuated a strand of inheritance, the entire past is at the poet's disposal; i.e. it is matter valid for him *qua* content. He can use that content partially or wholly. It is said that in the case of *The Anathemata* the mythos employed stops short just prior to the full flowering of our present technocracy. Again there is no space to discuss whether this is so or not, but, supposing it to be so, the 'nowness' or lack of it remains unaffected, because it is not the content as such,

[1] When this letter was written the *Granta* had temporarily ceased publication. A name in the letter is left blank as the person referred to had, of course, no opportunity to reply to what is said in the letter.

but the use made of it by the artist—a subjective matter, that determines the 'nowness' and that in turn will be infallibly betrayed by the resultant form—an objective matter.

For the artist the thing called 'the past' is very much what the thing called 'nature' is to him, viz.—something which he uses when he 'shows forth', 'recalls', 're-presents' and 'discovers'. For such is his task, whatever the mode, species or nature of the signs employed.

So the 'past' can no more than 'nature' be precluded from his data. *As an artist he stands or falls by what he does with this data.*

If we grant the foregoing we are then in some position to ask the crucial question: In what sense and to what degree have the last few decades cut us off from the last few millenniums and so from the many millenniums before them? Are a large part of our credits frozen or are they still available as the sinews of our war?

We have seen that *a* past is valid for *a* present. But in *our* present we are agreed that a metamorphosis has occurred affecting the liaisons with our past. It is precisely this situation which was my abiding dilemma during the writing of the whole of *The Anathemata*. It is this dilemma also which I call to the attention of the reader in my Preface.

There is a further but intimately related matter: Mr. ——— says that although I set out to integrate myself, as an artist, with my society I have not done so.

For the following reasons I find this statement puzzling. My contention stated in the Preface to *The Anathemata* and also hinted at in the Preface to *In Parenthesis* (1937) is that for a number of quite objective reasons over which we have no control, our present civilizational pattern in its essential and determining characteristics has occasioned a dichotomy which affects to some extent the 'doing' of man (Aristotle's *praxis*) and to a much larger extent all his 'making' (Aristotle's *poesis*) and which affects to a unique extent and in a special manner, those makings which involve certain specific arts, e.g. painting and poetry.

What I have suggested is that man-the-artist, finds himself, willy-nilly, un-integrated with the present civilizational phase. I regard this as a regrettable matter of fact. I also say that there have been civilizational phases when this was less marked and that there have been true culture-phases when this was not marked at all, when man-the-artist was as integral to the pattern as is man-the-mechanic or managerial man to our pattern today.

But this does not in any sense mean that the activity called, somewhat redundantly, 'making poetry' is irrelevant to our society. Still less that it cannot flourish in it and still less again that the maker is not conditioned by it. The works of Joyce, Picasso, Eliot and Britten, to take four names known to everybody, are quite sufficient to indicate what the Muses have managed to accomplish during the last few decades. The works of these four artists are as red-olent of 'now' as is an aero-engine, the Unitary State or nuclear physics; but with a difference. Each of these three phenomena is concerned only with some part of man's na-ture and is thus of only partial, and thence of passing, sig-nifiance. Whereas the arts as practised by those four con-temporary men are, for all their contemporaneity, *signa* of man as such. They show forth, recall, discover and re-present those things that have belonged to man from the beginning.

So that, in one sense, we have no complaints. Not only can the artist function in peculiar situations but certain works could not be but for those situations. Rather as the poetry of *Super fluminia Babylonis* resulted from the re-membrance of a deportation. By a coincidence that fa-mous psalm of exile provides also a clue: 'If I forget thee, O Jerusalem: let my right hand forget her cunning.' That is to say our making is dependent on a remembering of some sort. It may be only the remembering of a personal emotion of last Monday-week in the tranquility of next Friday fortnight. But a 'deed' has entered history, in this case our private history, and is therefore valid as matter for our poetry. For poetry is the song of deeds. But it seems to me that a deed that entered history a millennium, or fifty millenniums, ago and which has been assimilated into the mythos of whole groups of men, perhaps of the whole group called mankind, is, *other things being equal,* of even more validity for our poetry. But are the 'other things' equal? That, precisely, is our dilemma. We are back to the query discussed in my Preface. It is Mr. ———'s query also. It is the query of everybody who has given the matter thought.

No one intimately and contactually involved in the making of works today would underestimate the almost insuperable difficulties of how to make the signs available for today. We can, in my opinion, assert little with confidence, but I think we can assert that the poet is a 'rememberer' and that it is a part of his business to keep open the lines of communication. One obvious way of doing this is by handing on such fragmented bits of our own inheritance as we have ourselves received. This is the way I myself attempt. There are, no doubt, other ways. The artist is not responsible *for* the future but he is, in a certain sense, responsible *to* the future.

By way of allegory: If, from our shelled position, we tap out the code-word 'Helen', it may be we shall get no response—all the liaisons are phut. The barrage has done its work. Or it may be we get the reply that the de-coding officer with his book of words was blown up long since. We dare not give it in clear for that is forbidden and would in any case be of most value to the enemy. So we can do no more but hang on and await developments. Someone, sometime, will take over, even if it is no more than a burying-party and a salvage squad, or perhaps the personnel of an enemy War-Damage Investigations Department. But whoever they are they will find sufficient tokens of us to tell them what were still valid as signs, for some of us, when our whole front was finally rolled up.

And sooner or later they will decipher the legend scratched on the revetment: 'Mademoiselle she bought a cow', and the apparently inconsequent adjacent scrawl: 'I want the moon to play with.' And they will find on the fly-leaf of Pte. Slattery's pay-book the ejaculation 'Mary help!' and they will find the field-service post-card to someone called Cynthia at her Aventine address, Roma 13. And they will find an envelope addressed to a girl at the sea-side town of Kouklia in Cyprus and other correspondence to the same girl at various other addresses. And they will find on a torn scrap of the last mail to get through the barrage, the words 'Yours ever, Clio'. And they will most indubitably find on each leaf of the M.O.'s scattered dossier a reference to a blinded Theban King. And when they have understood what they have deciphered, those men of what will then be 'now' will use this fragmented *materia,* it will be valid content for their poetry. No matter how metamorphosed by a technocracy the full ramifications of which we cannot as yet guess, in so far as they are still men they will not altogether escape the things of man. They will not escape the world of the mammalia or of the hornèd moon. They will not escape Diana Nemorensis nor yet Venus: let us hope she will be for them a Venus Verticordia. And no less certainly than we ourselves will they be caught in the complex of Jocasta and her son. And if we are involved in what is indicated under the terms Theotokos and Logos, will not they be?

DAVID JONES

March 1953

If and Perhaps and But

BY DAVID JONES

Harrow-on-the-Hill.

Sir,

Unless I misconceive his meaning, Mr. Henry Reed, in his thoughtful talk printed in *The Listener* of June 18th, seems to imply that between the nineteen-twenties and today something happened whereby it is now possible for the poet to implement a 'formal artistic discipline *derived from the outside*' whereas this was not so three decades ago; and that what was 'inevitable for those days' does not apply to these present days.

I write only to ask what is the nature and the provenance of the thing which can have occasioned so radical a change. For such a change would seem to require some kind of civilizational change. For no 'external discipline' can be real, invigorating, and integrating unless it comes to us with the imperatives of a living tradition.

If the formal problems attaching to the making of poetry in 1923 were such that could not be solved by resort to 'external discipline' the same would seem to apply in 1953. Unless some radical change has indeed occurred, not in our own inclinations or wishes, but in the actual civilizational situation. But that situation, in so far as it conditions the making of works, seems not to have changed except in the sense of a considerable intensification and extension of its earlier characteristics. So that it would appear that the problems of the poet remain essentially the same, except that those problems are even more intensified and more complex.

I am constrained to write this letter of inquiry because the matter is of crucial importance to all of us who would try to understand the true nature of those problems inherent in the making of works of 'poetry', *under whatever mode,* in our particular epoch, in a late phase of a civilization with its many dichotomies both within and without.

Yours, etc.,

DAVID JONES

Aesthetics of Crisis

BY HAROLD ROSENBERG

Kenneth Burke once praised a piece of writing for being "rich in contradictions." This is the kind of wealth that distinguishes "Epoch and Artist," by David Jones. Jones not only holds inconsistent attitudes, he revels in displaying the contradictions of his "epoch." In theory, Jones is utterly opposed to the twentieth century; his position amounts to daring it to knock him down. An Anglo-Welshman now close to seventy, he is dedicated to his local culture and craft skills (he does copper engravings, illustrations for books, and watercolors). Back in the twenties he began to write, but before turning to the word he was converted to Catholicism and joined Eric Gill in the craftsmen's colony at the Guild of St. Joseph and St. Dominic, in Sussex. Jones's sensibility is steeped in liturgy and tradition and in imaginings of folk communities ruled by custom and sacred forms. To him, man is essentially an artisan. *Homo faber.* In modern times, Jones believes, man-the-maker has been debauched by the machine, and now his very nature as a molder of things is threatened by automation; thus, for the first time, a disparity exists between the artist and the culture that surrounds him, and he is forced to swim against the stream instead of being carried along by it. "Epoch and Artist" is largely composed of reflections on the author's native place and heritage: it is made up of talks delivered on the Welsh radio and short essays, many written for Catholic publications, on such subjects as "Wales and the Crown" (the first section of the book is almost entirely devoted to Wales), "Religion and the Muses," "Art and Sacrament," the old Roman roads in Britain, "The Arthurian Legend." An outlook and interests of this kind hardly hold out much promise for enlightenment about modern art.

Reprinted by permission; © 1964 The New Yorker Magazine, Inc. First appeared in the August 22, 1964 issue of *The New Yorker.*

Yet though to Jones the ways of this century are wretched, he is, oddly, an enthusiast of the time and of its artistic accomplishments, and his book contains some of the most acutely relevant writing on contemporary form and value to have appeared in years. That Jones has been involved in both painting and literature may have contributed to the breadth of his insights into current problems of creation. The decisive factor, though, it seems to me, is the difference between him and the usual elegist of cultural decline: while conscious of being surrounded by modern decadence, instead of devoting himself to denouncing examples of it, he takes pleasure in the questions this decadence raises for him. The twentieth century provides him with a unique intellectual stimulation, and for this he is grateful to it. He feels the present to be a trench of history, but the trench suits this ex-infantryman of the First World War to a "t." While he regards it as self-evident that Western civilization has entered a final crisis of values, the resulting bafflement itself seems to him a valuable means of orientation: "for let no one imagine that if they are not perplexed, and more than perplexed, when face to face—really and contactually face to face—with these questions, that they have so much as begun to know anything of the problems of the contemporary artist." Formed in the dual perspective of regret and possibility, his perceptions have an extraordinary solidity.

The literary figures most in Jones's mind are Hopkins and Joyce. In an introduction to Jones's first book, "In Parenthesis," a novel-poem about the First World War, T. S. Eliot noted that Jones's writing had "some affinity" with Joyce, the Pound of the Cantos, and his own, but he denied the presence of any significant influence. A major basis of resemblance is Jones's intense awareness that phenomena of the past are constantly showing through in what is happening now—the condition that Joyce and Karl Marx called "the nightmare of history." This historical consciousness belongs to the spirit of the age; it is as dominant in Picasso as in Freud or Thomas Mann. Jones displays the overlapping layers of time by a technique of jamming together data plucked from different cultural "moments," in a manner analogous to Picasso's "Las Meniñas" or to Tiresias in "The Waste Land" lamenting a seduction in a London flat. Jones, however, leans more to Joyce than to Eliot or Picasso in that besides being a good

European he is also a regionalist; his conviction that art must deal in particulars of the artist's environment and affections leads him to mix into his narrative (and into the critical pieces of "Epoch and Artist") references to local chronicles, place names, and folklore, and to sprinkle his rhetoric with Welsh phrases and locutions. He has also a love for odd words and an intensely personal prose rhythm. These, added to his responsiveness to the overtones of Church Latin and details of ecclesiastical history and ritual, help make him even more difficult of access to American readers than are Eliot and all but the latest Joyce. The result is that, at sixty-nine, Jones is for us a new writer: "In Parenthesis," which appeared in England in 1937, was first published in the United States in 1962 and by a beginning publisher. About his second book, "The Anathemata," an epic constructed upon an individual experience of the celebration of the Mass (I find it curiously parallel to Allen Ginsberg's "Kaddish"), Auden wrote that "without the copious notes which Mr. Jones provides it is unlikely that *anyone* except the author would be able fully to understand the poem." It was published here ten years after it saw light in England. Each of these works took a decade to compose, and Jones began by regarding his writings as things he was "making" for himself and that were not intended to be read by others. In sum, he is one of those artists who bear witness to the actuality of the cultural crisis by embodying the principle of difficulty in their work.

What has made this conservative, artisan-oriented folkic personage into an arch-vanguardist (as a writer, that is; the few illustrations I have seen of his artwork evince no tendency toward formal innovation) is his absolute conviction that there is no place for art to go but forward. Critics, historians, theoreticians may continue to construct aesthetic forms and contrive canons of taste out of the best art of the past; the maker of works knows beyond doubt that the Great Tradition long ago lost its ability to provide viable models. By 1914, Jones reminds his readers, even "academicism, let alone Tradition proper, was already moribund." The sacred words of the old aesthetics— "form," "shape," "composition," "represent"—were all in the process of shifting their inner meanings: "In the practice of an art," he writes, "whether of making a writing or making a drawing or making a wooden spoon, one learns

something of the surprising contradictions and metamor-
phoses which such words must be made to cover if they are
to be used other than in some narrow, arbitrary, conven-
ient-for-the-occasion, academic or superficial sense." The
collapse of traditional disciplines has produced a "civilizational situation" that forces the invention of hybrids. Nor
is this collapse going to be bridged over by a stabilization
of forms achieved through a change in aesthetic attitude.
In a letter in 1953 to the editor of *The Listener*, Jones
challenges a statement in an earlier issue that, in contrast
to the twenties, it had once more become possible to base
poetry on formal discipline. For the problems of poetry,
Jones points out, to have reached an objective resolution, a
radical change would have to have occurred "not in our
own inclinations or wishes but in the actual civilizational
situation." A new tradition would have had to arise, "for
no 'external discipline' can be real, invigorating, and integrating unless it comes to us with the imperatives of a living tradition." But, Jones concludes, the situation "in so
far as it conditions the making of works" has not changed
except that its earlier characteristics have been extended
and intensified. This one-page letter by Jones on the permanence of the cultural crisis says more about the character of art in our time than dozens of articles on "new"
turns by paintings or poets toward happier, taste-satisfying
work.

According to Jones's determinism (he has studied his
Spengler as well as neo-Catholic critics of modernism like
Maritain), the transformation of art in our time came
about not through the destructive will of artists or writers
but through their efforts to uphold the definition of man as
artist under historically impossible conditions. Reviewing
Berenson's "Aesthetics and History," Jones takes the con-
noisseur to task for misinterpreting the enforced experimentalism of modern art as a rebellion against the Italian
Renaissance. To one who instead of meditating on the
masterpieces of Florence and Venice considered what was
being taught in pre-1914 art schools, it was amply clear
that there had not been anything left to revolt against. In a
deft dig at latter-day humanists, Jones warns them against
succumbing to dogma in conceiving their aesthetic values
as eternal truths that contemporary art sinfully defies.
"When in the Liturgy is sung: 'Why do the gentiles rage
and the people devise vain things' there is posited an Ab-

solute Good against which a wicked raging and devising is directed. We should be careful not to infiltrate analogous sentiments into the matter under consideration." Art has not an ultimate form of perfection that must be sought by generation after generation. What counts is that the art activity shall be carried on genuinely in whatever way conditions permit. Aesthetic virtues that are no longer real ought to be eliminated as obstacles to performance. "There must be no mugging up, no 'ought to know' or 'try to feel;'" the artist "must work within the limits of his love."

Jones's pitting of the experience of the workman in the arts against the viewpoint of the standard-setting expert establishes a critical dividing line of immense importance in contemporary thinking about art. To investigate how art really manages to come into being in our technocracy, Jones proposes an exchange of reports among milliners, precision-tool makers, conveyor-belt tenders, and symbol-producers covering their "reconnaissances" into making. "The contactual is essential. You have to have been there. Ars is adamant about one thing: she compels you to do an infantryman's job. . . . Today most of us are staffwallahs of one sort or another. That may be why so much that is said concerning the things of Ars reminds one more of what the General's wife said to the cabinet minister concerning war-aims than of what is factually 'war' for those in the place of contact."

As a traditionalist without a tradition, or with a vanished one, Jones is ready to accept whatever features are imposed upon art by the anti-artistic drift of present-day civilization. For instance, given this century's intermixing of cultures, "extreme eclecticism was and is inevitable." At the same time, an opposing tendency "also was and is inevitable." That is, "this or that man pushing this or that notion as far as his sensitivities would allow him in this or that rather limited terrain"—which, Jones is quick to add, does not imply that the artist today believes in self-expression or is vainly striving to be original. In the abnormal situation of a traditionless civilization, each artist will endeavor to solve the general problems of art all by himself; in a word, he will create a "culture" of his own or the equivalent of one. If he had a choice, no artist, Jones least of all, would have it this way. But "art," as Turner said, "is a rum business," and you have to take it as it is. So, attached as he is to the craft ideal and warmly as he feels toward his friend Eric Gill, Jones is obliged to criticize him "because he sought to work as though a culture of some sort existed or, at all events, he worked as though one should, and could, *make* a culture exist."

Jones's own aesthetic envisions an individual equivalent of the kind of art that is typical of traditional cultures, in which the individual and his situation were entirely different from ours. There, each place, each community has its particular identity, a "thisness" that makes it different from other places: "there is an Etruscan 'thing' and that thingness has an aesthetic of its own." A work of art arising in such a communal entity, in which man and locale are one, participates in the shape of the whole, absorbing the facts of the collective experience into a language of signs that blends the actual and the sacred. The essential features of traditional art are expressed for Jones in certain terms that recur throughout his thought. Art is *anamnesis,* the recalling of past things, their re-presentation, or showing again, in a form that makes them everlastingly present. In giving form to the data of memory, the work of art transforms them into *signa,* which "show them forth" as more than mere fact; herein lies the "religiousness" that for Jones is inherent in all art, whatever its nature or intention. Experienced in their sacredness, or what he calls "otherness," things become *anathemata;* that is, set up or set apart (put "in parenthesis") and consecrated to a divinity, for that which is set up "can be set up only to the gods."

For Jones, recalling and setting up sacred signs are as much the business of the contemporary artist as they were of his forebears. In fact, they are even more urgently his affair, in view of the rapid assimilation of centuries-old communities by the spread of industry and the estrangement of the times from symbol and sacrament. Faced with this ruin of separateness and denuding of meaning, the contemporary artist must see to it that of the cultural "deposits" of the past none shall be lost but "all must be safely gathered in."

Yet everything that Jones so passionately points out about our expanding "shapeless cosmopolis" demonstrates that art can no longer fulfill the ancient conserving functions of epic tales and public monuments. Apart from its direct effects upon his own work, the chief value of his aesthetic program lies in his consciously pushing to their extremes the dilemmas of art today. For instance, if art is a language of signs, these signs, Jones knows, are constantly being invalidated by the speedy rhythms of cultural change and interchange. Locality and particularity are the substance of aesthetic reflection, but the forms of our world are universal and abstract. And though art must display the sacred otherness of fact, our minds and spirits have been shaped by science to treat fact as fact and nothing more.

What is fine about Jones is that he seeks neither to obscure these dilemmas nor to find a way out for himself and his work. (He is that rare anomaly, a regionalist who defends abstract art.) Nor, as has been noted, does he abhor the epoch that inflicts these dilemmas upon him. It is his faith, held against all evidence, that no alteration in man's condition will eliminate his sign-making proclivity; come what may, man will remain man-the-artist. To support that faith, Jones would rather take impossibilities upon himself than follow the logic of his ideas and close the door to creation. "It may be that the kind of thing I have been trying to make is no longer makeable in the kind of way in which I have tried to make it." To be sure, neither "In Parenthesis" nor "Anathemata" can be called a "making" at all in any traditionally accepted sense. "Ars," says Jones, "is concerned with the shape of a finished article." But "Anathemata," as its subtitle states, is "fragments of an attempted writing," and both it and "In Parenthesis" are arrangements of tentative insights and blocks of history without beginning or end, personal sorties into possibilities of language and feeling rather than works fashioned for the satisfaction of a pre-existing taste. They are formal embodiments of crisis, not as conceived in some ideological indictment but experienced "contactually" through the artist's attempt to organize the substance of his life: "One is trying to make a shape out of the very things of which one is oneself made." The result is about as good a general model of twentieth-century work as one can find: art that is "a series of fragments, fragmented bits, chance scraps really, of records of things, vestiges of sorts and kinds of *disciplinae*, that have come my way by this channel or that influence. Pieces of stuffs that happen to mean something to me and which I see as perhaps making a kind of coat of many colors, such as belonged to 'that dreamer' in the Hebrew myth."

To appreciate this Joseph's vision of art today, it is not necessary to agree with him about the nature of his Egypt or the causes of its crisis, to share his anti-urban feelings, or to regard machine production as a fall into subhumanity. (The manner of modern making may be more than compensated for by new social relations under which that making takes place; Jones himself wonders whether "our megalopolitan twilight" may not be showing forth a "Star of the Morning.") But however one interprets the existing cultural situation, Jones has formulated the axiomatic precondition for understanding contemporary creation: that one strip off "all defensive armour, so that the sharp contradictions and heavy incongruities may at least be felt. Vulnerability is essential."

10/23/56

Advance-guard Writing in America: 1900-1950

BY PAUL GOODMAN

Se quoque principibus permixtum agnovit Achivis,
Eoasque acies et nigri Memnonis arma.
—VIRGIL, *Aeneid*

An artist does not know that he is advance-guard, he must be told so or learn it from the reaction of the audience. *All* original composition—classical, standard, or advance-guard—occurs at the limits of the artist's knowledge, feeling, and technique. Being a spontaneous act, it risks, supported by what one has already grown up to, something unknown. The action of all art accepts an inner problem and concentrates on a sensuous medium. Obviously if one has an *inner* problem, one does not know beforehand the coming solution of it; and concentrating on the medium, one is surprised beyond oneself. Art-working is always just beyond what one can control, and the thing "does not turn out the way I planned." (In the best cases it is *just* beyond what one can control, and one has indeed learned to control the previous adventures up to that point, has acquired, as the ancients used to say, the habit of art that now again, in act, is in a present and therefore novel urgency.) Thus, whatever the subsequent social evaluation of a work—it may be quite traditional—to the creative artist as he makes it, it is always new and daring, and he cannot be morally or politically responsible for it. How could he be responsible, if he does not know what it will be? And further, the more powerfully spontaneous the working, the more he himself as a moral being will resist and disclaim it; a poet says what he does not wish to hear said. (Of course he is responsible artistically, to let the coming figure form with the utmost clarity and unity.)

For the most part, the products of such countless acts

Appears in *Utopian Essays and Practical Proposals*. Reprinted by permission of the author.

of artistic daring have been acceptable works, not far-fetched at all, but animating or perhaps troubling. The ir-responsible adventure turns out to be another proof of the common sensibility of mankind. The "inner problem" ac-cepted with reluctance by the artist is after all some uni-versal problem that now, thanks to the responsible art-working, has new words, a new image, a new facet. The audience accepts the work as genuine art. Sometimes, to be sure, if the effort has been extremely profound or sub-tle, or the problem has been new or idiosyncratic, the product does not find a ready or large audience. Neverthe-less, it is accepted as genuine, but perhaps "not for us," being too deep, decadent, or so forth.

But now there are also these other works that are indig-nantly rejected and called not genuine art, but insult, outrage, *blague, fumiste,* willfully incomprehensible, or, more favorably, with our childlike American docility, ex-perimental. And what is puzzling is that they are not iso-lated pieces, but some artists persistently produce such pieces, and there are whole schools of such "not-genuine" artists! What to make of this? In this case, the feeling of the audience is sound—it is always sound—there *is* insult, willful incomprehensibility, experiment; and yet the judg-ment of the audience is wrong—it is often wrong—for this is genuine art.

This seems to be a contradiction. For we defined the art-act as accepting the inner problem and concentrating on the sensuous medium; yet now we speak of a rhetorical attitude toward the audience, e.g., insult, and of an experi-mental handling of the medium, as still being genuine art. The explanation of this apparent contradiction gives us the nature of advance-guard and tells us its recent history and present direction.

Within the advance-guard artist, the norms of the audi-ence, of "society," exist as an introjected, unassimilated mass; it is their irk that is his special inner problem. It is his spontaneous attempt to vomit up or destroy and assim-ilate this irksome material that results in products that, as if willfully, offend, insult, or seek to disintegrate these same social norms. ("Introjects" are other people's stand-ards that one is forced to identify with as one's own.) All creative work occurs at the limits of knowledge and feel-ing, and the limits here are the risky attack on the unassim-

ilated, and perhaps unassimilable, as if to say, "Until I
get rid of this, I cannot breathe."

We may distinguish immature and mature advance-
guard. If the undigested mass is indeed digestible to those
of experience in society as a whole, then the advance-
guard offense is not taken as offensive, but as brash re-
belliousness which, if the offender is youthful, is considered
hopeful and charming. But if the undigested norms are
generally really indigestible, though socially accepted—
that is, if the standards of society in fact make everybody
unhappy—then the offense is insulting and "dangerous,"
and is met with social sanctions. Having caused offense
and being punished, the artist first knows that he is an advance-guard artist. Secondarily, then, he may as a moral
and political act appoint himself to this thankless career
and engage programmatically in the offense originally suggested by his creative work. Such a vocation of advance-
guard is not only insulting to the audience but a threat to
established institutions.

Consider as an example how France has been, up to
now, the native home of *avant-garde*. (I presume that the
military term comes from the disgusted generation of the
Restoration after the Congress of Vienna.) A stable land-
rooted bourgeois morality, an official "Cartesian" culture
of peculiar uniformity, and a sentimental Catholicism
were calculated to impress themselves on a growing mind
as the norms of all sense, reason, and charm; one could
not help swallowing them whole, without criticism. But
therefore, if one had any intellect and spirit, the subsequent inner nausea was bound to be early and total: bohemian, antisyntactical, and social-revolutionary. But therefore again, the French *avant-garde* always turns out to be
very "Cartesian," with proofs and manifestoes all in order,
and a keenness to proselytize and make uniform in the
latest cut. The French way of being a very great writer with
world-wide influence has usually been to invent a new
method or broach a new subject; writers of other lands
have had to write great books.

Whenever the mores are outmoded, anti-instinctual, or
otherwise counter to the developing powers of intelligent
and sensitive persons, there will be advance-guard work.
Yet, to repeat, advance-guard is not a direct attack on the
inhibiting mores, except secondarily. On the contrary, it is
precisely the intelligent and sensitive who, when they were

precocious children, most absorbed and identified themselves with the accepted culture, with whatever value it
had. It is only afterward that the nausea and anger set in,
inwardly, unknown, pervading the creative work. If advance-guard were a direct attack, it would not be genuine
art at all, and it would not ultimately become part of the
stream of tradition; but as the response to an inner irk, it
corrodes and pulverizes with creative work, it suffers the
conflict through, and it prepares the integrated normal
style of the next generation. Again, if advance-guard were
a direct attack, the response of the audience would be
angry defense and counterattack, instead of the peculiar
"outrage" which indicates that the members of the audience have the same inner difficulty but are unwilling to
recognize it; they are somehow "threatened."

Thus, if we want to retain the concept of "alienation,"
—e.g., to speak of artists "alienated" in having no social
status and having dissident values—we must be careful not
to mean simply that there are rival warring camps between
society and the artists—a sociological absurdity. But we
must mean (1) that society is "alienated" from itself, from
its own natural life and growth, and its persons are estranged from one another; but most members of society
do not feel their estrangement; (2) the artists, however,
feel it and regard themselves as estranged; and (3) society responds to them not with snobbery and incomprehension, as
to foreigners speaking a foreign tongue, but with outrage,
embarrassment, and ridicule, as to an inner threat. "Alienation" is primarily self-estrangement—this is, by the way,
how Marx used the term—and the advance-guard tries to
disgorge the alien culture.

Advance-guard periods are unsuited for the creation of
perfect works "exemplary to future generations," as Kant
would have said. The unassimilated culture prevents the
all-round development of the artist, it prevents him from
achieving a habit, and he spends too much energy in merely destroying what is not nourishing. Advance-guard works
tend to be impatient, fragmentary, ill tempered, capricious.
(Whether they are not thereby nearer to the human truth
is another question.) Perfect works are not fostered, either, by periods of "stability," whatever that means. They
are fostered by periods of expansion, for these nourish the
ongoing adventurous creative powers. If a period of expansion is followed, as Matthew Arnold said, by a period

of criticism that standardizes and popularizes the achievement, then, to the creative spirit, such a period is stagnant
and will be followed by a disgusted advance-guard. The
only healthy stability is an even growth.

2. Naturalism

I have set down these academic remarks in order to be
able to say something about the American advance-guard
from 1900 to 1950. During that period there was a deepening cultural crisis, and a deepening literary response,
going from an advance-guard of subject matter to an advance-guard of form to an advance-guard questioning the
worth of the art itself and its relation to the audience. By
the end of the period we can see shaping the lineaments of
our present writing. (May I ask the reader's indulgence if,
in treating so broad a subject, I speak in terms of decades
and mention "styles" and symbolical historical landmarks,
instead of individual works and real molecular changes.)

The advance-guard of the beginning of the century introduced offensive subject matter, in novels about the
seamy side of accepted morals, economics, and politics.
Contemporary with these were direct muckraking exposés
of the same subjects—so that advance-guard and reform
politics seem very close, but their approach is quite different. In an important sense this advance-guard succeeded, for, just as previously on the Continent, the factual account of sexuality and sexual misery, and poverty, exploitation, and graft has become standard literary content.
That is, what was achieved was the destruction not of the
institutions but of the hypocrisy and reticence concealing
them.

What gave to these early works a peculiar passion, quite
absent from later stories about this same subject matter, was the passionless and precise reportage, the naturalism of the telling. And contrast these creative works with
the muckraking journalism (and novels) of the same period. The journalism was indignant with the infamy. If the
novels, apparently having the same aim, had adopted the
same tone, they would not have outraged, though they
might have been banned as dangerous. For the muckraking tone accepts the same moral attitude as the audience's,
saying, "We attack what we consider evil, and this is an
evil overlooked by you." If the artists had said this, they
would have been worthy moral opponents. Instead they

offered the detailed image without evaluation and without the selection and arrangement that, according to the taste of that time, implied evaluation. What was the meaning of this naturalism?

The avowed aim of naturalism is familiar; to attack and reform by letting the facts speak for themselves, without style, as if to say, "There you see our world, damn it!" But of course naturalism is a highly artificial style. Its lack of selectivity is an icy selection from the common speech which abounds in evaluation. Naturalism is an icily hostile withdrawal from the audience, it will not share in their moral sense; it says in effect, "There is the world you have made for me, damn you. *I* abjure it. Put up with it if you can." This is an inward reaction to an introjected moral attitude, as if to say, "To be a person at all, to make evaluations, is to be like you, a hypocrite."

We may see the creative, self-curative use of such a response to an inward pathological situation if we bear in mind that naturalism is fundamentally a detailed stream of consciousness without evaluation. This is the means used in psychotherapy to recover a traumatic image; the detail provides associations, the suspension of evaluation prevents censorship. Now, it seems to me that, far from poets' having a conception of the abuse and attacking it, it was only by their method of naturalism that they were able to call up the scene of horror and overcome the hypocrisy in themselves. Secondarily they added on a program of reforms.

We, who have a different acquaintance with the kind of subject matter they broached, might find it hard to conceive their difficulty. Yet, to give a great example, it is hard otherwise to understand how so masterly an intellect as Ibsen could have hamstrung himself with his theatrical naturalism. It was *only* so, by making the scene real before his eyes, that he could believe the magnitude of his dissent from the mores.

In a Mallarmé, the anamnestic naturalism is pure and wonderfully total; he does nothing but notice and he notices, in principle, everything. Our novelists were more limited in what they noticed; and, more important, they at once confused their noticing with muckraking and moralizing. The reason for this confusion was that they made the assumption that a mere institutional change—sexual reform, socialism, etc.—would heal the inner irk, or, what is the same thing, create a society they could breathe in. Hypocrisy overcome, the truth out, everything good would follow. This assumption, which makes them seem close to the political reformers, was an illusion. The irk that brought them to a naturalistic handling of the subject matter could not be healed by merely altering the subject matter. However it was, even before the First World War, the advance-guard was already shifting away from the offensive subject matter to the offensive form and style, a much bolder effort of a much deeper dismay.

The audience reacted to the naturalistic offense with the specific sanction of censorship, on moral and political grounds. Yet this was obviously not a police measure of defense, to protect the children, but a reaction of outraged sensibility. There had to be spectacular trials to affirm the faith of the audience in itself. If there had been an objective danger, e.g., warmblooded pornography, the sales would have been wider and the police measures more quiet. The naturalistic scenes were socially harmless, the sales were small; but they were insulting, outrageous. That is, the audience felt perfectly well the icy hostility and froze, and rationalized the outrage as best it could.

3. The Revolution of the Word

The 'twenties, the aftermath of the war, was the golden age of advance-guard, and this kind of art was almost able to transform itself into integrated art. From that time on, the advance-guard has been international. It was an advance-guard of method, form, style.

A golden flowering of advance-guard is a paradox, but the paradox was in the times. People were stunned by the surprising barbarism of the First World War—how far we have come since then! The troubles in Western society, it was clear, were far deeper than could be cured by the intelligent practical reforms of its most social-minded physicians. History had gone beyond the revelations of the naturalists, and an artist could feel that if mankind dared so much, he could justifiably dare much further to solace his inner distress. At the same time, it was a period of hope and buoyancy. There was a general conviction that peace would be permanent—the nations outlawed war as "an instrument of national policy." The world became spectacularly international, and there was, after a short interim of reconstruction, an enormous economic production, scientific innovation, and technological application. It was a period of expansion, calculated, if it lasted, to produce modern masterpieces.

To understand the golden age of advance-guard, we must bear in mind the contrary facets: (1) the profound dismay at the breakdown of "civilization," and the inner disbelief in the previous programs of institutional change; the need to corrode the inner irk with a more thorough destructiveness; but (2) the buoyant hope and material prosperity, and the half-willingness of people in the victorious countries to venture a change—just as the vanquished were driven into a change. The first factor explains the advance-guard; but if we omit the second, we cannot understand the quantity and depth of the experiments, and the almost popularity achieved by the bizarre products. For advance-guard always rouses anxiety, but in conditions of expansion it is possible to tolerate the anxiety and allow the creative excitement to approach an integrated solution.

The advance-guard of the 'twenties was a concentrated attack on the formal attitudes of literature, the vocabulary, syntax, genre, method of narration, judgment of what is real and what is fantasy; everything, in short, that goes by the name Revolution of the Word. This revolution had begun earlier on the Continent, but now all forces joined and came to a climax and a self-consciousness. What is its meaning as a creative response to introjected norms?

The syntax and style of speech convey character, the so-called system of defenses and projections. Consider, as an analogy, the Rorschach test. In this test of "personality-type," the most important indices are not the content of what is seen in the blots, but the form of perception, e.g., whether color is seen or overlooked or there is shock at seeing color; whether color is seen free or in delineated areas; whether large details, small details, the whole are seen, and in what order; whether what is seen is on the periphery, in the center, down the middle line, always on the surface or sometimes in depth; whether the white spaces are seen as well as the inked ones; whether movement is projected, and so forth. It is these formal differences that project the type of feeling, the "personality." And so in literature. It is the formal actions, the structure, texture, diction, syntax, mood and tense, trope and image, concreteness and abstraction, directness and periphrasis, and so forth, that deeply communicate the character. To experiment with these things is the same as saying, "Not only do I disagree with you, but I am trying to make myself a different kind of person from what you made me, or what you are." Considered genetically, it is a going back to the time one first learned to speak and be a "person" at all. At the same time there is still the attempt to communicate by using the accepted machinery of communication, orthography, books, publication, as if to say, "Won't you become a different person? Try to understand me if I speak this new way."

Just as the previous naturalism was a kind of recovery of the traumatic scene, the Revolution of the Word was what later came to be called "character analysis." The parallel nonartistic movement of the time was medical psychoanalysis and progressive education, attempts to heal not institutions but personality disorders. And the secondary politics of the advance-guard tended to be the "permanent revolution," the expression of a worsening crisis in a period of expansion.

The insulted audience ridiculed the artists and charged them with bad faith and willful incomprehensibility. This meant that the audience felt that it was being not so much hostilely assaulted as disregarded. And this was indeed a correct feeling, for the artists were not regarding the audience as "persons"; it was the personality they shared with the audience that they were trying to disgorge. Alternately, the audience called the artists irresponsible children and felt that they themselves were bewildered children, and this was indeed the ambiguous nature of the case, for both were experimenting in learning to speak.

Unlike the grimness of naturalism, the Revolution of the Word was playful, euphoric, libidinous, dreamy, barbaric, exotic. To attack the institutions and ideology as the naturalists did, was to be infected with the guilt and punishment of instinct that had first resulted in the introjections. But to "pierce the character-armor" as did the Revolution of the Word, was to release pent-up drives. In principle such release is accompanied by intense anxiety. Nevertheless, as long as the period was economically booming and politically hopeful, it was possible to achieve wide toleration of the anxiety, especially by regarding the innovations as sophisticated (extremely "grown-up") and superficial (not "meant"). However it was, just as the standard literature of the 'twenties and 'thirties accepted the earlier advance-guard subject matter, so the 'forties consolidated much of the Revolution of the Word, especially in poetry, and the 'fifties have played with it still more freely, using it as a lingua franca for dissidents.

4. *Social Solidarity and "Irresponsibility"*

With the Depression and the looming of another war after all, the buoyancy vanished and the general anxiety became intolerable. In such circumstances, surface defenses are tightened and no inward adventure is possible. At once the advance-guard seemed to vanish from the scene. In the opinion of most critics twenty years later, it vanished for good and my history has no further relevance. But I shall show how in this continually deepening anxiety there has always been an advance-guard reaction, begun in the 'thirties and running afoul, and now—at the end of the 'fifties and into the 'sixties—beginning to affirm itself strongly, though not yet hitting on the right course. (If indeed the advance-guard had vanished in the 'thirties, we should have to reconcile ourselves to having no genuine literature at all—as seems to have been almost the case for two decades!—for it is impossible to *accept* the norms of anxiety, a clinging to security, and still create something.) But let us proceed step by step.

In the 'thirties, the Revolution of the Word began to be called "irresponsible"; and its obscurity, which had previously been shared in as entertaining and challenging, was rebuffed as Ivory Tower and of no consequence. To the artist this meant that now indeed he had no social role and he could call himself "alienated" or estranged, with what profound effect we must soon discuss. There was, however, an immediate reaction in the tightened circumstances of the anxious surface.

This was the literary manner of so-called "Socialist Realism"; for the most part it was merely reactive and without creative meaning, but if we carefully anatomize it, we can see that it contained something new. (1) The socialist-realists fully accepted the early-century program of reform, and with a deadly monotony reiterated the naturalistic subject matter. (2) They couched it in a banal dramatic manner, full of standard evaluation, that made the old-fashioned message quite reactionary in effect (as Trotsky, for instance, was quick to point out). (3) With this, however, there was a new sentiment: the solidarity of the artist and audience; that art is a solidary action; the artist is not physically or culturally isolated from the audience, though he may purposely attack it. This sentiment, which still has vitality, went back to such different advance-guard roots as Dada, the theater of participation, and the Bauhaus. But (4) instead of finding a creative expression of solidarity, the sentiment at once degenerated into opportunistic propagandizing of party formulas, first of the minority then of the majority.

The valuable new sentiment of solidarity—which we expect to appear in a crisis of fear, and which did appear— was debauched by the miserable pretense of the art, which renounced the artistic responsibility of inventing something new. It was a pretense, for whereas the naturalists had suffered an illusion, that their society, which they accepted at face value, could be reformed, these artists did not inwardly believe it at all. And outwardly, as it turned out, they eventually migrated to Hollywood or advertising or government service, there to endure ulcers, Stalinism, sinusitis, and such other complaints as come from aggressing against oneself and laying the blame elsewhere. The charge of "irresponsibility" was a projection; it was they who were irresponsible to their own creative selves. And finally, when the Second World War broke out, it was the official spokesmen who used the word "irresponsible" and took up the call for social solidarity.

Let us review the situation as it passed into the 'forties and toward our present day. On the one hand the norms that a young person perforce introjected were now extraordinarily senseless and unnatural—a routine technology geared to war, a muffled and guilty science, a standard of living measured by commodities, a commercial art, a moral "freedom" without personal contact: it is not necessary to go over this familiar ground. Then we should have expected the activity of artists of the late 'forties and the 'fifties to have been more than ever advance-guard. But the general anxiety and their own anxiety were such that there could be no audience recognition of any product of inward daring, if anyone could dare to produce it. (I think some of us continued.) What an artist would say spontaneously would now seem hopelessly irrelevant, likely even to himself, and he would have no means to communicate it, nor perhaps even incentive. This was a clinch.

The tendency of some artists would therefore be to fall silent, to accept their estrangement—and this seems to have been the case. (Instead of writers, we got the epidemic "revivals" of Melville, Henry James, F. Scott Fitzgerald, etc., even Nathanael West. This is too pathetic to dwell on.)

But of course the silence—the "silence, cunning, and exile"—is a physiological impossibility. Creative vitality simply expresses itself. The advance-guard action, then, took the form of concern neither with the subject matter nor the method, but with the use, and attitude, of being an artist at all. In the language of the accompanying philosophy, this was the "existential" problem for the artist: not what to think nor what kind of person to be; but how to persist at all, being an artist. (As usual, the advance-guard problem has slightly anticipated the current general problem: how to persist, being alive.) The literary revival—in America it was a discovery—of Kierkegaard made sense, for the age was again very like the Congress of Vienna.

The problem we faced—how to be an artist at all—was different from that blithely tackled by Dada in the early 'twenties, for at that time, in buoyant circumstances, it was possible to decide that art was pointless and to take revenge with irksome acts of anti-art; but in straitened circumstances one cannot allow himself such luxuries.

5. Aftermath of World War II

One would not call the aftermath of World War II buoyant and confident of progress. Probably one should not even call it an age of anxiety, as Auden did. Rather, from the clinical point of view, we have seen the phenomena of shell shock, a clinging to adjustment and security of whatever quality, and a complete inability to bear anxiety of any kind, to avoid panic and collapse. For instance, in 1948 I lectured on Kafka to a college audience composed of ex-soldiers. This audience unanimously insisted, with frantic emphasis, that Kafka was a freak whose psychotic vision had no relevance to anything in "real life." Where there was such insecurity as this, as not to allow even the possibility that all might not be well, we could expect little creativity of any kind.

Correspondingly, for at least a decade after the war, the literary atmosphere for the reception of any deepspringing art, advance-guard or otherwise, was miserable.

Beginning at about 1945 the start of front occured in PS; are outlant

Certainly the literary magazines were never so poor in forty years in this country. In the interest of a secure academism, including an academism of the 'twenties, they printed nothing that could arrest attention (although some things that were fine and solid). Perhaps no new things were submitted. At least the impression was created among young persons, who get incentive from such periodicals, that nothing astonishing was being done and nothing could be done. One felt, indeed, that this was the intention of the editors.

 It is the thesis of this essay that advance-guard is only one species of art and is, in principle, not the best art. Yet it comes to be the case that where the literary climate is unfavorable to the destructive élan of advance-guard, there is little genuine creation of any kind. The best period is one in which every new work destroys the convention of its predecessors, yet, advancing to just the next step—the result of an achieved habit and assimilated tradition—it carries its audience along. The possible, and usual, period is one in which the integrated artist employs productively the destructive work of an immediately previous advance-guard—and this is common within an artist's own career, his own youth being his advance-guard. But where the advance-guard dies, the language dies.

6. *New Directions Apparent Around 1950*

Now consider, as we have been doing, the introjection of the norm of shell shock, equivalent to clinging to security. Genetically this takes us very far back, to the infantile fright of total abandonment. The average person feels it as a lack of concern and a passionless going about one's business. (Hannah Arendt has well described this indifference and excessive busyness in the spectacularly guilty and shell-shocked Germans post Hitler; but the ill has been much more universal than she seems to be aware of.) A self-aware person feels the introjected shell shock as his estrangement. The advance-guard artist, however, unwilling to accept this introject as his own, revives from the fright of total abandonment, begins to wail and reach out—to the audience, for a new possibility. He becomes first a cry baby, then an unwanted lover. That is, to persist at all, being an artist, the advance-guard artist tries to create a new relation of artist and audience. The art of the artist is to invent ways needfully to throw himself on the mercy of the audience. By this aggression he saves the audience from its numb shock. To explore this, let me describe three advance-guard tendencies apparent around 1950, and that still are working themselves out. Let me call them the direction of Genet, of Cocteau, and of a writer who proceeds from a remark of Goethe.

(1) Conscious of estrangement, serious standard writers, in their self-portraits and choice of protagonists, have more and more been describing marginal personalities— criminals, perverts, drunkards, underground people—or persons in extreme situations that make them "existent" rather than universal. Their artist no longer considers himself an accuser or advocate, an explorer or a radical, but as one beyond justification, as if to say, "Your judgment is indifferent to me." In plot, the melodrama of the sensational popular writer is now the sober content of the standard writer. The meaning of it is, clearly, the assertion of the repressed vitality in despite of the lifeless or shell-shocked norms, but it accepts the normal judgment and fails to create a new valuation. This is, of course, to give up the possibility of humane synthesis altogether. Therefore, one kind of possible advance-guard action would be to assert the marginal as the central and to prove its justification, thereby demolishing the norm.

This is what Genet has tried. In a famous speech on delinquency, he explains himself succinctly. He says that as a man he has little sense of moral values, they do not concern him. His only contact with life is the act of writing. But when he comes to write about the law-abiding or the esteemed, his pen stands still, his images do not soar, the rhythm limps. As soon as he takes up his criminal types, however, he has plenty to say, his style warms up. Therefore he must, he does, present the criminals in a more heroic light; and therefore he has come to understand that they are the superior people. Genet uses the action of art, that is, his existential role, to find vital norms, necessarily offensive and alone, for him, justifying. (Naturally, they are the norms of his own inner problem, which seems to be a conflict between accepted castration and flaming exhibition. It is interesting to contrast this with the almost similar conflict of our Hemingway, accepted castration and stoical endurance, which has made him the classical writer for the serious young men of the Organized system.)·

Genet pursues his prophetic role with a careful calculation of his audience. E.g., in *Les Pompes Funèbres* the chief person is at once introduced as honorably glorying in a masochistic idolatry for a Nazi soldier occupying Paris, with whom he happily performs what the audience will consider the ugliest possible sexual act. Yet Genet manages to keep confronting the reader with such fullness of affection and of desire to be accepted—and profound thought and remarkable language—that finally the normal valuation is indeed swept away, and there is confusion, grief, and contact.

As the shock of the infantile fright of total abandonment relaxes, the first creative act is to wail, "Help! I am abandoned." This puts it up to the listener. What the method says is this, "I have proved we are *both* lost; therefore, instead of your clinging to a false adjustment, let us cling together." The audience must respond to it by trying to annihilate the outcry, as if it had not been heard, or to prevent others from hearing it. The snub that the audience administers is not, then, one of outrage but of embarrassment before a poor relation, as in the joke where the millionaire tells his butler, "This beggar is breaking my heart, throw him out!"

(2) To an academic critic, the later plays and films of Jean Cocteau seem to bear out the rule mentioned above, that an artist's early work is the advance-guard that is consolidated in his later, standard work. The only problem would be how from such a likely sowing comes such poor fruit. But Cocteau himself has explained his intentions otherwise, and has given his theory of the right direction for advance-guard. We must attend to it, for during this century he has been the advance-guard's chief philosopher.

It is inadmissible, he says in *Foyer des Artistes*, for the poet to allow his audience to be lost to commercial entertainers. The heat of the audience is necessary for the persistence of the artist. Now, what attracts the audience is, in principle, corn, vulgar sentiment. Therefore the artist must at present, with all the honor and truth of genuine art, convey this corn, and so Cocteau has chosen to do. That is, what seems to be curiously stupid standard work is really a daring advance-guard effort to answer the crucial question of how to unmake alienation.

Nevertheless, the works are stupid. "Precisely," the creator might say; "they were not made for you." Perhaps the problem is too hard and the poet is suffering an illusion and undergoing a kind of (profitable) martyrdom. The corn in these works of Cocteau is still alien to himself, he cannot energize it with feeling. To put it bluntly, it is not yet low enough to be quite uncorrupted. (Let me say that in the film *Orphée* Cocteau fortunately gave up the noble program for which he was unprepared, and again made something fine. Plastically and poetically, *Orphée* is by no means equal to *Le Sang d'un Poète* of which it is the sequel, but the grim honor with which it treats its subject—what it means to be the youth-thieving poet now "stinking with money and success"—makes a very poignant work.)

Anyone who chooses this direction, of seducing the audience, must without talking down find a level of subject matter so elementary that he and the audience really share it in common, meaning by it the same thing. There must be such common subject matter, for all of us walk on the ground, breathe, and so forth, and these things are common and not subject to the corruption of self-alienation. Somewhere between this level and the level of shell shock and commercialized sentiment, there must be a border line of subject matter felt by the artist and not quite devitalized in the audience. It is here that the advance-guard must operate. (Is this the intention of the *Nouvelle Vague?*)

As the shock of total abandonment relaxes, the infant reaches out with coaxing and flattery, or with teasing and being nasty, saying, "How can I please you? How can I annoy you?" Trying still to please at too adult a level, Cocteau merely flatters the normal audience without offense. The sanction of the audience against him is to make him a commercial success and appoint him to the French Academy. The advance-guard artist must invent something more direct and childish that will win a smile or a slap of which all are at once ashamed.

(3) But finally, the essential aim of our advance-guard must be the physical re-establishment of community. This is to solve the crisis of alienation in the simple way. If the persons are estranged from one another, from themselves, and from their artist, he takes the initiative precisely by putting his arms around them and drawing them together. In literary terms this means: to write for them about them personally, and so break the roles and format they are huddled in. It makes no difference what the genre is,

whether praise or satire or description, or whether the style is subtle or obscure, for anyone will pay concentrated attention to a work in which he in his own name is a character. Yet such personal writing can occur only in a small community of acquaintances, where everybody knows everybody and understands what is at stake; in our estranged society it is just this intimate community that is lacking. Of course it is lacking! Then give up the ambitious notion of public artist. The advance-guard action is to create such community, starting where one happens to be. The community comes to exist by having its culture; the artist makes this culture.

We know that for various moral and political reasons such movements toward community have occurred widely, sporadically, since the war. But no such community can flourish on moral, economic, or political grounds alone, for—whatever its personal satisfactions—its humane integration cannot compete with the great society, however empty it is. As a friend to all such places, I would urge them to attach to themselves their artists and give them free rein, even at the risk of the *disruptive* influence of these artists.

As soon as the intimate community does exist—whether geographically or not is not essential—and the artist writes for it about it, the advance-guard at once becomes a genre of the highest integrated art, namely Occasional poetry, the poetry celebrating weddings, commencements, and local heroes. "Occasional poetry," said Goethe, "is the highest kind"—for it gives real and detailed subject matter, it is closest in effect on the audience, and it poses the enormous problem of being plausible to the actuality and yet creatively imagining something unlooked-for.

An aim, one might almost say the chief aim, of art is to heighten the everyday, to bathe the world in such a light of imagination and criticism that the persons who are living in it without meaning or feeling find that it is meaningful and feelingful to live.

Obviously, if the artist, responsible to his art, commits himself to his bold insight and genuine feeling, and brings it home inevitably to the audience by writing man to man *ad hominem,* the Occasional poetry that he creates is not likely to flatter or comfort. Rather it will always have the following ambiguous effect: on the one hand it is clearly an act of love, embarrassing in its directness, for to give one's creative attention to anyone is a gesture of love; on the other hand, given the estrangement of the aliens from one another, it will always seem, and be, an act of hostility, an invasion of privacy, a forcing of unwanted attention. To the extent, then, that this advance-guard does not succeed in welding a community secure enough to bear criticism and anxiety—and how can a single-handed poet accomplish much?—the sanction against it is absolute and terrible: exclusion from the circle of frightened acquaintances.

7. The Nature, Advantages, and Disadvantages of Advance-Guard

Let me now review the course of this argument as a whole. We started by distinguishing advance-guard as a species of genuine art with a social-psychological differentia: that an important part of the advance-guard artist's problem is the destruction of introjected social norms. This explains the peculiar offense of advance-guard to the audience. Tracing the history of the introjected norms and the advance-guard response, we singled out three phases: the phase of the rejection of institutions by naturalistic revelation and hostile withdrawal of feeling; the phase of the rejection of normal personality by experiments on the language (character analysis), arousing anxiety; and the phase of the rejection of self-alienated adjustment by direct contact with the audience, rousing the embarrassments of offered but unwanted love.

We are now in a position to restate more fundamentally the difference between integrated art and advance-guard. What, psychologically, is the meaning of an art that has a sociological differentia in its definition?

We must say, with Otto Rank, that the action of art asserts immortality against the loss, waste, and death in oneself and the world; and the artist appoints himself to the recreation—who else will do it? Now the advance-guard artist is essentially concerned with the immortal perfection of the particular society of which he is a member, whereas the more integrated artist, taking his environment for granted, is concerned with the universal human condition as embodied in his own problem.

Here too the usual opinion is just the contrary of the truth. The advance-guard artist is considered as going his own irresponsible way, heedless of his audience, and dwelling in an ivory tower. But the truth is that his relation to his audience is his essential plastic medium—so that he is often careless with the material medium; he is excessively socially responsible. On the other hand, the usual sentiment is accurate, for standard art the audience can take or leave, but advance-guard is irritating and obstrusive and cannot be disregarded; it is a loving and hostile aggression on the audience.

In the little history we have sketched, we have seemed to come full circle: in the beginning it was the naturalistic artist who withdrew, in the end it is the shell-shocked audience that withdraws. But throughout there is the attractive and repulsive tampering of the artist and audience with one another. In order to reconstitute a better society within himself, the artist destroys the existing society. This is naturally resisted. Yet people, too, are dissatisfied with their state and want to get on, and they are fascinated by any new direction.

What are the peculiar advantages and disadvantages of advance-guard? We have pointed out that an advance-guard artist must divert energy to an internal problem that is not constructively his own, but only destructively; this hinders an ease of flow and symmetry of form. (In the best cases the parts of an inner conflict are fused and transformed in the coming solution; in advance-guard there are some elements that are merely to be attacked and destroyed.) On the other hand, there is no doubt that his concern for the destruction and reconstruction of society as a part of his art draws on powerful energies of its own, unavailable to standard artists: both the memory of a very early time of satisfactory interpersonal peace—an "age of gold"—and the present-day revolutionary ferment. It is impossible for any artist to ignore the problem of social renovation. In the best, expansive period, all the agents of society are engaged in the renovation, and the artist need not particularly concern himself with it, it "takes care of itself"; that is, he need not inquire where he is man, where artist, where citizen. In other ages, the advance-guard artist "wastes himself" on the social problem —it is his vocation, for it exists within him; but the standard artist ignores it at the price of losing the glancing brilliance of actual relevance (I do not mean the slick shine of commercial relevance), and he may soon become merely academic.

From the point of view of society, again, it is certainly
no advantage to be manipulated "for its own good" by artists, and it is even worse when the aim is to make society
into a work of art. Yet there is, in life, an important factor that can be called "the art of life"—concern and distress for the style we live—and in a disintegrated culture
like our own, very few are busy with it, and among these
is the advance-guard artist. And from the point of view of
the artist, again, in a shell-shocked society like ours there is
a general estrangement, and the artist is estranged, in the
sense especially that he feels helplessly without status. But
being more conscious of his estrangement, he is really less
estranged than the others, and he is used to inventing
means of communication, patterns, irritants, bridges; this
is his forte.

An artist feeds on fame. It is only this, to quote Rank
again, that alleviates his "guilt of creation" by gaining him
accomplices. Here the advance-guard artist is in an ironical situation. More than others, he needs accomplices, not
only *post factum,* but as collaborators *in delictu,* in con-
structing the social art-object in a rebellious atmosphere.
Yet his hardly veiled hostility and embarrassing love diminish his chance of personal fame and drive off his collaborators. On the other hand, he is less lonely. He more
easily identifies himself, with pain, with the whole social
framework; and with hope, with its future in young persons.

In America, as we proceed further into the 'sixties,
there seems to be plenty of advance-guard writing again;
just as for the previous twenty years there seemed to be
none. But these judgments of audiences and critics are
pretty illusory: they depend on the degree of the audience's own anxiety. When anxiety is very strong, oblivion
is a characteristic sanction of the outraged audience; the
advance-guard offense is present, felt, and "annihilated,"
excluded from the possibility of being real. The artists go
underground, and when they reappear they bring with
them the underground.

The Fate of the Avant-Garde

BY RICHARD CHASE

It is the custom nowadays to pronounce the avant-garde dead. But the fact seems to be that under modern conditions the avant-garde is a permanent movement. Far from being merely the isolated band of highbrows and sterile academicians many Americans think it is, the vanguard of writers and artists has been, for more than one hundred and fifty years, a necessary part of the cultural economy, and the health of culture depends upon its recurring impulse to experimentation, its search for radical values, its historical awareness, its flexibility and receptivity to experience, its polemical intransigence.

Historically the avant-garde is the heir to the aristocratic coterie or court circle of artists and intellectuals. But whereas the aristocratic coterie of Medieval and Renaissance times had no commitment except to itself and posterity and consequently felt free to cultivate the distinterested pursuit of art and ideas apart from the rest of society, history has imposed upon the modern avant-garde the duty not only of disinterestedly cultivating art and ideas but of educating and leading an aimless body of philistine taste and opinion.

The historical role of the avant-garde was thus necessitated by the breakdown of the aristocratic class and by the spread of literacy. After the eighteenth century, the democratization of culture and the new literacy confronted the advanced intelligence with a newly arisen welter of taste and opinion which, left to itself, found no other standards than the conformism, at once aggressive and complacent, of the bourgeoisie. In this situation the dissident intellectual, himself characteristically a bourgeois, found his mission. The mediocrity and, as it were, histori-

From *Partisan Review,* Summer 1957, Volume XXIV, Number 3, pp. 363-375. © 1957 by *Partisan Review.* Reprinted by permission.

cal helplessness of his class in matters of art and ideas were an open invitation to his powers of discrimination and foresight. At the same time, his instinct for self-preservation and his powers of polemic were animated and challenged by the hostility with which his efforts were met.

In America especially, official middle-class opinion is always relegating its avant-garde to the ash-can, but the phoenix rises again. The death of the avant-garde could only come about if all expressions of taste and opinion were reduced to standardized commodities, such as are purveyed by mass culture. If this should happen there would be so little openness of mind, so little variability of preference and commitment, that not only the avant-garde but all significant activities in arts and letters would cease to be. But there does not seem to be any immediate danger of this, despite the enormous influence of the mass media. The vital dialectics of American culture still have room to operate.

Any cultural vanguard must have roots in its native soil, yet it is freer of nationalism than the rest of middle-class opinion and feels its ties with foreign intellectual movements. The dissident intelligentsia, if one may use so grand a term, is therefore international as well as national and has a unity of purpose apart from local economic and political conditions. Thus one may find inspiration and hope in the continuing identity of the restive avant-garde in communist countries, like Poland and Hungary, where the cultural commissar exerts a crushing influence in imposing conformist values on artists and thinkers, values which are in so many ways indistinguishable from those of the middle-class philistine in non-Communist countries.

But if the avant-garde is not dead, it remains true that its recent phase of "modernism" and experimentalism in the arts is, after forty years of struggle, finally exhausted. Why should it not be exhausted?—considering that, as Joseph Frank says, "we are now at the tail-end of the greatest flowering of American arts and letters since New England transcendentalism—a flowering that far surpasses the earlier one in force and originality." Without the concerted effort of the free spirits of the time, in the flow and upsurge of their power, this flowering would not have come about. We now inevitably find ourselves in a period of suspended animation and cultural confusion. If we are ever to set the ball rolling again, we have got to be clear first about the traditional significance of the avant-garde in its international and its native aspect and, second, about the cultural dialectic which in the past it has articulated and vivified in this country.

Although it is obviously not so, many intelligent people persist in the belief that the avant-garde is self-appointed, that it is historically gratuitous and irrelevant. It is accused of perversely *alienating itself* from what is vaguely referred to as the broad healthy mainstream of culture. Philip Rahv has commented on this attitude in a passage which, since it should be classic in this discussion, I quote at length:

> The neo-philistines make an opportune kind of optimism their credo; they are impatient to assume the unchallenge-able reality of the "world," and while reconciled to mass-culture they are inclined to deprecate the traditional atti-tudes of the literary and artistic avant-garde—attitudes said to arise out of negativism pure and simple and willful in-dulgence in "alienation." Now the avant-garde is of course open to criticism. It has the typical faults of its incon-gruous position in a mass-society, such as snobbery and pride of caste. It is disposed to take a much too solemn and devotional view of the artist's vocation. Its distortions of perspective result from its aloofness and somewhat inflexible morality of opposition. But to accuse it of having invented alienation is ludicrous. For what the avant-garde actually represents historically, from its very beginnings in the early nineteenth century, is the effort to preserve the integrity of art and the intellect amidst the conditions of alienation brought on by the major social forces of the modern era. The avant-garde has attempted to ward off the ravages of alienation in a number of ways: by means of developing a tradition of its own and cultivating its own group norms and standards, by resisting the bourgeois in-centives to accommodation, and perforce making a virtue of its separateness from the mass. That this strategy has in the main been successful is demonstrated by the only test that really counts—the test of creative achievement. After all, it is chiefly the avant-garde which must be given credit for the production of most of the literary masterpieces of the past hundred years, from *Madame Bovary* to the *Four Quartets;* and the other arts are equally indebted to its ven-turesome spirit.

The French Encyclopedists showed many of the character-istics of the avant-garde, but probably, as Mr. Rahv sug-gests, a more distinctly modern form of cultural advance was to be seen in the German and English, and later in the French romantic movements. The Wordsworth-Coleridge group was avant-garde in the modern sense, and in various countries and under varying conditions their kind of insurgence has been repeated in waves of forward-moving and receding energy.

It should be noted in passing that although we see in Wordsworth and Coleridge and later in Keats, Shelley and Byron two phases of cultural insurgence, the dialectics of English culture are somewhat misleading when the attempt is made to apply them to American culture. This analogy is always made by middlebrow writers in their effort to cut the ground out from under the vanguard. They tell us that sometimes there is no need for a dissident intelligentsia, and in support of this argument they point to the Victorian age, when not only inferior writers but the great writers of the time won more or less immediate public esteem and authority. It is true that this happened in England, but it did not happen in America, where the great writers were not the popular ones. The great writers, like Melville, Whitman, and James, had to content themselves with a fugitive notoriety and long neglect. By comparison with America England is an organic and continuous culture. What has not been sufficiently seen is that American culture shows far more enduring contradictions and discontinuities than does English culture—or if this has been seen, its consequences have not yet been understood. American civilization, happily similar to English in many ways and particularly in its political character, tends, in the quality of its cultural movements, to resemble French and Russian civilization, at least in the sense that it shows very disparate extremes of taste and opinion. The statement that French culture is a long dialectical argument between Pascal and Montaigne is an inevitable and significant truth. Van Wyck Brooks' idea that American culture is similarly typified by the difference between Jonathan Edwards (the "highbrow") and Benjamin Franklin (the "lowbrow") is also a far-reaching truth. But English cultural history offers no such clear-cut polarities. At certain periods of its history England had evolved an admirable middle culture, a main body of taste and opinion, into which the avant-garde, never radically alienated in the first place, could be temporarily absorbed, without detriment to the cultural life of the nation. This has never happened in America, where all the great things have been done by lowbrows or by highbrows and where the middle culture, beginning with Howells, has been mediocre, has too easily found its motives in commercialism and academic conformity, has incongruously patterned itself on the English model, and has thus fundamentally misunderstood and feared the really definitive characteristics of American culture.[1]

Mr. Rahv says that the avant-garde tends to develop "a tradition of its own" and to cultivate "its own group norms and standards." And herein lies the paradox, for like all traditions and standards, these are subject to calcification and are therefore in need of perpetual change and renewal. Indeed, one must admit that the cultural vanguard is more subject to calcification than are other traditions. Its necessary extremism and its intensely articulated polemical attitude not only give it dynamism but lay it open to rigidification and sterility, whereas the very aimlessness of conventional culture saves it from these extremes.

The insurgent movement in this country which defended "modernism"—that is, the aesthetic experimentalism and social protest of the period between 1912 and

[1] I am well aware that this will sound to some readers too abstract and willful, too gratuitously intransigent. I am aware too of the genuine middlebrow virtues which were articulated and defended by Howells, pale and derivative as they are compared with English middlebrowism. It is true that enlightened publishers and professors are for the moment hospitable to talents of high order—of the sort which formerly in this country they would take seriously only after resisting a long avant-garde campaign. For example, Dylan Thomas quickly gained such popularity as comes to serious poets, without much intervention by avant-garde critics. The paperback classics, old and new, appear really to have discovered a fairly large audience of discerning readers. The general complacency that most people feel these days about the middle culture and the favorable situation of the writer and artist in America may actually turn out to have some justification. It is possible that history has in store for us a more organic and continuous culture than we have had in the past. Perhaps the new suburban, totally-populated, bureaucratized, and other-directed America is already rendering historically archaic the kind of culture critique which, following writers like Tocqueville and the early Brooks, I have been bringing to bear on the problem of the avant-garde. Perhaps there has already evolved a fundamentally new situation which has brought to a conclusion not only the modernist phase but the whole history of our culture from the seventeenth century down to 1950. It may be, in short, that the kind of critique suggested in these pages applies only (to go on with Riesman's handy terms) to the older Calvinist, production-oriented, inner-directed America. In the new America there may be no need for the avant-garde spirit—or for culture. Meanwhile, although the future is obscure, we have one clear option before us: we can at least try to understand the past and the present.

1950—has expired of its own success. Until recently the avant-garde writer, who made it his mission to promote "modernism," could feel that he was (in Van Wyck Brooks' phrase) "employed by civilization." Now he is more likely employed only by a university or a publishing house. The university and the publishing house have accepted Joyce, Pound, Eliot, Melville, James, Hemingway, and Faulkner—authors the avant-gardist once touted in vain—just as conclusively as Tennyson was ever accepted. And it appears that civilization no longer offers the insurgent intellectual or artist a job, or if it does, it is not the same job, and the particular tastes, ideas, and purposes it calls for are by no means clear. Still, the erstwhile insurgent modernist who believes that one phase of the avant-garde movement is dead but that the stratagem of avant-garde activity is of permanent value in America may at least look into the past, partly with the hope of catching a glimpse of the future.

As we have been told at length, the serious writer of the nineteenth century was painfully on his own. We are not surprised to find two of the most isolated of these writers pleading for what we should call an avant-garde movement. Thus Melville begs his contemporaries to "confess" immediately the greatness of Hawthorne without waiting for the slow judgment of posterity, which, whatever it may be, will do neither Hawthorne nor his generation any good, at least not while they still have the power of further accomplishment. "By confessing him," in Melville's well-known words, "you thereby confess others; you brace the whole brotherhood. For genius, all over the world, stands hand in hand, and one shock of recognition runs the whole circle round." Yet Melville's plea had no more effect than the similar plea in Henry Adams' letter of 1862 to his brother Charles Francis: "What we want is a *school*. We want a national set of young men like ourselves or better, to start new influences not only in politics, but in literature, in law, in society, and throughout the whole social organism of the country—a national school of our own generation." As it turned out, Adams' broadly based insurgent intelligentsia was even less possible than Melville's more purely literary "brotherhood."

There was, to be sure, sporadic insurgent activity in the nineteenth century. The Concord transcendentalists were a genuine avant-garde movement. There were tenuous and momentary groups like the "young America" writers of the 1830s who contributed to the *Democratic Review*. Walt Whitman, himself in one sense a member of the transcendentalist group, was a kind of one-man vanguard with a number of sadly inferior disciples around him, such as O'Connor and the Pfaff beer-cellar wits and bohemians. But Whitman's plea in *Democratic Vistas* for a new school of "literatuses" who would combat the conventional, genteel writers of the day and prophesy and articulate a radical American culture reminds us that during his middle and old age no such movement appeared and that, despite his disciples, Whitman was nearly as isolated as Melville and Adams.

However, about 1912 a genuine vanguard movement emerged in this country, in dramatic response both to the historical demands and possibilities of American culture and in response to the international movement of "modernism." The tremendous energy liberated by this upsurge of creativity and criticism, despite the disasters that successively overtook it in the form of two world wars and a great depression, lasted for nearly forty years. There seems to be no generally accepted name for the six years or so after 1912 when the character of the modern movement in arts and letters was defined and the cultural energy we have been drawing on ever since was finally able to break through the conventional surface of American life. "Resurgence" is perhaps the most accurate word. The movement did not happen in a vacuum; it had been prepared (to look no farther back) by the social critics of the second half of the last century, notably Whitman, Adams, Howells, Bellamy, and Veblen. The ground had been laid, too, by the European heralds of modern times, such as Marx, Arnold, Shaw, Freud, and Nietzsche (whose writings constitute a philosophy and psychology of avant-garde action). It was the first time since the transcendentalist period that the barriers of provincialism were broken down and the most important minds of Europe were felt immediately, without being bowdlerized and filtered through the medium of genteel or middle-brow criticism.

Although it had a sense of a common purpose, the Resurgence was a many-sided affair, including the prophetic literary nationalism of Brooks and his associates, the poetic *risorgimento* of Ezra Pound and his group, the political-literary liberalism of Walter Lippmann and Herbert

Croly in the *New Republic,* the pragmatism of Dewey, the New History of Beard and James Harvey Robinson, the popularized Nietzschean iconoclasm of Mencken, and so on. Despite the discontinuity of taste and opinion that characterized the three decades after 1920—so that a writer who felt culturally at home in 1920 might feel totally at sea in 1930 and at sea all over again but in a different way in 1940—one could still draw on the emotional and intellectual capital of the Resurgence. This was true not only of the avant-garde but of the liberal middlebrow critics who soon began to oppose everything radical and extreme in modern culture, and it was true also of such momentary "Counter-revolutionary" groups as the New Humanists.

Yet nowithstanding this continuity of energy in the midst of bewildering historical changes, there was a tragic wastefulness in the modern movement. The impact of the First World War fragmented and dispersed the Resurgence into the brilliant but unstable individual performances of the writers and artists of the 1920s. The economic pressures of the 1930s brought about a revival of the social concerns of 1912, but the generous and hopeful (and in some ways, it must be admitted, unrealistic) reform programs of the Resurgence were reduced to forms of doctrinaire politics, whether of the left or the right, which could not stand the test of time. The dispersal of energies in the 1920s and the reductive and repressive consolidations of the 1930s, historically inevitable as they may have been, left little cultural capital in the bank and failed to open up any significant new sources of renewal and recoupment.

The literary academicism of the 1940s was on the whole a fairly tame movement, although I cannot refrain from expressing my feeling that that period has been much maligned. The unintimidated critic is still wanting who will prove brave enough to defend a decade which saw the emergence of writers like Saul Bellow, Randall Jarrell, Robert Lowell, Ralph Ellison, Alfred Kazin, Isaac Rosenfeld, Mary McCarthy, and Leslie Fiedler, among many others—a decade which, furthermore, if it was too academic, nevertheless came to understand American culture and its "usable past" much more accurately than they were ever understood before.

In general, one may say that all the clamoring spirits of

1912-1918 were avant-garde, Van Wyck Brooks as much so as Ezra Pound. After the war, however, a large segment left the avant-garde and, like Brooks himself, fell back on the cultural middle ground that had been prepared by Howells, the protean Howells, who had his complacent as well as his radical side. Brooks abdicated from modern culture about 1925, drawing back in horror from the genie whose bottle his early polemics had helped to unstopper. For behold! among the great writers who really spoke for the present and the future were Eliot, Joyce, Proust, Gide, Hemingway, and Pound, and they all seemed to Brooks culturally dangerous—they were, he said, undemocratic, highbrow, coterie writers.

Ever since Brooks' abdication, one of the main debates of American intellectual life has been that between the middlebrow and the highbrow (both claiming an affinity with or disowning the intellectually inarticulate lowbrow as it suited their purposes). The middlebrow claims to swim in the main stream of life and of culture and accuses the highbrow of irrelevance, ignorance, and sterility. The highbrow retorts that the middlebrow's "main stream of life and culture" is more than likely only the backwaters of history, or the stagnant waters of conventional success.

Pound and Brooks have been in many ways the typical symbols of our modern cultural debate. From a historical point of view, they seem oddly alike, especially in their early days. This is a fact of more than passing interest, as was pointed out by C. G. Wallis a long time ago. Both Pound and Brooks claim a descent from Whitman. Both launched about 1915 a program for the radical revision of taste and opinion. Both assume a vigorous pedagogic tone, alternately iconoclastic and prophetic. Both plead for a concerted intelligentsia. They are both against puritanism, Babbittry, and gentility and in favor of the new realism. They evolve their different but complementary versions of the "usable past" and come up with a rather narrow canon of sacred texts; with Pound it is Dante, Guido, Sappho, Arnaut, Chaucer; with Brooks, it is Ruskin, Ste.-Beuve, William Morris, Taine, Nietzsche. They share a strong but not too clear idea of the high office of the Poet as a social force. They both stress the cultural poverty of America, Pound speaking of "poets astray in the villages" and Brooks of "the ordeal of Mark Twain." Mr. Wallis points out that they are both examples of "the self-educated man

whose urge to moralize outstrips his taste and judgment,"
that "neither of them is much good at discursive reason-
ing," that "both writers have worked hard at perfecting a
pastiche style; more than a third of the *Cantos* is translation or paraphrase; the fabric of Brooks' New England
books is largely paraphrase or quotation without quotation
marks."

Without trying to make too much out of these broad
similarities, one can see that they do suggest once again
the well-known fact that cultural battles are always bitter-
est between antagonists who are in some ways alike. They
also suggest a good deal of immaturity, insecurity, and
provincialism on both sides of the fence. And in fact the
continuing virulence of the highbrow-middlebrow debate
in this country bespeaks what is in many ways a still raw
civilization.

Thus it was alternately disheartening and amusing to
find the now Olympian Brooks descending into the arena
again, as he did recently in an essay in the *Times Book
Review,* in order to attack the avant-garde. My innocent
response, on picking up Brooks' article was something like
this: If only Van Wyck Brooks, who throughout his long
career has done so much great work and has meant so
much to all of us, would say something disorderly, like the
aging Whitman, or the aging Yeats, or even the aging Howells—instead of launching one more dull attack on the
highbrows. But no—he still complains that Pound
"chucked out" Virgil and Thucydides and that Joyce "sa-
tirized out of existence so many of the greatest writers,"
and so on. Brooks' idea that at present "avant-garde circles" stretch "from one end of the country to another,"
each submitting itself to the "party line" is of course the
sheerest fantasy. It is an example of the tactic of those
who say that the "critics" and the quarterly magazines
now maintain a tight reactionary grip over the cultural life
of America. The second step in this generally bogus argument is to present the reigning middlebrowism of our time
as if it were a form of rebellion instead of what it actually
is—namely, the most successful form of cultural complacency in the Age of Eisenhower. Where and what is "the
parent intellectual body" with which Brooks says the
avant-garde should restore its ties? Where and what is
"the mainland of American thinking" from which the
"magic island" of the advanced intellectuals is detached?

Not that these are necessarily meaningless concepts—but what *do* they mean?

The concern of the critic at present should be exactly this alleged middle ground of culture, this more or less mythic center of taste and opinion—on the assumption, that is, that the duty of the critic is always to concern himself with whatever looks like the most powerful form of obscurantism and the most self-interested and successful kind of cultural mystique and polemic at any given time. There is no service in attacking the avant-garde critics, as everyone, including most of the critics themselves, are doing these days. It is all too clear what is wrong with them. Or if not, let me repeat: their specifically polemical task of the last forty years has expired with the success of the movements they championed. They have not yet clearly formulated what their duties in this interim period are. Meanwhile, they suffer from the well-known maladies of the avant-gardist, especially on the ebb tide of his influence: sterility, academicism, willful and excessive intellectuality.

But although the most forward-looking critics of the day should be trying to keep alive such imperfect dialectics as have been evolved in the effort to understand American culture, although they should be asking what is meant by "the parent intellectual body" and "the mainland of American thinking," the familiar attitude is quite different. William Barrett has recently expressed the widespread feeling of intellectuals by saying: "since I have left the world of the highbrow, the terms 'highbrow' and 'lowbrow' do not seem to me to clarify human issues as much as I once thought they did." There is much to be said for this attitude, suggesting, as it does, two things—first, that the goal of the relaxed and enlightened man should be a flexibility of taste and, second, that the terms "highbrow" and "lowbrow" only imperfectly correspond to realities. But to this latter argument I am always moved to reply that, imperfect as they are, they refer broadly to the main fact of our culture—its discontinuity and inner contradiction. These terms, or something like them, are therefore not dispensable, unless historically realistic statements about American culture are also dispensable.

Yet the tendency of the best critical minds of the time is to try to achieve a flexible receptivity which breaks down distinctions and allows the critic to be highbrow, lowbrow, middlebrow all at once. The best critics find an article like that of Brooks in the *Times,* or a highbrow reply to Brooks which uses the same terms, to be artificial. In other words, their ideal is to contain and express the contradictions of culture, rather than to take a stand on one side or another. Edmund Wilson, for example, was once a hero of radical intransigence; now he is most admired for his flexibility and variousness.

William Phillips' description of the modern artist as "a suspended man" who "keeps the balance of opposing forces" fits not only the artist but the present-day ego-ideal of many critics. The artist "seems to be suspended," says Mr. Phillips, "between tradition and revolt, nationalism and internationalism, the aesthetic and the civic, and between belonging and alienation. Hence any movement to line him up on one side or another over-simplifies his role and limits his creative function."

In a much-quoted passage, Lionel Trilling applies the same idea specifically to American writers. He is disputing Parrington, who thought of American culture as a flow of two currents, one of liberals and one of reactionaries (and Mr. Trilling's comments would apply as well to writers like the early Brooks, who thought of our culture as a flow of two currents, one of highbrows and one of lowbrows). Culture, writes Mr. Trilling,

> is not a flow, nor even a confluence; the form of its existence is struggle, or at least debate—it is nothing if not dialectic. And in any culture there are likely to be certain artists who contain a large part of the dialectic within themselves, their meaning and power lying in their contradictions; they contain within themselves, it may be said, the very essence of the culture, and the sign of this is that they do not submit to serve the ends of any one ideological group or tendency. It is a significant circumstance of American culture, and one which is susceptible of explanation, that an unusually large proportion of its notable writers of the nineteenth century were such repositories of the dialectic of their times—they contained both the yes and the no of their culture, and by that token they were prophetic of the future.

This is a simple but profound formulation. How indeed shall we understand Cooper, Melville, Hawthorne, Whitman, Faulkner and the rest unless we see how inexhaustibly they embody the contradictions of their culture? That we now understand them in this way is the surest sign of

our general advance over the older simplifications and par-
tialities of historical criticism.

But does it follow from the fact that our great novelists
and poets have succeeded by embodying the contradictions
of our culture that the rest of us should try to do the
same? Mr. Trilling does not say so, and yet if he did, he
would be right—if he should add that this image of the
versatile, or as Mr. Phillips says, "suspended" man is the
proper and inevitable image for this interim period of our
cultural history. Shouldn't one be able to enjoy *both* Whitman and Eliot, *both* Pound and Brooks, *both* Faulkner
and J. P. Marquand, *both* Wallace Stevens and Sherwood
Anderson?

What has happened to the avant-garde in our "suspended" culture of the 1950s is a psychological equivalent of
what has happened to it sociologically. Sociologically it
has been institutionalized by the universities and the
publishers, which by definition means that in its modern
phase it has to come to an end. At the same time, it has
been internalized, so to speak, in the flexibly dialectical
mind of contemporary criticism. In this withdrawal from
the field of action it finds a possibility of continued life.
The resiliency of the best critical minds must be counted
on to keep the avant-garde attitude alive during periods
which have no immediate task for its polemical mission.

Yet the task of the temperamental or born avant-garde
critic is not limited to the polemical purpose of converting
the philistines to art. He is also perennially the disinterested student and historian of culture, looking into the past
and the present for the radical and not merely the contingent and incidental facts. The past convinces him that discontinuity and contradiction have always been of the essence of American culture. The present convinces him that
among critics only the most powerful and resilient of "suspended" minds are capable of keeping alive the avant-
garde spirit, or any spirit, or of embodying cultural contradictions of any sort without collapsing under the great
strain into a formless middle way of feeling and thought.
Who can doubt that this formless middle way of feeling
and thought, with its increasing moralism and convention-
ality, is hardening into the new "cake of custom"? As for
the future, one can only believe that the end of the present
interim period will be marked by a new resurgence from

the uneasy subliminal depths of our culture, in the classic manner of avant-garde action—provided, that is, that 1950 marks the end of a phase of American culture as we have known it, and not the end of that culture itself.

The End of the Line

BY RANDALL JARRELL

What has impressed everyone about modernist poetry is
its *differentness*. The familiar and rather touching "I like
poetry—but not modern poetry" is only another way of
noticing what almost all criticism has emphasized: that
modernist poetry is a revolutionary departure from the romantic poetry of the preceding century. Less far-reaching
changes would have seemed a revolutionary disaster to
"conventional" poets, critics, and readers, who were satisfied with romantic poetry; a revolutionary improvement to
more "advanced" poets and critics, who disliked romanticism with the fervor of converts. *Romantic* once again,
after almost two centuries, became a term of simple dero-
gation; correspondingly, there grew up a rather blank cult
of the "classical," and poets like Eliot hinted that poets like
Pound might be the new classicism for which all had been
waiting.

All this seems to me partially true, essentially false. The
change from romantic poetry was evolutionary, not revolutionary: the modernists were a universe away from the
great-grandfathers they admired; they *were* their fathers,
only more so. I want to sketch this evolution. But if the
reader understands me to be using *romantic* as an unfa-
vorably weighted term, most of what I say will be distorted. Some of the tendencies of romanticism are bad;
some of the better tendencies, exaggerated enough, are
bad; but a great deal of the best poetry I know is romantic. Of course, one can say almost that about any of the
larger movements into which critics divide English poetry;
and one might say even better things about the "classical
tradition" in English poetry, if there were one. (It is not
strange that any real movement, compared to this wax

From *The Nation*, Volume CLIV (February 21, 1942), pp. 222-
228, by permission of the publisher.

monster, comes off nowhere; but it is strange that anyone should take the comparison for a real one.) If I pay more attention to unfortunate or exaggerated romantic tendencies, it is because these are the most characteristic: the "good" tendencies of movements are far more alike than the "bad" ones, and a proof that two movements are essentially similar needs to show that they share each other's vices.

Modernist poetry—the poetry of Pound, Eliot, Crane, Tate, Stevens, Cummings, MacLeish, et cetera—appears to be and is generally considered to be a violent break with romanticism; it is actually, I believe, an extension of romanticism, an end product in which most of the tendencies of romanticism have been carried to their limits. Romanticism—whether considered as the product of a whole culture or, in isolation, as a purely literary phenomenon—is necessarily a process of extension, a vector; it presupposes a constant experimentalism, the indefinite attainment of "originality," generation after generation, primarily by the novel extrapolation of previously exploited processes. (Neo-classicism, in theory at least, is a static system.) All these romantic tendencies are exploited to their limits; and the movement which carries out this final exploitation, apparently so different from earlier stages of the same process, is what we call modernism. Then, at last, romanticism is confronted with an impasse, a critical point, a genuinely novel situation that it can meet successfully only by contriving genuinely novel means—that is, means which are not romantic; the romantic means have already been exhausted. Until these new means are found, romanticism operates by repeating its last modernist successes or by reverting to its earlier stages; but its normal development has ended, and—the momentum that gave it most of its attraction gone—it becomes a relatively eclectic system, much closer to neo-classicism than it has hitherto been. (A few of these last romanticists resort to odd varieties of neo-classicism.) If this account seems unlikely to the reader, let me remind him that a similar course of development is extremely plain in modern music.

A good many factors combine to conceal the essentially romantic character of modernist poetry. (1) A great quantitative change looks like a qualitative one: for instance, the attenuation or breaking-up of form characteristic of romanticism will not be recognized or tolerated by the average romantic when it reaches its limit in modernist poetry. (2) The violent contrast between the modernist limits of romantic tendencies and the earlier stages of these tendencies, practiced belatedly and eclectically by "conventional" poets, is an important source of confusion. (3) Most of the best modern criticism of poetry is extremely anti-romantic—a poet's criticism is frequently not a reflection of but a compensation for his own poetry; and this change in theory has helped to hide the lack of any essential change in practice. (4) Modernist poems, while possessing some romantic tendencies in hypertrophied forms, often lack others so spectacularly that the reader disregards those they still possess; and these remaining tendencies may be too common for him to be conscious of them as specifically romantic. (Most of the romantic qualities that poetry has specialized in since 1800 seem to the average reader "normal" or "poetic," what poetry inescapably is.) (5) Romanticism holds in solution contradictory tendencies which, isolated and exaggerated in modernism, look startlingly opposed both to each other and to the earlier stages of romanticism. (6) Both modernist and conventional critics have been unable to see the fundamental similarities between modernist and romantic poetry because they were unwilling to see anything but differences: these were to the former a final recommendation, and to the latter a final condemnation.

We can understand modernist poetry better by noticing where and how it began. The English poetry that we call *fin de siècle*—the most important tendency of its time—was a limit of one easily recognizable extension of romanticism. These "decadent" poets were strongly influenced by Baudelaire, Verlaine, and similar French poets. Rimbaud, Laforgue, and Corbière—who had already written "modern" poetry—had no influence on them. Why? Because a section of French poetry was developing a third of a century ahead of English poetry: Rimbaud wrote typically modernist poetry in the 1870's; in the '90's a surrealist play, Jarry's *Ubu Roi*, scared the young Yeats into crying: "After us the Savage God!" France, without England's industrial advantages and enormous colonial profits, had had little of the Victorian prosperity which slowed up the economic and political rate of change in England—had still less of that complacent mercantile Christianity the

French dismissed as "English hypocrisy." And—if we stick
to a part of the culture, literature—the rate of change
could be greater in France because romanticism was more
of a surface phenomenon there. English poetry was not
ready to be influenced by French modernism for many
years. Meanwhile there were two movements particularly
suited to criticism. Accompanying the triumph of prose
naturalism there was a prosy, realistic, rather limited reaction against "decadent" poetry (it included Robinson,
Frost, Masters, Masefield, some of the Georgians, etc.).
The other movement, Imagism, carried three or four romantic tendencies to their limits with the perfection of a mathematical demonstration.

French modernist poetry first influenced poetry in English through Americans who, lacking a determining or con-
fining tradition of their own, were particularly accessible
and susceptible: Pound and Eliot (like Picasso, Stravinsky,
and Joyce) were in some sense expatriates in both space
and time. They imported modernism into English rather
more deliberately and openly than Wordsworth and Coleridge had imported romanticism; but all Pound's early ad-
vice to poets could be summed up in a sentence half of
which is pure Wordsworth: Write like prose, like speech—
and *read French poetry!* The work of this most influential
of modern poets, Ezra Pound, is a recapitulation of the development of our poetry from late romanticism to modernism. His early work is a sort of anthology of romantic
sources: Browning, early Yeats, the *fin de siècle* poets, Vill-
on and the troubadours (in translations or imitations that
remind one of Swinburne's and Rossetti's), Heine. *His*
variety of imagism is partly a return to the fresh beginnings
of romantic practices, from their diluted and perfunctory
ends; partly an extension to their limits of some of the
most characteristic obsessions of romanticism—for instance, its passion for "pure" poetry, for putting everything
in terms of sensation and emotion, with logic and generalizations excluded; and partly an adaptation of the exotic
procedures of Chinese poetry, those silks that swathe a
homely heart. When Pound first wrote poems that are
modernist in every sense of the word, their general "feel" is
reminiscent of what one might call a lowest common denominator of Corbière, Laforgue, and Rimbaud; but Heine
had by no means disappeared; and the original Cantos I
and II, gone now, were still full of Browning. But if Eliot

was willing to base his form on Browning's (the dramatic monologue is primarily a departure from the norm of ordinary poetry; but in modernist poetry this departure *itself becomes the norm*), he had no interest in Browning's content and manner; in even his earliest poems one is seeing romanticism through Laforgue, and one can reconstruct this romanticism, in the pure form in which it had once existed, only from Eliot's remarks about his early feelings for Rossetti and Swinburne. . . . All during this time the Irish expatriate Joyce was making his way from late-romantic lyrics (in verse, though there is much that is similar in his early prose) to the modernist poetry (in prose) that crops up here and there in *Ulysses,* and that is everywhere in *Finnegans Wake.*

But it would take fifty or a hundred pages to write about this development in terms of specific poets. One can indicate the resemblances of romanticism and modernism more briefly, by making a list of some of the general characteristics of modernist poetry:

(1) A pronounced experimentalism: "originality" is everyone's aim, and novel techniques are as much prized as new scientific discoveries. Eliot states it with surprising naïveté: "It is exactly as wasteful for a poet to do what has been done already as for a biologist to rediscover Mendel's discoveries." (2) External formlessness, internal disorganization: these are justified either as the disorganization necessary to express a disorganized age or as new and more complex forms of organization. Language is deliberately disorganized, meter becomes irregular or disappears; the rhythmical flow of verse is broken up into a jerky half-prose *collage* or *montage.* (3) Heightened emotional intensity; violence of every sort. (4) Obscurity, inaccessibility: logic, both for structure and for texture, is neglected; without this for a ground the masses of the illogical or a-logical lose much of their effectiveness. The poet's peculiar erudition and allusiveness (compare the Alexandrian poet Lycophron) consciously restrict his audience to a small, highly specialized group; the poet is a specialist like everyone else. He intimidates or overawes the public by an attitude one may paraphrase as: "The poet's cultivation and sensibility are of a different order from those of his readers; even if he tried to talk down to them —and why should he try?—he would talk about things they have never heard of, in ways they will never under-

stand." But he did not despair of their understanding a slap in the face. (5) A lack of restraint or proportion: all tendencies are forced to their limits, even contradictory tendencies—and not merely in the same movement but, frequently, in the same poet or the same poem. Some modernist poetry puts an unparalleled emphasis on texture, connotation, violently "interesting" language (attained partly by an extension of romantic principles, partly by a more violent rhetoric based on sixteenth and seventeenth century practices); but there has never before been such prosaic poetry—conversational-colloquial verse without even a pretense at meter. (6) A great emphasis on details—on parts, not wholes. Poetry is essentially lyric: the rare narrative or expository poem is a half-fortuitous collocation of lyric details. Poetry exploits particulars and avoids and condemns generalizations. (7) A typically romantic preoccupation with sensation, perceptual nuances. (8) A preoccupation with the unconscious, dreams, the stream of consciousness, the irrational: this *surréaliste* emphasis might better have been called *sousréaliste*. (9) Irony of every type: Byronic, Laforguian, dryly metaphysical, or helplessly sentimental. Poetry rejects a great deal, accepts a little, and is embarrassed by that little. (10) *Fauve* or neo-primitive elements. (11) Modernist poets, though they may write about the ordinary life of the time, are removed from it, have highly specialized relations with it. The poet's naturalism is employed as indictment, as justification for his own isolation; prosaic and sordid details become important as what writers like Wallace Stevens and William Carlos Williams somewhat primitively think of as the *anti-poetic.* Contemporary life is condemned, patronized, or treated as a disgraceful aberration or special case, compared to the past; the poet hangs out the window of the Ivory Tower making severe but obscure remarks about what is happening below—he accepts the universe with several (thin) volumes of reservations. What was happening below was bad enough; the poet could characterize it, truthfully enough, with comparative forms of all those adjectives that Goethe and Arnold had applied to their ages. But its disasters, at least, were of unprecedented grandeur; it was, after all, "the very world, which is the world/Of all of us,—the place where, in the end,/ We find our happiness or not at all"; and the poet's rejection or patronizing acceptance of it on his own terms—

and, sometimes, what terms they were!—hurt his poetry more than he would have believed. (12) Individualism, isolation, alienation. The poet is not only different from society, he is as different as possible from other poets; all this differentness is exploited to the limit—is used as subject-matter, even. Each poet develops an elaborate, "personalized," bureaucratized machinery of effect; *refine your singularities* is everybody's maxim. (13) These poets, typically, dislike and condemn science, industrialism, humanitarianism, "progress," the main tendencies of Western development; they want to trade the present for a somewhat idealized past, to turn from a scientific, commercial, and political world-view to one that is literary, theological, and personal.

This complex of qualities is essentially romantic, and the poetry that exhibits it is the culminating point of romanticism.

It is the end of the line. Poets can go back and repeat the ride; they can settle in attractive, atavistic colonies along the railroad; they can repudiate the whole system, *à la* Yvor Winters, for some neo-classical donkey-caravan of their own. But Modernism As We Knew It—the most successful and influential body of poetry of this century—is dead. Compare a 1940 issue of *Poetry* with a 1930 issue. Who could have believed that modernism would collapse so fast! Only someone who realized that modernism is a limit which it is impossible to exceed. How can poems be written that are more violent, more disorganized, more obscure, more—supply your own adjective—than those that have already been written? But if modernism could go no further, it was equally difficult for it to stay where it was: how could a movement completely dynamic in character, as "progressive" as the science and industrialism it accompanied, manage to become static or retrogressive without going to pieces? Among modernist poets, from 1910 to 1925, there was the same feeling of confident excitement, of an individual but irregularly cooperative experimentalism, of revolutionary discoveries just around the corner, that one regularly sees at certain stages in the development of a science; they had ahead of them the same Manifest Destiny that poets have behind them today. Today, for the poet, there is an embarrassment of choices: young poets can choose—do choose—to write anything from surrealism to imitations of Robert Bridges; the only thing they

have no choice about is making their own choice. The
Muse, forsaking her sterner laws, says to everyone: "Do
what you will." Originality can no longer be recognized
by, and condemned or applauded for, its obvious experimentalism; the age offers to the poet a fairly heartless
eclecticism or a fairly solitary individuality. He can avoid
being swept along by the current—there is no current; he
can congratulate himself on this, and see behind him, glit-
tering in the distance of time, all those bright streams
sweeping people on to the wildest of excesses, the unlike-
liest of triumphs.

For a long time society and poetry have been developing in the same direction, have been carrying certain tendencies to their limits: how could anyone fail to realize that
the excesses of modernist poetry are the necessary con-
comitants of the excesses of late-capitalist society? (An example too pure and too absurd even for allegory is Robinson Jeffers, who must prefer a hawk to a man, a stone to a
hawk, because of an individualism so exaggerated that it
contemptuously rejects affections, obligations, relations of
any kind whatsoever, and sets up as a nostalgically-await-
ed goal the war of all against all. Old Rocky Face,
perched on his sea crag, is the last of *laissez faire;* Free
Economic Man at the end of his rope.) How much of the
modernist poets disliked their society, and how much they
resembled it! How often they contradicted its letter and
duplicated its spirit! They rushed, side by side with their
society, to the limits of all tendencies. When, at the beginning of the '30's, these limits were reached, what became
of these individualists? They turned toward anything collective: toward Catholicism, communism, distributism, social credit, agrarianism; they wrote neo-classical criticism
or verse; they wrote political (Marxist or fellow-traveller)
criticism or verse; they stopped writing; and when they
read the verse of someone like E. E. Cummings, as it
pushed on into the heart of that last undiscovered continent, *e. e. cummings,* they thought of this moral impossibility, this living fossil, with a sort of awed and incredu-
lous revulsion.

I have no space to write of later developments. Auden
was so influential because his poetry was the only novel
and successful reaction away from modernism; and a few
years later Dylan Thomas was so influential—in England
—because his poetry was the only novel and successful

reaction away from Auden. But his semi-surrealist experimentalism could be as good as it was, and as influential as
it was, only in a country whose poets had never carried
modernism to the limits of its possibilities. No one can understand these English developments if he forgets that,
while we were having the modernism of Pound, Stevens,
Williams, Moore, Eliot, Tate, Crane, Cummings, and all
the rest, England was having the modernism of the Sit-
wells.

I am afraid that my hypothesis about romanticism and
modernism, without the mass of evidence that can make a
theory plausible, or the tangle of extensions and incidental
insights that can make it charming, may seem improbable
or unpleasant to some of my readers. It is intended to be
partial: I have not written about the hard or dry or "classical" tendencies of some modern verse—what Empson
and Marianne Moore have in common, for instance; and I
have not listed the differences between modernism and romanticism that everybody has seen and stated. But I hope
that nobody will dislike my article because he thinks it an
attack on romanticism or modernism. This has been description, not indictment. Burke said that you can't indict
a whole people, and I hope I am not such a fool as to indict a century and a half of a world. Besides, so far as its
poetry is concerned, it was wonderful. Wordsworth and
Blake and Heine, Baudelaire and Corbière, Hardy and
Yeats and Rilke—the names crowd in; and there are dozens more. That some of these poets were, sometimes, as
strange as they were wonderful; that some of the successors were, alas, rather stranger: all this is as true as it is
obvious. But the "classical" prejudice which hints that
these poets were somehow deceived and misguided as
(say) Dryden and Valéry were not, seems every year more
grotesque. One repeats to oneself, *Whom God deceives is
well deceived,* and concludes that if these poets were not
classical, so much the worse for classicism.

Part Two

TWO MANIFESTOES

This section provides two brief examples of modernist literary manifestoes. The first was composed by a group of Italian writers connected with the Futurist movement, one of the many avant-garde groups which sprung up and then died in the early 1920's. The second is an essay by the Russian writer Evgeni Zamyatin, published in Russia in 1924. Author of the anti-utopian novel *We*, Zamyatin defiantly asserted the need for heresy in literature. He was expressing, in compact and sometimes cryptic form, many of the notions current among the young Russian writers of the 1920's, before they were silenced or destroyed by the Stalin dictatorship.

A Manifesto of Italian Futurism

1. We want to sing the love of danger, the habit of danger and of temerity.

2. The essential elements of our poetry will be courage, daring, and revolt.

3. Literature having up to now magnified thoughtful immobility, ecstasy, and sleep, we want to exalt the aggressive gesture, the feverish insomnia, the athletic step, the perilous leap, the box on the ear, and the fisticuff.

4. We declare that the world's wonder has been enriched by a fresh beauty: the beauty of speed. A racing car with its trunk adorned by great exhaust pipes like snakes with an explosive breath . . . a roaring car that seems to be driving under shrapnel, is more beautiful than the *Victory of Samothrace.*

5. We want to sing the man who holds the steering wheel, whose ideal stem pierces the Earth, itself launched on the circuit of its orbit.

6. The poet must expend himself with warmth, refulgence, and prodigality, to increase the enthusiastic fervor of the primordial elements.

7. There is no more beauty except in struggle. No masterpiece without an aggressive character. Poetry must be a violent attack against the unknown forces, summoning them to lie down before man.

8. We stand on the far promontory of centuries! . . . What is the use of looking behind us, since our task is to smash the mysterious portals of the impossible? Time and Space died yesterday. We live already in the absolute, since we have already created the eternal omnipresent speed.

9. We want to glorify war—the only hygiene of the

world—militarism, patriotism, the anarchist's destructive
gesture, the fine Ideas that kill, and the scorn of woman.

10. We want to demolish museums, libraries, fight
against moralism, feminism, and all opportunistic and utilitarian cowardices.

11. We shall sing the great crowds tossed about by
work, by pleasure, or revolt; the many-colored and poly-
phonic surf of revolutions in modern capitals; the noctur-
nal vibration of the arsenals and the yards under their violent electrical moons; the gluttonous railway stations
swallowing smoky serpents; the factories hung from the
clouds by the ribbons of their smoke; the bridges leaping
like athletes hurled over the diabolical cutlery of sunny
rivers; the adventurous steamers that sniff the horizon; the
broad-chested locomotives, prancing on the rails like great
steel horses curbed by long pipes, and the gliding flight of
airplanes whose propellers snap like a flag in the wind,
like the applause of an enthusiastic crowd.

It is in Italy that we launch this manifesto of tumbling
and incendiary violence, this manifesto through which
today we set up *Futurism,* because we want to deliver
Italy from its gangrene of professors, of archaeologists, of
guides, and of antiquarians.

Italy has been too long a great secondhand brokers'
market. We want to rid it of the innumerable museums
that cover it with innumerable cemeteries.

Museums, cemeteries! . . . Truly identical in the sinister
jostling of bodies that do not know each other. Great
public dormitories where one sleeps forever side by side
with beings hated or unknown. Reciprocal ferocity of painters and of sculptors killing each other with line and color
in the same gallery.

They can be visited once a year as the dead are visited
once a year. . . . We can accept that much! We can even
conceive that flowers may once a year be left for *la Gioconda!* . . . But we cannot admit that our sorrows, our fragile
courage, our anxiety may be taken through there every
day! . . . Do you want to be poisoned? Do you want to
rot?

What can one find in an old painting beside the embarrassing contortions of the artist trying to break the barriers
that are impassable to his desire to wholly express his
dream?

To admire an old painting is to pour our sensitiveness into a funeral urn, instead of throwing it forward by violent casts of creation and action. Do you mean thus to waste the best of you in a useless admiration of the past that must necessarily leave you exhausted, lessened, trampled?

As a matter of fact the daily frequentation of museums, of libraries and academies (those cemeteries of wasted efforts, those calvaries of crucified dreams, those catalogues of broken impulses! . . .) is for the artist what the prolonged tutelage of parents is for intelligent young men, drunk with their talent and their ambitious will.

For the dying, the invalid, the prisoner, it will do. Since the future is forbidden them, there may be a salve for their wounds in the wonderful past. . . . But we want nothing of it—we the young, the strong, the living *Futurists!*

Let the good incendiaries come with their carbonized fingers! . . . Here they are! Here they are! . . . Set the library stacks on fire! Turn the canals in their course to flood the museum vaults! . . . There go the glorious canvases, floating adrift! Take up the picks and the hammers! Undermine the foundations of the venerable cities!

The oldest among us are not yet thirty; this means that we have at least ten years to carry out our task. When we are forty, let those younger and more valiant than us kindly throw us into the waste basket like useless manuscripts! . . . They will come after us from afar, from everywhere, prancing on the light rhythm of their first poems, clawing the air with their crooked fingers, sniffing at academy gates the good scent of our rotting intellects already intended for the catacombs of libraries.

But we shall not be there. They will find us at last, on some winter night, out in the country, under a sad hangar on which the monotonous rain strums, crouching by our trembling planes, warming our hands over the miserable fire of our books of today gaily blazing under the scintillating flight of their images.

They will gather in a mob around us, panting with anguish and spite, and all exasperated by our untiring courage will bound forward to kill us with the more hatred for the love and admiration in their hearts. And Injustice, strong and wholesome, will glitter radiantly in their eyes. For art can be nothing but violence, cruelty and injustice.

The oldest among us are not yet thirty and yet we have already squandered great treasures, treasures of energy, of love, of courage and eager will, hastily, deliriously, countlessly, breathlessly, with both hands.

Look at us! We are not out of breath. . . . Our heart is not in the least tired! For it feeds on fire, on hatred, on speed! . . . You find it surprising? That is because you do not even remember having lived!—Up on the crest of the world, once more we hurl our challenge to the stars!

Your objections? Enough! Enough! I know them! Fair enough! We know well enough what our fine, false intelligence asserts.—We are only, it says, the summary and the extension of our forebears.—Perhaps! Let it be so! . . . What does it matter! . . . But we don't want to listen! Beware of repeating these imfamous words! Rather, look up!

Up on the crest of the world, once more we hurl our challenge to the stars!

On Literature, Revolution, and Entropy

BY EVGENI ZAMYATIN

> Tell me what is the final integer, the one at the very top, the biggest of all.
>
> But that's ridiculous! Since the number of integers is infinite, how can you have a final integer?
>
> Well then how can you have a final revolution?
>
> There is no final revolution. Revolutions are infinite.
>
> —Evgeni Zamyatin, *We*

Ask the question point-blank: What is revolution? You get a variety of replies. Some people will answer in the style of Louis XIV: *La révolution, c'est nous.* Others turn to the calendar, giving you the day and the month. Still others spell it out letter by letter. But if we go one stage beyond the alphabet and articulate our answer, this is what we get:

Two dead, dark stars collide with a deafening but unheard crash and spark into life a new star: that's revolution. A molecule breaks loose from its orbit, invades a neighboring atomic universe, and gives birth to a new chemical element: that's revolution. With one book Lobachevsky[1] cleaves the centuries-old walls of the Euclidean world and opens the way to the infinities of non-Euclidean space: that's revolution.

Revolution is everywhere and in all things; it is infinite, there is no final revolution, no end to the sequence of integers. Social revolution is only one in the infinite sequence of integers. The law of revolution is not a social law, it is immeasurably greater, it is a cosmic, universal law—such as the law of the conservation of energy and the law of

[1] Nikolai Lobachevsky (1793-1856), Russian mathematician who pioneered non-Euclidean geometry.

the loss of energy (entropy). Some day an exact formula will be established for the law of revolution. And in this formula nations, classes, stars—and books will be expressed as numerical values.

Red, fiery, death-dealing is the law of revolution; but that death is the birth of a new life, of a new star. And cold, blue as ice, as the icy interplanetary infinities, is the law of entropy. The flame turns from fiery red to an even, warm pink, no longer death-dealing but comfort-producing; the sun ages and becomes a planet suitable for highways, shops, beds, prostitutes, prisons: that is a law. And in order to make the planet young again, we must set it afire, we must thrust it off the smooth highway of evolution: that is a law.

The flame, true enough, will grow cold tomorrow or the day after tomorrow (in the Book of Genesis days are years and even aeons). But already today there should be somebody who can foresee that; there should be somebody today to speak heretically of tomorrow. Heretics are the only (bitter-tasting) remedy for the entropy of human thought.

When (in science, religion, social life, art) a flaming, seething sphere grows cold, the fiery molten rock becomes covered with dogma—with a hard, ossified, immovable crust. In science, religion, social life, and art, dogmatization is the entropy of thought; what has been dogmatized no longer inflames, it is merely warm—and soon it is to be cool. The Sermon on the Mount, delivered beneath the scorching sun to upstretched arms, and rending sobs, gives way to slumberous prayer in some well-appointed abbey. Galileo's tragic *"E pur si muove"* gives way to calm calculations in some well-heated office in an observatory. On the Galileos the epigones build—slowly, coral upon coral, forming a reef: this is the path of evolution. Till one day a new heresy explodes and blows up the dogma's crust, together with all the ever so stable, rocklike structures that had been erected on it.

Explosions are not comfortable things. That is why the exploders, the heretics, are quite rightly annihilated by fire, by axes, and by words. Heretics are harmful to everybody today, to every evolution, to the difficult, slow, useful, so very useful, constructive process of coral reef building; imprudently and foolishly they leap into today from tomorrow. They are romantics. It was right and proper that in 1797 Babeuf [2] had his head cut off: he had leaped into 1797, skipping one hundred and fifty years. It is equally right and proper that heretical literature, literature that is damaging to dogma, should also have its head cut off: such literature is harmful.

But harmful literature is more useful than useful literature: because it is anti-entropic, it militates against calcification, sclerosis, encrustedness, moss, peace. It is utopian and ridiculous. Like Babeuf in 1797 it is right one hundred and fifty years later.

We know Darwin, we know that after Darwin came mutations, Weismannism, neo-Lamarckism. But these are only penthouses and balconies while Darwin is the building itself. And the building contains not only tadpoles and toadstools, it also contains man. Fangs grow sharp only if there is someone to gnaw on; the domestic hen's wings serve only to flap with. Ideas and hens obey the same law: ideas which feed on minced meat lose their teeth just as civilized men do. Heretics are necessary to health. If there are no heretics, they have to be invented.

Live literature does not set its watch by yesterday's time, nor by today's, but by tomorrow's. Live literature is like a sailor who is sent aloft; from the masthead he can descry sinking vessels, icebergs, and maelstroms which are not yet visible from the deck. You can drag him down from the mast and put him to work in the boiler room or on the capstan, but that won't change a thing: the mast is still there and from the masthead another sailor will be able to see what the first sailor has seen.

In stormy weather you need a man aloft. And right now the weather is stormy. SOS signals are coming in from all directions. Only yesterday the writer was able to stroll calmly on deck, taking snapshots of "real life"; but who wants to look at pictures of landscapes and scenes from daily life when the world has taken on a forty-five-degree list, when the green waves are threatening to swallow us and the ship is breaking up? Right now we can look and

[2] François Babeuf (1760-1797), French revolutionary who demanded a program of egalitarianism and practical socialism after the Thermidorian reaction. He was executed for plotting to overthrow the government by force.

think only as men do in the face of death: we shall die—
and what then? How have we lived? If we are to live all
over again in some new way, then by what shall we live,
and for what? Right now we need in literature the vast
philosophical horizon, the vast sweep from the masthead,
from the sky above, we need the most ultimate, the most
fearsome, the most fearless "Whys?" and "What nexts?"

Those are the questions that children ask. But children
are after all the boldest of philosophers; they come into
life naked, not covered by one single small leaf of dogma
or creed. That is why their questions are always so ridicu-
lously naïve and so frighteningly complicated. The new
people, who are right now coming into life, are naked and
fearless as children, and they too, like children, like Scho-
penhauer, Dostoevsky, Nietzsche, are asking their "whys"
and "what nexts." Philosophers of genius, children, and
ordinary people are equally wise, because they ask equally
stupid questions—stupid for civilized man who possesses a
well-furnished apartment, with a magnificent bathroom,
and a well-furnished dogma.

Organic chemistry has blurred the dividing line between
living and dead matter. It is a mistake to divide people
into the living and the dead: there are live-dead people
and live-live people. The live-dead people also write, walk,
talk, act. But they do not make mistakes; only machines
produce without mistakes, but they produce only dead
things. The live-live people are all mistakes, searchings,
questions, torments.

So too what we write also walks and talks, but it can be
live-dead or live-live. The genuinely live, stopping at nothing, brooking no obstacle or hindrance, searches for the
answers to foolish, "childish" questions. The answers may
be wrong, the philosophy erroneous—but errors are of
greater value than truths: truth is machinelike, error is
alive, truth reassures, error unsettles. And even if the
answers are quite impossible, so much the better: to ask
answered questions is the privilege of minds constructed
on the same principle as the cow's stomach, which is ideal-
ly suited, as well we know, to chewing the cud.

If there were in nature something fixed, if there were
truths, all this would, of course, be wrong. But happily all

truths are erroneous. This is precisely the significance of the dialectic process: today's truths become tomorrow's errors; there is no final integer.

This (one and only) truth is only for the strong: weak-nerved minds unfailingly require a finite universe, a final integer; they require, as Nietzsche said, "the crutches of assurance." The weak-nerved do not have the strength to include themselves in the dialectic syllogism. True, this is difficult. But it is the very thing that Einstein did succeed in doing: he managed to remember that he, Einstein, with watch in hand observing motion, was also moving; he succeeded in looking at the earth's movements *from outside*.

That is precisely how great literature—literature that knows no final integer—looks at the earth's movements.

The formal characteristic of live literature is the same as its inner characteristic: the negation of truth, that is, the negation of what everyone knows and what I knew up to this moment. Live literature leaves the canonical rails, leaves the broad highway.

The broad highway of Russian literature, worn shiny by the giant wheels of Tolstoy, Gorky, Chekhov, is realism, real life: consequently we must turn away from real life. The rails, sanctified and canonized by Blok, Sologub, Bely, are the rails of symbolism—symbolism which turned away from real life: consequently we must turn toward real life.

Absurd, isn't it? The intersection of parallel lines is also absurd. But it's absurd only in the canonical, plane geometry of Euclid; in non-Euclidian geometry it's an axiom. The one essential is to cease to be flat, to raise above the plane. Today's literature has the same relation to the plane surface of real life as an aircraft has to the earth: it is nothing more than a runway from which to take off and soar aloft from real life to reality, to philosophy, to the realm of the fantastic. Leave the carts of yesterday to creak along the great highways. The living have strength enough to cut off their yesterdays.

We can put a police officer or a commissar in the cart, but the cart will still remain a cart. And literature will still remain the literature of yesterday, if we drive real life—even "revolutionary real life"—along the well-traveled highway—even if we drive it in a fast troika with bells.

What we need today are automobiles, airplanes, winged flight, seconds, dotted lines.

The old, slow, soporific descriptions are no more. The order of the day is laconicism—but every word must be supercharged, high-voltage. Into one second must be compressed what formerly went into a sixty-second minute. Syntax becomes elliptical, volatile; complicated pyramids of periods are dismantled and broken down into the single stones of independent clauses. In swift movement the canonical, the habitual eludes the eye: hence the unusual, often strange symbolism and choice of words. The image is sharp, synthetic, it contains only the one basic trait which one has time to seize upon from a moving automobile. The lexicon hallowed by custom has been invaded by dialect, neologisms, science, mathematics, technology.

There is a rule, if you can call it a rule, that the writer's talent consists in making the rule the exception; but there are far more writers who turn the exception into the rule.

The business of science and art alike is the projection of the world onto co-ordinates. Differences in form are due to differences in the co-ordinates. All realist forms involve projection onto the fixed, plane co-ordinates of the Euclidean world. These co-ordinates have no existence in nature. This finite, fixed world does not exist; it is a convention, an abstraction, an unreality. And therefore realism —be it "socialist" or "bourgeois"—is unreal; immeasurably closer to reality is projection onto fast-moving, curved surfaces—as in the new mathematics and the new art. Realism which is not primitive, not *realia* but *realiora,* consists in displacement, distortion, curvature, nonobjectivity. The lens of the camera is objective.

A new form is not intelligible to all; for many it is difficult. Maybe. The habitual, the banal is of course simpler, pleasanter, more comfortable. Euclid's world is very simple and Einstein's world is very difficult; nevertheless it is now impossible to return to Euclid's. No revolution, no heresy is comfortable and easy. Because it is a leap, it is a rupture of the smooth evolutionary curve, and a rupture is a wound, a pain. But it is a necessary wound: most people suffer from hereditary sleeping sickness, and those who are sick with this ailment (entropy) must not be allowed to sleep, or they will go to their last sleep, the sleep of death.

This same sickness is common to artists and writers:

they go contentedly to sleep in their favorite artistic form which they have devised, then twice revised. They do not have the strength to wound themselves, to cease to love what has become dear to them. They do not have the strength to come out from their lived-in, laurel-scented rooms, to come out into the open air and start anew.

To wound oneself, it is true, is difficult, even dangerous. But to live today as yesterday and yesterday as today is even more difficult for the living.

Part Three

A FEW MODERNIST MOVEMENTS

It was characteristic of the modernist impulse in literature, especially in its early and more assertive period, that it should break up into a variety of "movements"—some of them self-created and self-named, others designated retrospectively by literary critics or historians. Some of these movements, such as Symbolism, have been of incalculable importance; others, like Dadaism, have been momentary diversions. Here are a few brief reflections on some of these movements.

Symbolism

BY GRAHAM HOUGH

Symbolism as a literary term has no clear meaning. It is a radiant blur rather than a delimited area. However, it covers a bundle of tendencies that have powerfully affected poetry and critical thought since the middle of the last century. Among these tendencies are the assimilation of poetry to music (Poe, Verlaine, Pater); to dream (Poe, Baudelaire); to an unattainable and inexpressible ideal (Poe, Mallarmé); to magic and the occult (Rimbaud, Yeats). We find repeated assertions of the power of 'symbols' over the mind, symbols being verbal or visual presentations regarded as realizing complexes of experience otherwise inapprehensible. Sometimes this symbolic power is connected with a mysterious system of correspondences supposed to be present in Nature, as in Baudelaire's sonnet; or with the action of spiritual powers, as in Yeats. Later, with Pound and his school, the symbol is disenchanted and called an image. It is then supposed to be efficacious simply by its own configuration. Symbolist ideas are often expressed in outrageous or challenging irrational terms; but they may appear more demurely, as when Eliot regards the meaning of a poem as a mere sop to the reader's intellect, to keep it quiet while the poetry does its work on him.[1] And they may appear disguised as linguistic science, as in Owen Barfield's identification of poetic diction with a primitive, undifferentiated state of language when the object and its associations are still undistinguished;[2] perhaps in I. A. Richards's denial of referential purport to what appears in poetry as statement.

In all these manifestations there is a common thread. It is the tendency to exalt the non-discursive element in poet-

Reprinted from *An Essay on Criticism* by Graham Hough by permission of W.W. Norton & Company, Inc. Copyright © 1966 by Graham Hough.

[1] *The Use of Poetry and the Use of Criticism*, 1933, p. 151.
[2] Owen Barfield, *Poetic Diction*, 2nd edn., 1952.

ry; to remove the language of poetry as far as possible from its referential or representational functions.

In a wider sense symbolism is a fundamental activity of the human mind—the power of actualizing inarticulate experience in some apprehensible sensory form. The operation of this symbolising power has been most fully analysed by Cassirer.[3] He sees it as the central, typical, universal human faculty, at work impartially in myth, religion, language, art and science, creating the human reality by giving it symbolic form. As far as art is concerned this seems in a sense obvious; what else could art be doing? But it has not in fact been the most prevalent way of looking at the matter in our culture. It has been more usual to think of art as *reproducing* experience already more or less available in other forms—to think of it in fact mimetically. Cassirer accordingly admits the prevalence of a mimetic theory up to the middle of the eighteenth century. It is then largely replaced by an expressive theory. Art does not imitate the external world, it expresses the feelings of the artist. But this is hardly more than a mimetic theory in another guise; instead of reproducing the outer world art reproduces the inner life, the life of the affections and emotions.[4] Cassirer would substitute for these the view of art as essentially *formative*. It does not reproduce pre-existing reality. There is no reality for man until he has created it in symbolic form. Art is one of the systems of symbolic form.

At bottom this is a Kantian view of art—an unreachable *Ding an sich* is apprehended only under the necessary forms given to it by human activity.

'The Parthenon frieze of a Mass by Bach, Michelangelo's Sistine Chapel, or a poem of Leopardi, a sonata of Beethoven or a novel of Dostoevsky are neither merely representative nor merely expressive. They are symbolic in a new and deeper sense.'[5] And symbolic, we must add, in their own way. Art is a special mode of apprehending reality, a symbolic system different from that of science

---

[3] Ernst Cassirer, *The Philosophy of Symbolic Form*, Berlin, 1933; English trans. New Haven, 1953. For the literary student Cassirer's thought is more easily accessible in his shorter works, *An Essay on Man*, New Haven, 1944; 2nd edn., New York, 1956; *Language and Myth*, New York, 1946; and in the work of Suzanne Langer.

[4] *Essay on Man*, 1956 edn., pp. 177–81. For the replacement of mimetic by expressive theory see also M. H. Abrams, *The Mirror and the Lamp*, New York, 1956.

[5] *Essay on Man*, p. 187.

and pragmatic manipulation, but equally valid and with its
own rights.

This attitude, or something like it, has never been wholly absent from aesthetic theory, but in former times it has
commonly been expressed as an honorific or hortatory
supplement to an essentially mimetic way of thinking. Cassirer's massive and elaborately documented presentation of
art as symbolic form amounts virtually to a new insight.
Cassirer enables us to give a clearer meaning to
Baumgarten's notion of art as a heterocosm, another
world. Art is not a fanciful supplement to the world of science and practical activity, or to the 'truths' of religion. It
is another world in the sense that it is an alternative mode
of apprehending the world, one of the organs by which
man creates his reality.

But we have wished in this essay to avoid general aesthetics and to narrow our consideration to the specific conditions of literary art. And the art of literature exhibits certain fundamental differences from the other arts—music,
painting and the dance. A sequence of musical notes *need*
not represent anything. It may represent the song of the
cuckoo, or suggest sadness or passion; but it need not do
any of these things. It is the same with painting, though
we are only misled by the generally mimetic tradition of
European painting. A mark on canvas need not represent
anything. It may represent the Cross or a woman's face,
but it need not do anything of the sort. It can be merely
thick or thin, vertical or horizontal. The media employed
by these arts—sounds and visual marks—are not essentially signs. They are themselves, they need not represent anything else. But the medium of literature is verbal. Literature is made of words. And words are already signs. They
stand for something, they represent something already, before literature takes them over. So literature makes use of
a medium that is itself already a product of the symbolizing, formative activity. Literature is a symbolic form only
in a secondary, derivative sense, for it makes use of a system of symbolic forms that is already in existence—the
system that we call language. The world already called
into existence by language is used as raw material by
literary art. Literature can therefore never be a wholly autonomous symbolic system as music and painting are.

Whatever view we may take of the nature and origin of
language, by the time literature gets hold of them words

Lit signifies, states, leads to   PS ≡

are already signs, representational counters. Literature is therefore essentially mimetic as music and painting are not. There cannot be anything in literature corresponding to non-figurative painting. And this is why mimetic theories of literature have been so obvious and so prominent.

We should be unwise to quarrel with the mimetic orientation of traditional criticism, since it is based on a manifest truth. But we may need to qualify it. An obscure sense that it needs qualifying has been endemic in criticism from the beginning. Poetry is more philosophical than history; it submits the shows of things to the desires of the mind, etc. These and a host of similar pronouncements are all attempts at seeing poetry as in some sense an autonomous symbolic system.

In what sense can this be maintained? To what extent do conventional mimetic assumptions need to be modified or supplemented?

(a) Literature does not work entirely with mimetic or referential methods. The meaning of a poem is its whole complex of structures, not simply its reference. Literature uses words, and words are signs; but in literature they are used as something more than signs. Literature exploits other properties of words besides their referential ones; e.g. their capability of being organized into rhythmical groups, their auditory and muscular suggestions, their fortuitous kinships with other words. Latent and undeveloped in ordinary language, these qualities become decisive in literature. And they fuse with the referential, mimetic properties of words to make of literature a new symbolic system, different from the symbolic system of non-literary language.

(b) Literature uses words, and words are signs, standing for things that we already know in other ways. But literature (indeed language itself) uses these signs with great freedom. It can combine them in ways that are quite foreign to the nature of the things signified. In literature mouths can be blind, light can creak, a man may cross a rainbow bridge, and romantic love can last for ever. Visionary and imaginative experience, 'the irregular combinations of fancy', are part of the substance of literature. The verbal signs, by themselves tied to objects with fixed properties and relations, acquire in literary combination a new freedom of action. In this sense too literature offers a quasi-independent symbolic system.

But this independence is never complete. Literature is never in the position of music or the visual arts in making a solitary, unassisted raid on the inarticulate. It works with material that has been articulated already. The numerous attempts, particularly numerous in the last hundred years, to see literature as precisely analogous to the other arts, as an independent symbolic system, collectively comprise the literary theory known as symbolism.

Traditional literary theory sees literature working in the same way as non-literary discourse. The statements of literature are fictions, but within the fictional parenthesis all the ordinary kinds of discourse occur in the ordinary ways. The organizing principles of literature are narrative, description, argument, exhortation and the expression of feeling. And these all involve *saying* something. We can *word* distinguish literature in this respect from ritual or music, which can objectify a complex of experience without *saying* anything.

Symbolist theory tries to assimilate the work of literature to a ritual or a piece of music. 'A poem should not mean but be.'

It is a brave attempt and it needed to be made. But it is an ideal limit, not an actuality. It is only by saying something that a poem can do more than say. It is only through its meaning that a poem can be at all. *Probably true*

It was necessary to make the symbolist attempt in the nineteenth century for a variety of related reasons, all of them familiar enough.

The rationalizing tendencies of neo-classicism had reached an impasse. Their possibilities were exhausted and literature could only continue by exploring other methods. The increasing power and prestige of the scientific consciousness threatened to engulf all others, and literature obscurely and instinctively revolted. We see it doing so in German and English romanticism.

But the literature of the early nineteenth century, Romantic literature, was still deeply dedicated to hopes of political and social progress. As the century went on political disenchantment tended to deprive it of this source of vitality; and the unbroken march of science and technology threatened to narrow its sphere of action still farther. Symbolism both intensifies the Romantic revolt and seeks to provide it with an unassailable esoteric philosophy. Hence the exaltation of dream, of various forms of magic and occultism, of non-discursive arts like music and the dance, of non-discursive literary effects such as the symbol (whatever that means) and the image.

Symbolism, seeking to vindicate the claims of literature to be a genuine mode of apprehending reality with its own rights, maximizes those claims. It either tries to cut words loose from their reference altogether—*De la musique avant toute chose,* etc.; or it tries to use the references as talismans and charms (symbols) or as pictures (images).[6]

Poetry regarded in this light has a different relation to words from that which is recognized in traditional criticism. It does not use words in the same way; 'même elle ne s'en *sert* pas du tout; je dirai plûtot qu'elle les sert'. A brilliant sketch of the symbolist view of poetry is given by Sartre in the passage, already cited earlier, from which these words are taken. He reconciles this with his highly functional view of literature by distinguishing sharply between *poésie* and *littérature,* between *le poète* and *l'écrivain.* This rather dubious piece of casuistry serves his purpose; and at any rate we know what he means. 'L'écrivain [as distinct from the poet] c'est aux significations qu'il a affaire. Encore faut-il distinguer: l'empire des signes, c'est la prose; la poésie est du côté de la peinture, de la sculpture, de la musique.'[7] But no pre-symbolist critic would have made this distinction. In traditional criticism poetic diction is a matter of selection, refinement or vividness, not of some non-significative quality.

Symbolist criticism then makes a sharp break with former critical theory: it is one of the few major turning-points in our literary thought. What are we to make of it?

There is no need either to vindicate or to dispute the creative power that symbolism has released. *Les Illuminations, Byzantium,* and *The Waste Land* provide their own testimony. But does post-symbolist criticism account only for symbolist poetry, or has it changed the way we look at poetry in general?

To a large extent it has. It has at least given a new tendency, a new direction to most modern literary interpreta-

6 See A. G. Lehmann, *The Symbolist Aesthetic in France,* Oxford, 1950; Guy Delfel, *L'Esthétique de Stephane Mallarmé,* Paris, 1951; Maurice Bowra, *The Heritage of Symbolism,* 1951; Joseph Chiari, *Symbolisme from Poe to Mallarmé,* 1956; Edmund Wilson, *Axel's Castle,* 1931, chap. I; Frank Kermode, *Romantic Image,* 1957; G. Hough, *Image and Experience,* 1960.
7 'Qu'est ce que la litterature?', *Situations,* II, 63.

tion. In the consideration of poetry and prose (Chapter XV) I found myself instinctively adopting, though with some qualifications, the symbolist point of view, feeling as I did so that this was only to say what most modern critics would agree to. How has this worked out in actual critical practice?

The shortest answer is provided by the wide currency of Archibald MacLeish's aphorism, 'A poem should not mean but be.' This implies that the referential content of a poem is only a small part of its totality. No doubt this was always felt and was always implicit in much traditional discussion of poetry. But it was never before so emphatic or so self-aware. And the sense that the total structure of a poem is infinitely more than its referential paraphrasable content has become so vivid in post-symbolist criticism that it has become necessary to provide a far fuller and more intelligible account of the other structural elements and the way they go to form the totality of the work. And because it was necessary it has become possible.

Symbolisme from Poe to Mallarmé

BY JOSEPH CHIARI

. . . These remarks point to the fact that by the last quarter of the nineteenth century the idea of a new relationship between man and the universe, an idea whose development can be traced as far back as Plato and Pythagoras, had become part of the clear consciousness of the arts, instead of the vague implicitness which it had assumed previously with English romanticism. The gist of this idea is that the mind cannot apprehend reality separated from it, but can only apprehend its phenomenal aspects in an experience which unites subject and object, and involves the unified sensibility of the subject; that means that the artistic experience which, in the Cartesian world of knowledge through mind, could be grasped and described in its entirety, here becomes on the contrary a process of discovery, an adventure which, lacking the *a priori* concepts upon which to stand, is a journey towards the unknown in search of something—the 'thing-in-itself' or the inner reality which can be hinted at but can never be discovered. The whole excitement is in the journey, and for the writer the media employed are the words, but this time not used in order to clothe concept, whether purely mental or emotional, but as a means to try to suggest, through all their aspects representing the whole being involved in the process, the imaginative graph of the experience which the artist lived in the course of his journey to knowledge. Since knowledge is no longer an act of the cogitating mind centralising and therefore intellectualising all sensory processes, but an apprehension through senses and mind of the phenomenal aspects of a hidden reality, the senses and the mind are both fully and organically engaged in the attempt to register the fleeting reactions of a subject making progressive contacts with an object or with the outside world. That is why the various sensuous aspects of lan-

gauge—the musical and the pictorial, together with rhythm
and logical meaning—are all involved in a new formula
based on the attempt, not to describe, but to suggest or to
register the moving tension towards an ever-receding core.
"Creation", as Collingwood said, "is the act of imagination; an artist paints or writes to help himself to discover
what he imagines, what he tries to see with his imagination. Art for the creative mind lives in the mind, its interest is there, not on canvas or paper." The work of art, as
Kant said, has no purpose, it is merely purposive. The
whole work of art does not exist in the mind of the artist,
it comes into existence by experimenting with the parts;
the poet proceeds not from idea to expression but from
expression to idea—source. Art is the realisation of the individuality of the artist through progressive self-discovery
in action, without preconceived ideal or set purpose—social, religious or otherwise; and least of all is it art for
art's sake; it is obeying one's inner laws, the laws the individual was made for, which are to reveal his own aspect
of truth, part of the great Truth. Knowledge is no longer
subjective intellectualism, that is to say the work of an
over-powerful ego which draws to itself as a magnet the
elements of static materiality, but on the contrary receptivity, enquiry, tension towards some elusive unknowable reality which the devout might reach through grace and the
mystic in acts of complete surrender which are the foundations of true knowledge. Knowledge is consciousness,
the true aim of poetry, but consciousness in our time is no
longer a Cartesian entity, but a kind of Bergsonian continuous becoming. What Descartes called the 'Je', now only is
and knows itself in the act of consciousness, and the rest
of the time it remains, as Husserl put it, 'in parenthesis'.
Consciousness is not a concept or a starting point as Boi-
leau suggested, but an end, the goal of the journey from
non-being and darkness to being and light. 'Le rêve' of
Baudelaire or Valéry is not the subconscious of Freud and
the surrealists, but on the contrary a state in which mental
and perceptual activities take place not according to a
willed conceptual pattern, but as a growth whose strength
and range vary according to genius, towards consciousness
and knowledge. Consciousness, the inextricable combination of experience and awareness of experience, breaks
gently like dawn from darkness, then it increases in
strength, penetrates underwoods and deep valleys, until it

finally illuminates mountains and sky in the glory of the
day—which is the completed work or poem.

These views of knowledge illumine all the theorising of
the symbolist movement; one can easily understand how
the words, used like Tom Thumb's pebbles in his journey
through the wood of memory or the past, will be arrayed
according to their capacity to suggest this very fleeting experience, and not as a firm receptacle of an already existing core; they will be essentially transient and fleeting, and
their symbolic value, I mean their referential value to logical meaning, will be reduced to the minimum. They will
be, as much as words can stand it, what they are in themselves, the organic notations of an experience. In two respects, in respect of fleetingness and transience, and in respect of being essentially themselves, they resemble musical notes, which, at best, should be what they are and
nothing else. The new way of presenting the poetic experience also resembles music in the fact that structural
rhythm plays an essential part in suggesting the poetic experience and the emotion which underlies it. We shall see
later how a good deal of Mallarmé's insistence on poetry
as music, which was taken by many as being the result of
Wagner's influence, was in reality due to the very nature
of the poetic experience which, in its fluidity, had drawn
nearer to music. Life in all its aspects, from the most minute to the cosmological level, from the most static matter
to feelings and all aspects of the human psyche, is now
conceived as movement and timelessness. The novel, based
on sequential time, has its last great representative in
Flaubert; after him Gide, Proust, Joyce concerned themselves not with telling stories conveying through characters
a criticism of the society to which these characters belonged, but rather aimed at conveying the moment of
present experience and intensity which, whether it embraces twenty-four hours or two-score of years, brings together the simultaneity of events which form the duration
of a human consciousness. Whitehead describes that moment as the "creativity of the world which is the throbbing
emotion of the past hurling itself into a new transcendent
fact." It is the search for time lost and time regained of
Proust, it is the abolition of time and matter of Dostoevski
and the moment of dénouement of Gide. *L'Après-midi
d'un Faune, La Jeune Parque, Ulysses,* and, later on, *Four
Quartets,* are above all the records of journeys of discover-

ies across various *états-d'âme;* centred round a story, as is the case with *Ulysses* and *L'Après-midi d'un Faune,* a myth in the case of Valéry, and concrete experiences in the case of Eliot, with whom the structure of the poem approximates most to the structure of a musical composition.

Considerations on Symbolism

BY MARCEL RAYMOND

M. G. Bonneau, author of a book on French symbolism, has drawn an amusing comparison between the symbolist movement and the dragon of Alca in the second book of *Ile des Pingouins,* which none of those who had allegedly seen him could describe. Symbolism embraces a number of diverse trends and individual efforts; what they all have in common would seem to be, essentially, their protest against modern society and positivistic philosophy. A sense of the deep life of the spirit, a certain intuition of mystery and of a reality transcending the phenomenal world, a new will—at least in France—to grasp the essence of poetry and to free it from didacticism and sentimentalism: such are the elements generally underlying the activity of the poetic generation of 1885.

In connection with the term "symbol"—one of those fetishist words that are all the more suggestive because they are charged with complex meanings difficult to define—it is very important to avoid misunderstandings on a capital point which concerns the poetry of today as much as that of yesterday; for the symbolist mode of thought and expression does not characterize any specific historical period.

It seems that the human mind, in dreams, daydreams, or even in waking hours, is endowed with the faculty of autonomous creation, and that it freely imagines fables, figures, images in which the deep emotional life of the self is projected. This spontaneous symbolism is restrained among civilized men by the various organs of censorship, but it functions almost uninhibited among so-called primitive peoples, or in the dreams of the sophisticated. Thus arise the myths and other fabulous constructions which

From Marcel Raymond, *From Baudelaire to Surrealism,* Book I, Chapter I, pp. 43-50. Documents of Modern Art, Volume 10, reprinted by permission of George Wittenborn, Inc., New York 10021.

common-sense denounces as unreal, but which are true
psychologically (and can also be true otherwise) because
on the level of the imagination they correspond to the
feelings and thoughts which engendered them. As a result
of this correspondence, the subject comes to feel that the
image mystically partakes of the psychic reality it symbol-
izes.

We are familiar with this notion of correspondence or
equivalence. It is applicable to the poet who entrusts images with the mission of expressing or embodying a state
of mind. The work of elaboration in which he engages and
the elementary, direct process that we have just defined are
naturally related; the two coincide when the poet eschews
thought and construction and passively yields to dreaming.
This activity of the mind reduced to its own forces, which
builds up a story that is the mind's own history, enables us
to perceive the phenomenon of creative imagination in the
raw, prior to any kind of aesthetic arrangement or intention.

However, if we may say that any fable, any association
of images emerging into consciousness tends to organize itself into a symbol, there is no question here of a two-term
relation between a clearly perceived feeling or thought and
the images into which it is projected. For the genuine symbol results from a direct adherence of the mind to a *naturally* figurative form of thought; and, as Jean Baruzi says,
"since it is never a translation, it can never be translated."
This is an essential fact, often ignored; it follows that the
symbols of dreams and of nondirected daydreams are
"polyvalent" as the psychologists say, that is, they represent a complex state, which is, moreover, in process of
transformation. Consequently, such symbols will as a rule
have several "values"; furthermore, these are interconnect-
ed by affective links, and none of them can be reduced to
a simple formula. This fact is overlooked by many readers
and commentators who, when confronted by a modern
poem cannot rest until they have ascribed to its symbols a
logical *meaning* that precludes any other interpretation.
There is no doubt that many works produced in the course
of the last fifty years, whose elements took shape in an obscure area of consciousness, are polyvalent.*

If anyone argues that this conception of the symbol also

---

* As early as 1901, M. G. Pelissier voices similar views in *Revue
des Revues* (March issue).

applies to poets who are quite unlike the symbolists of the late nineteenth century, we shall readily agree; if anyone declares that it does not apply to the symbolists because most of them deliberately resorted to an indirect method of expression and grouped images which they invested with a quite precise meaning (at least for them), we shall answer that we have no intention of denying that the intellect is capable of becoming aware of the spontaneous process we have described, and of associating a representation with a psychic reality, state of mind, feeling, or idea. It is quite true that the symbolists often did proceed in that way. One might conclude that it is for the very reason that they were for the most part intellectuals and artists devoid of innocence and extremely civilized, that they came to substitute an effort of auscultation, analysis, and synthesis, for the natural movement of alogical thought. (It has often been observed that the more a man knows himself, the less active he is, that he has greater difficulty in performing a psychological function once he has understood its mechanism.) The deliberate effort to express oneself symbolically may considerably decrease the authenticity of the symbol, which then becomes something it is not when the mind is left to itself: an indirect mode of expression, in which, through choice, the signifying object supplants the signified object.

It must be noted that the foregoing remarks rather simplify the actual state of affairs. Actually, there are a host of intermediary positions between the unconscious and the conscious, a number of relations between thought and symbol. Originally, we are confronted with the free activity of the mind, accompanied by the mystical presence of reality in the image; in the end we obtain, on the level of the intellect, the symbol as it has been defined by Jules Lemaître: "an extended comparison, of which we are given only the second term, a system of consistent metaphors."

According to Paul Valéry, "what was baptized symbolism may be summed up very simply in the intention, common to several families of poets (incidentally hostile to one another), to recover their property from Music." (Foreword to *Connaissance de la Déesse*, by Lucien Fabre.) It is unlikely that the situation is as simple as all that, that the poets—from Ronsard to Racine, Chénier, Hugo—had ever allowed themselves to be expropriated, and that the music of musicians can be assimilated to that of poets. Nevertheless, it is true that one of the capital articles of symbolist aesthetics was to put the musical resources of language to deliberate use.

But the musicality—in the full sense of the term—of poetry, like that of prose, is not measured in quasi-mathematical terms by more or less sonorous combinations of words considered as a pure system of sounds. Many verses are harmonious to the ear, but their resonance ends with the last syllable and they fail to leave a musical impression on the mind. This elementary observation suffices to invalidate the thesis of the aestheticians who attempted to explain the secret of a musical verse by simple sound relations, overlooking the possible power of psychological suggestion in words. In reality this phenomenon is much subtler, and the "musical" poet must be capable of feeling the affinities existing between the world of sound and the world of thought. Here again, the problem is to bring out mysterious "correspondences"; certain syllables, thanks to an infinitely subtle accord with the meaning of the word which they compose, by virtue of the confused memories evoked by this word even more than by its sonorous charm, actually "move" the mind, magnetize it in a specific direction. But in no case can the psychological value of the word and its virtual treasury of images and associations be considered independently of its sonorous qualities. Consequently, the "music" of words can be distinguished only arbitrarily from their meaning—in the broadest sense —and a certain "inner music" must always be placed above a quasi-material harmony, which is pleasing only to the ear.

One of the symbolists' greatest merits was their awareness of the complexity of these phenomena. "In my writing I arrange the great flow of words musically, placing them on the orchestral staves: here are the strings and the woods, there the brasses and the percussion instruments. . . ." These graphic words of Saint-Pol Roux show us that a virtue carried to the extreme can defeat itself. The systematic application of the principle resulted, it would seem, in a new servitude and in two errors of capital importance. First of all, the symbolists often sacrificed inner musicality to the mere juggling of sonorities—hence their abuse of "strings" and "brasses." Then, although they were rightly concerned with the relations between sound and thought, they—at least some of them, and particularly René Ghil—made the mistake of neglecting individual divergencies for the pleasure of formulating laws, principles, prescriptions that are largely fanciful. These errors were patent enough, and they served as a warning to the successors of the symbolists. For the last thirty years the dream of the "merger of the arts" has ceased to haunt the imagination of our poets. And the representatives of the young schools have sought to ally themselves with painters rather than with musicians.

As for free verse, which was born partly, it would seem, of a desire to express one's thought "without deforming it" (this was the intention of Laforgue who rather embodies the "decadent" spirit), and partly from musical preoccupations (G. Kahn and the symbolists), it originated in the nineteenth century, and the poets of today have only inherited an instrument forged by their predecessors, sometimes transforming and abusing it. The passions that it aroused have long since calmed down, and many an illusion has perhaps been dispelled; free verse has not succeeded in killing regular verse nor in *radically* differentiating itself from rhythmic prose. So many automatisms of so many kinds lurk in wait for the writer, that deliberately accepted restrictions have in some quarters come to be regarded as a favorable condition for the exercise of poetic thought.

On the other hand, it has been realized that the French language is not devoid of accentuation, and that every text in prose, and above all, any spoken utterance, is naturally articulated in rhythmic feet, with several atonal syllables preceding each accented syllable. Ultimately, free verse is characterized only by the small number of syllables in each rhythmic foot and the intensification of the cadence, which, it is true, considerably modifies the *tone* of the discourse. Moreover, we shall see that in the eyes of many modern poets verbal rhythm tends to merge with psychological rhythm, and that a weakly accented "verse" is nothing but a proposition, an ideological unit. Gradually, an absolute individualism, partly reflecting the general trend of the century, achieved dominance in the domain of prosody. The "emancipated" verse, blank verse, the symbolist free verse (of which several styles should be distinguished), the verset, prose arranged in lines, "consecutive" prose—all these "forms" do not deter the strictest regular verse from continuing its course of development. Such variety borders on anarchy, and one need hardly emphasize its dangers, but to those who keep in mind the diversity of the poets' intentions, it will be apparent that this great diversity could not have been avoided.

"The symbolist school," writes Bernard Fay, "was a misunderstanding. These young men seduced by Verlaine, enthusiastic admirers of Rimbaud and Mallarmé, did not see that in reality their masters wished them to engage in a crusade, a 'spiritual' hunt. These young men engaged in literature and sought to found groups, when they should have worked on themselves. . . ." This judgement is severe, and in its bald form, even unjust; the symbolists of 1885 and 1890 were, on the whole, anything but careerists. Nevertheless it is true—and this is essential—that Baudelaire, Mallarmé, and Rimbaud had boldly raised poetry to a vital plane; they had made it a transcendent activity; while the majority of their disciples—unwittingly in many cases—brought it back to the literary plane. I am quite aware that there was a certain wisdom in asking of literature only what it can give, and in keeping away from insoluble problems. Yet how is it that these problems are the only ones that still deserve to be raised, in the eyes of certain men, among them those poets whom Nietzsche calls "the expiators of the spirit"?

As men of letters and artists, the symbolists came to consider questions of form *for their own sake*. That is why they searched for a suggestive imagery, resorted to mythology, legend and folklore, and tended to conceive of the symbol as an idea that is subsequently clothed in what Moréas described as "the sumptuous simars of external analogies," that is, as a two-term relation similar to the allegory or emblem. To be sure, the images of fauns, sirens, swans, and dream-women are so full of human and aesthetic meaning that they easily lend themselves to the play of the imagination; still, one must go deep down into oneself if one is to come close enough to the source of these dreams to embody in them something of one's own life. This also explains the need (another heritage of the Parnassus) to dwell upon "beauties of detail," which sometimes resulted in the so-called "coruscating" style, brilliant with ornaments and gems, heavy and over-refined, and terribly outmoded today.

The cult of the Beautiful ends in aestheticism. In his ar-

True but nec [handwritten margin note]

ticle *"L'Ecole paienne"* Baudelaire had already declared that "the exclusive passion of art is a canker which devours everything else." Often art safeguards itself only by renouncing itself. As for culture, it is well known that it can become a means of escaping from life, of protecting oneself against ideas and feelings, a means of self-betrayal. And the religion of the Beautiful, grafted on an extensive culture, was a prominent characteristic of most of the symbolists. If we also recall that they possessed an extremely flexible and lucid intelligence, we shall be able to grasp the truth paradoxically formulated by Jacques Rivière who ventured an abstract definition of the spirit of the symbolist poet: "An intellect that goes straight to the end, that finds no resistance in the things it invents, but flows right through them, and is so fluid, keen, and penetrating that it reaches the extremity of its subject at one stroke. Everything in the work of the symbolists bears the mark of an ultra-conscious creator."

All this leads us to conclude that in a number of cases a kind of discordance prevailed between the goal that the poets set for themselves and the education they had received, between their refined sensibility, their discernment, and the artistic resources they brought into play. Symbolism offered the spectacle of a poetry which attempted to express the "soul" of things and the profound stirrings of life, yet resulted from a painstaking effort of analysis; of poets who wished to "suggest mystery," yet, out of dilettantism or a taste for the precious and the enigmatic, turned their back on the real mysteries in order to invent others. On the other hand, there is Laforgue who had studied Hartmann's work on the *Unconscious* and sought to silence his reason: "Create living life in the raw, and drop the rest," he exclaimed. In reality, nothing is more deliberate than the "lifelike" incoherence of his *Complaintes,* while the "incongruous marriages" of his verbal associations strike one rather as laboratory products. The real Laforgue, the Laforgue who is so moving, must be sought elsewhere. In passages of this kind we seem to perceive an over-subtle intellect vainly spending itself in attempts to mimic the movements of the unconscious.

Good Manuscript Time [handwritten margin note]

The foregoing remarks on symbolism are by no means intended as an appreciation of the positive contribution of the School of 1885. We have merely indicated why it did not live up to the example and ambitions of its masters, in order to make possible a better understanding of what took place around 1900. At that time French poetry tried to renew itself by going back to older (romantic) sources and models, and proceeded to draw sustenance from the works of Baudelaire, Mallarmé and Rimbaud, and from a closer contact with the spirit of the times, a spirit of revolt and adventure.

Dada

BY MARCEL RAYMOND

No doubt a great event, the war, was needed to create some enthusiasm for Rimbaud's desire to "change life" and to make young men look upon revolt against morality, literature, self-evident truths, and the everyday course of things, as the only acceptable attitude. Those who refuse to see in the dada movement anything but a Parisian scandal characterized by violence and buffoonery, will never understand the intense moral crisis of the 1920's and the current of anarchistic individualism, the refusal to be useful, that upset so many traditional slogans and age-old beliefs.

Without attempting to tell the whole story, let us recall that dadaism had at least three points of origin—(1) in the United States, with Marcel Duchamp and Francis Picabia; (2) in Zurich, where Tristan Tzara founded in 1916 a group which he called "Dada," a name that means absolutely nothing; (3) finally, in Paris, where in 1919 these men established contact with a few young writers who had been brought together by their universal suspicion and had just published (in March) the first issue of a magazine entitled, by antiphrasis, *Littérature.* The original purpose of Tzara and his friends seems to have been to organize an "enormous" mystification (aimed at the past, present, and future literary schools), employing the modern resources of publicity in behalf of a school whose intentions were entirely negative, "Ubuesques." Nevertheless, the ideas and sentiments of dada—and in saying this we do not underestimate what André Breton called "Tristan Tzara's admirable spirit of revolt"—seem rather

From Marcel Raymond, *From Baudelaire to Surrealism,* Book III, Chapter XIV, pp. 269-275. Documents of Modern Art, Volume 10, reprinted by permission of George Wittenborn, Inc., New York 10021.

French in origin, although the post-war psychosis saw the hand of Germany in the plot.

The contributors to *Littérature*—at least the younger ones, for the magazine at first opened its pages to Valéry, Gide, etc.—were on an average twenty years of age in 1917, which in France was perhaps the grimmest of the war years. Life itself undertook to destroy whatever illusions they might have had about the "real" world—: the regimentation of morals, the distortion of religious feelings, a science that had celebrated its greatest triumphs in the calculations of ballistics, the greatest "trahison des clercs" (betrayal of the intellectuals) that mankind had ever seen—there was ample ground for disillusionment. As for literature, it has fallen a prey to military chroniclers. "We civilizations know that we are mortal," Valéry said a short time later (in *La Crise de l'Esprit*). Can dadaism be called a wrecking enterprise? In the eyes of André Breton, Louis Aragon, Philippe Soupault, everything had already been torn down; dadaism could be only an inventory of the ruins, and a declaration of the failure, or more accurately, the death of a civilization.

Dada thus appears as a desperate systematic skepticism leading directly to total negation. Man is nothing. "Measured by the scale of eternity, any activity is futile," says Tzara. And André Breton: "It is inadmissible that man should leave a trace of his passage on earth." Everything is of equal insignificance. "What is beautiful? What is ugly? What is great, strong, weak? What is Carpentier, Renan, Foch? Don't know. What is myself? Don't know. Don't know, don't know, don't know." These words by Georges Ribemont-Dessaignes are saluted by Breton as an act of great humility. To utter any judgement, to claim to distinguish the true from the false, is a mark of ridiculous presumption, for actually nothing can be contradicted. At about the same time Einstein's theory was encouraging people to believe that everything was relative to circumstances, to man, and that nothing in the world had any importance at all.

One may deplore these negations as paradoxical, puerile, insane, inhuman; but it must be realized that at a certain moment they were, "philosophically" speaking, logical and legitimate. Moreover these opinions were in tune with the humorists of the Jarry school, such as Jacques Vaché, whom André Breton met at Nantes in 1916, and whose

shadow seems to have presided secretly over the development of dada. Vaché defined humor as "a sense of the
theatrical and joyless futility of everything, when one
knows." In most cases, the idea of the infinite, which is
always present, and the certainty that convention or arbitrariness governs all our actions suffice to convince man of
the absurdity of himself and his life.

One of the essential preoccupations of the dadaists was
to draw up an indictment of literature. According to them,
the best literature is always imitation; the most sincere
writers have always been dependent on others, have been
prisoners of tyrannical traditions and, above all, of reason.
It is impossible to know oneself, and the most clearsighted
man imagines himself, composes and betrays himself before his mirror. Some of Paul Valéry's aphorisms seemed
to justify the attitude of these young people who had admired the author of *La Jeune Parque* at a time of intellectual impurity and scarcity, and had been even his friends
for a few seasons. "A work of art is always a forgery (i.e.
it is a fabrication without any relation to an author acting
under the influence of a single impulse). It is the product
of a collaboration of very different states of mind." Or:
"the slightest erasure is a violation of spontaneity." To this
the ungrateful disciples soon retorted: "Let us then choose
spontaneity, authenticity, let us act on one impulse, and
renounce writing 'works'." For the time being, dada con-
tented itself with acquiescing in such declarations of
Valéry as the following: "The striving for a rhythmical,
measured, rhymed, alliterated language comes up against
conditions entirely alien to the pattern of thought (*Entre-
tiens avec Fr. Lefèvre*)."

If every work of art is a forgery, it is not only because
the man who composes it cannot possibly be sincere. In
addition to the constraints of art, ordinary language is "the
worst of conventions" because it imposes upon us the use
of formulas and verbal associations which do not belong
to us, which embody next to nothing of our true natures;
the very meanings of words are fixed and unchangeable
only because of an abuse of power by the collectivity:
"one may very well know the word 'hello' and yet say
'good-bye' to the woman one meets again after a year's absence (André Breton, *Les Pas perdus*)." The "improper"
word may express a feeling in a way that is quite
satisfactory to the subject; in any event, its use is fully jus-

tified by the fact that it was spontaneously uttered. Even
before the war, Jean Paulhan had made this kind of observations in his magazine, *Le Spectateur*. Now it was time to
draw the consequences of these principles. As for the need
to be understood, it was of small importance; writing was
a private affair. And why write at all? The editors of
Littérature asked modern writers this question. Solemn or
pathetic answers were ridiculed; those approved were the
modest or ironical answers, like that of Valéry, "I write
out of weakness," or of Knut Hamsun, "I write to kill
time."

Needless to say, the public understood none of all
this. It demanded art, whatever it might be, and the most
modern art, too; it saw gestures, and heard obscure, insulting, blasphemous words. The most serious critics raised
the cry of madness, the more indulgent gently censured
these young people eager to sow their wild oats, while the
culprits themselves wallowed in "the aristocratic pleasure
of displeasing." But this pleasure, and all other pleasures
derived from the camaraderie and quarrels of Parisian literary life, could not suppress their sense of bitter joy, almost indistinguishable from despair—the joy of flaying a
society that crushes man for the greatest evil of all, a civilization whose wretchedness had been bared by the war, in
brief, a pseudo-reality which must immediately be proclaimed null and void. "Absolutely incapable of resigning
myself to my lot, wounded in my highest conscience by
the denial of justice which in my eyes original sin does not
excuse at all, I shall not adapt my existence to the absurd
conditions of all existence in this world. . . ." This haughty profession of faith opens André Breton's *Confession
dédaigneuse*. Whatever use literature after 1919 may have
made of these themes and this rhetoric—and fashion and
snobbery often debased them—we must not ignore the
tragic anguish they reflect. Even if all dadaist poetry were
to sink into oblivion, a few sentences would still deserve to
be rescued—sentences which are among the most striking
ever written to express the precariousness of man's fate
and the sorrow of him who is lost and cannot resign himself to his destiny.

Occasionally the writers of the group around *Littérature*
use simple language, even in their poems. For instance,
Louis Aragon whispers this *Air du Temps* to himself:

Est-ce que tu n'as pas assez de lieux communs
Les gens te regardent sans rire
Ils ont des yeux de verre
Tu passes tu perds ton temps tu passes
Tu comptes jusqu'à cent et tu triches pour tuer dix sec-
    ondes encore
Tu étends le bras brusquement pour mourir
N'aies pas peur
Un jour ou l'autre
Il n'y aura plus qu'un jour et puis un jour
Et puis ça y est
Plus besoin de voir les hommes ni les bêtes à bon Dieu
Qu'ils caressent de temps en temps
Plus besoin de parler tout seul la nuit pour ne pas enten-
    dre
La plainte de la cheminée
Plus besoin de soulever mes paupières
Ni de lancer mon sang comme un disque
Ni de respirer malgré moi
Pourtant je ne désire pas mourir
La cloche de mon coeur chante à voix basse un espoir très
    ancien
Cette musique. je sais bien mais les paroles
Que disaient au juste les paroles
Imbécile

Have you not had your fill of commonplaces
People look at you without laughing
They have glass eyes
You pass, you waste your time, you pass,
You count to a hundred and you cheat to kill ten more
    seconds
Abruptly you stretch out your hand to die
Don't be afraid
One day or another
There will be only one day to go and one day more
And then that's it
No more need to see men or the dear little beasts
They fondle from time to time
No need to talk to yourself at night to keep from hearing
The wail of the chimney
No need to raise my eyelids
Nor to hurl my blood like a discus
Nor to breathe in spite of myself

Yet I do not want to die
Softly the bell of my heart sings an ancient hope
I know the music well. But the words
Now what exactly were the words saying
Idiot.

(Le Mouvement perpetuel)

Is this a summons to silence, a summons to renounce all literature? Such was the teaching of Rimbaud. The idea of such a sacrifice is tempting, but it is difficult to carry it out, to cease protesting, to break one's pen. And then there was something else, something different from an absolute negation, which gradually came to light in the dada movement. After everything had been swept clean, a reality remained. To be sure, it was not reason or intelligence or feeling, but the obscure source of the unconscious which feeds our being and which governs even our loftiest actions, the spirit. The first slogans were soon enriched by the formula: dictatorship of the spirit. Zurich, the birthplace of dada, is the city of Bleuler and Jung, psychologists related to Freud; Louis Aragon and Breton had occasion to experiment with the methods of psychoanalysis. Here the essential is not the thesis of pansexualism, but the theory (that had been advocated by scientists such as Pierre Janet) according to which our conscious activities are only surface manifestations, most often determined by unconscious forces which constitute the substance of the self. And as Jacques Rivière said, Freud emphasized "the hypocrisy inherent in consciousness," the general tendency that "drives us to camouflage ourselves," to seek justifications of our words and acts, to cheat at all times in order to make ourselves look more beautiful or at least to "adjust" ourselves. His theory justified an attitude of systematic distrust which curiously confirmed Valéry's statements on "forgery" in literature and on the impossibility of being sincere. The influence of Freud on the dada movement has sometimes been contested; possibly it amounts to little, but the meeting of the Viennese philosopher and the poets on this common ground is nevertheless a significant symptom.

We are now in a position to formulate the problem of art, more accurately the problem of expression, as it appeared to the writers of the *Littérature* group: only the unconscious does not lie, it alone is worth bringing to light. All deliberate and conscious efforts, composition, logic, are futile. The celebrated French lucidity is nothing but a cheap lantern. At best the "poet" can prepare traps (as a physician might do in treating a patient), with which to catch the unconscious by surprise and to prevent it from cheating. The goal was clearly indicated by Jacques Rivière: "To grasp our being before it has yielded to consistency; to seize it in its incoherence, or better, in its primitive coherence, before the idea of contradiction has appeared and compelled it to reduce and construct itself; to replace its logical unity, which can only be acquired, by its absurd unity, which alone is innate." As for art, it was repudiated, or at least there was no more question of any activity aiming at the elaboration, however free, of anything reminiscent of a finished work. Is this the ultimate outcome of the great romantic adventure which began in France on the day when an enemy of reason, of society, of civilization, of reality, an apostle of primitivism, declared that the only "perfect and full" happiness consisted in being absorbed in those regions of the mind which had remained intact and "innocent"? *fonce innocence*

Surrealism and Revolution

BY ALBERT CAMUS

11/5/86

This is not the place to deal at length with Rimbaud. Everything that can be said about him—and even more, unfortunately—has already been said. It is worth pointing out, however, for it concerns our subject, that only in his work was Rimbaud the poet of rebellion. His life, far from justifying the myth it created, only illustrates (an objective perusal of the letters from Harrar suffices to prove this) the fact that he surrendered to the worst form of nihilism imaginable. Rimbaud has been deified for renouncing his genius, as if his renunciation implied superhuman virtue. It must be pointed out, however, despite the fact that by doing so we disqualify the alibis of our contemporaries, that genius alone—and not the renunciation of genius—implies virtue. Rimbaud's greatness does not lie in the first poems from Charleville nor in his trading at Harrar. It shines forth at the moment when, in giving the most peculiarly appropriate expression to rebellion that it has ever received, he simultaneously proclaims his triumph and his agony, his conception of a life beyond the confines of this world and the inescapability of the world, the yearning for the unattainable and reality brutally determined on restraint, the rejection of morality and the irresistible compulsion to duty. At the moment when he carries in his breast both illumination and the darkness of hell, when he hails and insults beauty, and creates, from an insoluble conflict, the intricate counterpoint of an exquisite song, he is the poet of rebellion—the greatest of all. The order in which he wrote his two great works is of no importance. In any case there was very little time between the conception of the two books, and any artist knows, with the certainty born of experience, that Rimbaud simultaneously carried the seeds of the *Season in Hell* (*Une Saison en Enfer*) and the *Illuminations* within him. Though he wrote them one after the other, there is no doubt that he experienced the suffering of both of them at the same time. This contradiction, which killed him, was the real source of his genius.

But where, then, is the virtue of someone who refuses to face the contradiction and betrays his own genius before having drunk it to the last bitter drop? Rimbaud's silence is not a new method of rebelling; at least, we can no longer say so after the publication of the Harrar letters. His metamorphosis is undoubtedly mysterious. But there is also a mystery attached to the banality achieved by brilliant young girls whom marriage transforms into adding or knitting machines. The myth woven around Rimbaud supposes and affirms that nothing was possible after the *Season in Hell*. But what is impossible for the supremely gifted poet or for the inexhaustibly creative writer? How can we imagine anything to follow *Moby Dick, The Trial, Zarathustra. The Possessed?* Nevertheless, they were followed by great works, which instruct, implement, and bear witness to what is finest in the writer, and which only come to an end at his death. Who can fail to regret the work that would have been greater than the *Season in Hell* and of which we have been deprived by Rimbaud's abdication?

Can Abyssinia be considered as a monastery; is it Christ who shut Rimbaud's mouth? Such a Christ would be the kind of man who nowadays lords it over the cashier's desk in a bank, to judge by the letters in which the unhappy poet talks only about his money which he wants to see "wisely invested" and "bringing in regular dividends." [1] The man who exulted under torture, who hurled curses at God and at beauty, who hardened himself in the harsh atmosphere of crime, now only wants to marry someone "with a future." The mage, the seer, the convict who lived perpetually in the shadow of the penal colony, the man-king on a godless earth, always carried seventeen pounds of gold in a belt worn uncomfortably round his stomach, which he complained gave him dysentery. Is this the

---

[1] It is only fair to note that the tone of these letters might be explained by the people to whom they are written. But they do not suggest that Rimbaud is making a great effort to lie. Not one word betrays the Rimbaud of former times.

mythical hero, worshipped by so many young men who, though they do not spit in the face of the world, would die of shame at the mere idea of such a belt? To maintain the myth, those decisive letters must be ignored. It is easy to see why they have been so little commented upon. They are a sacrilege, as truth sometimes is. A great and praiseworthy poet, the greatest of his time, a dazzling oracle—Rimbaud is all of these things. But he is not the man-god, the burning inspiration, the monk of poetry as he is often presented. The man only recaptured his greatness in the hospital bed in which, at the hour of his painful end, even his mediocrity becomes moving: "How unlucky I am, how very unlucky I am . . . and I've money on me that I can't even keep an eye on!" The defiant cry of those last wretched moments: "No, no, now I rebel against death!" happily restores Rimbaud to that part of common human experience which involuntarily coincides with greatness. The young Rimbaud comes to life again on the brink of the abyss and with him revives the rebellion of the times when his imprecations against life were only expressions of despair at the thought of death. It is at this point that the bourgeois trader once more rejoins the tortured adolescent whom we so much admired. He recaptures his youth in the terror and bitter pain finally experienced by those who do not know how to attain happiness. Only at this point does his passion, and with it his truth, begin.

Moreover, Harrar was actually foretold in his work, but in the form of his final abdication. "And best of all, a drunken sleep on the beach." The fury of annihilation, appropriate to every rebel, then assumes its most common form. The apocalypse of crime—as conceived by Rimbaud in the person of the prince who insatiably slaughters his subjects—and endless licentiousness are rebellious themes that will be taken up again by the surrealists. But finally, even with Rimbaud, nihilist dejection prevailed; the struggle, the crime itself, proved too exacting for his exhausted mind. The seer who drank, if we may venture to say so, in order not to forget ended by finding in drunkenness the heavy sleep so well known to our contemporaries. One can sleep on the beach, or at Aden. And one consents, no longer actively, but passively, to accept the order of the world, even if the order is degrading. Rimbaud's silence is also a preparation for the silence of authority, which hovers over minds resigned to everything save to the necessity of putting up a fight. Rimbaud's great intellect, suddenly subordinated to money, proclaims the advent of other demands, which are at first excessive and which will later be put to use by the police. To be nothing—that is the cry of the mind exhausted by its own rebellion. This leads to the problem of suicide of the mind, which, after all, is less respectable than the surrealists' suicide, and more fraught with consequences. Surrealism itself, coming at the end of this great act of rebellion, is only significant because it attempted to perpetuate that aspect of Rimbaud which alone evokes our sympathy. Deriving the rules for a rebellious asceticism from the letter about the seer and the system it implies, he illustrates the struggle between the will to be and the desire for annihilation, between the yes and the no, which we have discovered again and again at every stage of rebellion. For all these reasons, rather than repeat the endless commentaries that surround Rimbaud's work, it seemed preferable to rediscover him and to follow him among his successors.

Absolute rebellion, total insubordination, sabotage on principle, the humor and cult of the absurd—such is the nature of surrealism, which defines itself, in its primary intent, as the incessant examination of all values. The refusal to draw any conclusions is flat, decisive, and provocative. "We are specialists in rebellion." Surrealism, which, according to Aragon, is a machine for capsizing the mind, was first conjured up by the Dadaist movement, whose romantic origins and anemic dandyism must be noted.[2] Non-signification and contradiction are therefore cultivated for their own sakes. "The real Dadaists are against Dada. Everyone is a director of Dada." Or again: "What is good? What is ugly? What is great, strong, weak . . . ? Don't know! Don't know!" These parlor nihilists were obviously threatened with having to act as slaves to the strictest orthodoxies. But there is something more in surrealism than standard nonconformism, the legacy left by Rimbaud, which, in fact, Breton recapitulates as follows: "Must we abandon all hope at that particular point?"

An urgent appeal to absent life is reinforced by a total rejection of the present world, as Breton's arrogant statement indicates: "Incapable of accepting the fate assigned

---

[2] Jarry, one of the masters of Dadaism, is the last incarnation, peculiar rather than brilliant, of the metaphysical dandy.

to me, my highest perceptions outraged by this denial of justice, I refrain from adapting my existence to the ridiculous conditions of existence here below." The mind, according to Breton, can find no point of rest either in this life or beyond it. Surrealism wants to find a solution to this endless anxiety. It is "a cry of the mind which turns against itself and finally takes the desperate decision to throw off its bonds." It protests against death and "the laughable duration" of a precarious condition. Thus surrealism places itself at the mercy of impatience. It exists in a condition of wounded frenzy: at once inflexible and self-righteous, with the consequent implication of a moral philosophy. Surrealism, the gospel of chaos, found itself compelled, from its very inception, to create an order. But at first it only dreamed of destruction—by poetry, to begin with—on the plane of imprecation, and later by the use of actual weapons. The trial of the real world has become, by logical development, the trial of creation.

Surrealist irreligion is methodical and rational. At first it established itself on the idea of the absolute non-culpability of man, to whom one should render "all the power that he has been capable of putting into the word God." As in every history of rebellion, this idea of absolute non-culpability, springing from despair, was little by little transformed into a mania for punishment. The surrealists, while simultaneously exalting human innocence, believed that they could exalt murder and suicide. They spoke of suicide as a solution and Crevel, who considered this solution "the most probable, just, and definitive," killed himself, as did Rigaut and Vaché. Later Aragon was to condemn the "babblers about suicide." Nevertheless the fact remains that to extol annihilation, without personal involvement, is not a very honorable course. On this point surrealism has retained, from the *"littérature"* it despised, the most facile excuses and has justified Rigaud's staggering remark: "You are all poets, and I myself am on the side of death."

Surrealism did not rest there. It chose as its hero Violette Nozière or the anonymous common-law criminal, affirming in this way, in the face of crime, the innocence of man. But it also was rash enough to say—and this is the statement that André Breton must have regretted ever since 1933—that the simplest surrealist act consisted in going out into the street, revolver in hand, and shooting at

random into the crowd. Whoever refuses to recognize any
other determining factor apart from the individual and his
desires, any priority other than that of the unconscious,
actually succeeds in rebelling simultaneously against society and against reason. The theory of the gratuitous act is
the culmination of the demand for absolute freedom.
What does it matter if this freedom ends by being embodied in the solitude defined by Jarry: "When I'll have collected all the ready cash, in the world, I'll kill everybody
and go away." The essential thing is that every obstacle
should be denied and that the irrational should be trium-
phant. What, in fact, does this apology for murder signify
if not that, in a world without meaning and without
honor, only the desire for existence, in all its forms, is legitimate? The instinctive joy of being alive, the stimulus of
the unconscious, the cry of the irrational, are the only
pure truths that must be professed. Everything that stands
in the way of desire—principally society—must therefore
be mercilessly destroyed. Now we can understand André
Breton's remark about Sade: "Certainly man no longer
consents to unite with nature except in crime; it remains
to be seen if this is not one of the wildest, the most in-
contestable, ways of loving." It is easy to see that he is
talking of love without an object, which is love as experienced by people who are torn asunder. But this empty,
avid love, this insane desire for possession, is precisely the
love that society inevitably thwarts. That is why Breton,
who still bears the stigma of his declarations, was able to
sing the praises of treason and declare (as the surrealists
have tried to prove) that violence is the only adequate
mode of expression.

But society is not only composed of individuals. It is
also an institution. Too well-mannered to kill everybody,
the surrealists, by the very logic of their attitude, came to
consider that, in order to liberate desire, society must first
be overthrown. They chose to serve the revolutionary
movement of their times. From Walpole and Sade—with
an inevitability that comprises the subject of this book—
surrealists passed on to Helvétius and Marx. But it is obvious that it is not the study of Marxism that led them to
revolution.[3] Quite the contrary: surrealism is involved in

[3] The Communists who joined the party as a result of having
studied Marx can be counted on the fingers of one hand. They are
first converted and then they read the Scriptures.

an incessant effort to reconcile, with Marxism, the inevitable conclusions that led it to revolution. We can say, without being paradoxical, that the surrealists arrived at Marxism on account of what, today, they most detest in Marx. Knowing the basis and the nobility of the motives that compelled him, particularly when one has shared the same lacerating experiences, one hesitates to remind André Breton that his movement implied the establishment of "ruthless authority" and of dictatorship, of political fanaticism, the refusal of free discussion, and the necessity of the death penalty. The peculiar vocabulary of that period is also astonishing ("sabotage," "informer," etc.) in that it is the vocabulary of a police-dominated revolution. But these frenetics wanted "any sort of revolution," no matter what as long as it rescued them from the world of shopkeepers and compromise in which they were forced to live. In that they could not have the best, they still preferred the worst. In that respect they were nihilists. They were not aware of the fact that those among them who were, in the future, to remain faithful to Marxism were faithful at the same time to their initial nihilism. The real destruction of language, which the surrealists so obstinately wanted, does not lie in incoherence or automatism. It lies in the word *order*. It was pointless for Aragon to begin with a denunciation of the "shameful pragmatic attitude," for in that attitude he finally found total liberation from morality, even if that liberation coincided with another form of servitude. The surrealist who meditated most profoundly about this problem, Pierre Naville, in trying to find the denominator common to revolutionary action and surrealist action, localized it, with considerable penetration, in pessimism, meaning in "the intention of accompanying man to his downfall and of overlooking nothing that could ensure that his perdition might be useful." This mixture of Machiavellianism and Augustinism in fact explains twentieth-century rebellion; no more audacious expression can be given to the nihilism of the times. The renegades of surrealism were faithful to most of the principles of nihilism. In a certain way, they wanted to die. If André Breton and a few others finally broke with Marxism, it was because there was something in them beyond nihilism, a second loyalty to what is purest in the origins of rebellion: they did not want to die.

Certainly, the surrealists wanted to profess materialism. "We are pleased to recognize as one of the prime causes of the mutiny on board the battleship Potemkin that terrible piece of meat." But there is not with them, as with the Marxists, a feeling of friendship, even intellectual, for that piece of meat. Putrid meat typifies only the real world, which in fact gives birth to revolt, but against itself. It explains nothing, even though it justifies everything. Revolution, for the surrealists, was not an end to be realized day by day, in action, but an absolute and consolatory myth. It was "the real life, like love," of which Éluard spoke, who at that time had no idea that his friend Kalandra would die of that sort of life. They wanted the "communism of genius," not the other form of Communism. These peculiar Marxists declared themselves in rebellion against history and extolled the heroic individual. "History is governed by laws, which are conditioned by the cowardice of individuals." André Breton wanted revolution and love together—and they are incompatible. Revolution consists in loving a man who does not yet exist. But he who loves a living being, if he really loves, can only consent to die for the sake of the being he loves. In reality, revolution for André Breton was only a particular aspect of rebellion, while for Marxists and, in general, for all political persuasions, only the contrary is true. Breton was not trying to create, by action, the promised land that was supposed to crown history. One of the fundamental theses of surrealism is, in fact, that there is no salvation. The advantage of revolution was not that it gives mankind happiness, "abominable material comfort." On the contrary, according to Breton, it should purify and illuminate man's tragic condition. World revolution and the terrible sacrifices it implies would only bring one advantage: "preventing the completely artificial precariousness of the social condition from screening the real precariousness of the human condition." Quite simply, for Breton, this form of progress was excessive. One might as well say that revolution should be enrolled in the service of the inner asceticism by which individual men can transfigure reality into the supernatural, "the brilliant revenge of man's imagination." With André Breton, the supernatural holds the same place as the rational does with Hegel. Thus it would be impossible to imagine a more complete antithesis to the political philosophy of Marxism. The lengthy hesitations of those whom Artaud called the Amiels of revolution are easily explained. The surrealists were more different from Marx than were reactionaries like Joseph de Maistre, for example. The reactionaries made use of the tragedy of existence to reject revolution—in other words, to preserve a historical situation. The Marxists made use of it to justify revolution—in other words, to create another historical situation. Both make use of the human tragedy to further their pragmatic ends. But Breton made use of revolution to consummate the tragedy and, in spite of the title of his magazine, made use of revolution to further the surrealist adventure.

Finally, the definitive rupture is explained if one considers that Marxism insisted on the submission of the irrational, while the surrealists rose to defend irrationality to the death. Marxism tended toward the conquest of totality, and surrealism, like all spiritual experiences, tended toward unity. Totality can demand the submission of the irrational, if rationalism suffices to conquer the world. But the desire for unity is more demanding. It does not suffice that everything should be rational. It wants, above all, the rational and the irrational to be reconciled on the same level. There is no unity that supposes any form of mutilation.

For André Breton, totality could be only a stage, a necessary stage perhaps, but certainly inadequate, on the way that leads to unity. Here we find once again the theme of All or Nothing. Surrealism tends toward universality, and the curious but profound reproach that Breton makes to Marx consists in saying quite justifiably that the latter is not universal. The surrealists wanted to reconcile Marx's "let us transform the world" with Rimbaud's "let us change life." But the first leads to the conquest of the totality of the world and the second to the conquest of the unity of life. Paradoxically, every form of totality is restrictive. In the end, the two formulas succeeded in splitting the surrealist group. By choosing Rimbaud, Breton demonstrated that surrealism was not concerned with action, but with asceticism and spiritual experience. He again gave first place to what composed the profound originality of his movement: the restoration of the sacred and the conquest of unity, which make surrealism so invaluable for a consideration of the problem of rebellion. The more he elaborated on this original concept, the more irreparably he separated himself from his political companions, and at the same time from some of his first manifestoes.

André Breton never, actually, wavered in his support of

surrealism—the fusion of a dream and of reality, the sublimation of the old contradiction between the ideal and the real. We know the surrealist solution: concrete irrationality, objective risk. Poetry is the conquest, the only possible conquest, of the "supreme position." "A certain position of the mind from where life and death, the real and the imaginary, the past and the future . . . cease to be perceived in a contradictory sense." What is this supreme position that should mark the "colossal abortion of the Hegelian system"? It is the search for the summit-abyss, familiar to the mystics. Actually, it is the mysticism without God which demonstrates and quenches the rebel's thirst for the absolute. The essential enemy of surrealism is rationalism. Breton's method, moreover, presents the peculiar spectacle of a form of Occidental thought in which the principle of analogy is continually favored to the detriment of the principles of identity and contradiction. More precisely, it is a question of dissolving contradictions in the fires of love and desire and of demolishing the walls of death. Magic rites, primitive or naïve civilizations, alchemy, the language of flowers, fire, or sleepless nights, are so many miraculous stages on the way to unity and the philosophers' stone. If surrealism did not change the world, it furnished it with a few strange myths which partly justified Nietzsche's announcement of the return of the Greeks. Only partly, because he was referring to unenlightened Greece, the Greece of mysteries and dark gods. Finally, just as Nietzsche's experience culminated in the acceptance of the light of day, surrealist experience culminates in the exaltation of the darkness of night, the agonized and obstinate cult of the tempest. Breton, according to his own statements, understood that, despite everything, life was a gift. But his compliance could never shed the full light of day, the light that all of us need. "There is too much of the north in me," he said, "for me to be a man who complies entirely."

He nevertheless often diminished, to his own detriment, the importance of negation and advanced the positive claims of rebellion. He chose severity rather than silence and retained only the "demand for morality," which, according to Bataille, first gave life to surrealism: "To substitute a new morality for current morality, which is the cause of all our evils." Of course he did not succeed (nor has anybody in our time) in the attempt to found a new morality. But he never despaired of being able to do so. Confronted with the horror of a period in which man, whom he wanted to magnify, has been persistently degraded in the name of certain principles that surrealism adopted, Breton felt constrained to propose, provisionally, a return to traditional morality. That represents a hesitation perhaps. But it is the hesitation of nihilism and the real progress of rebellion. After all, when he could not give himself the morality and the values of whose necessity he was clearly aware, we know very well that Breton chose love. In the general meanness of his times—and this cannot be forgotten—he is the only person who wrote profoundly above love. Love is the entranced morality that served this exile as a native land. Of course, a dimension is still missing here. Surrealism, in that it is neither politics nor religion, is perhaps only an unbearable form of wisdom. But it is also the absolute proof that there is no comfortable form of wisdom: "We want, we shall have, the hereafter in our lifetime," Breton has admirably exclaimed. While reason embarks on action and sets its armies marching on the world, the splendid night in which Breton delights announces dawns that have not yet broken, and, as well, the advent of the poet of our renaissance: René Char.

11/5/86

Looking Back on Surrealism

BY THEODOR W. ADORNO

The generally current theory of surrealism—as laid down in the manifestos of Breton, and also as most commonly expressed in the secondary literature—connects it with the dream, and with the unconscious, even with the Jungian archetypes, which (so runs the theory) found in collage and automatic writing their pictorial language, freed from the trimmings added by the conscious ego. Thus dreams are thought to deal arbitrarily with the elements of reality as well as with its *modus operandi*. If however, no art is required to understand itself—and one is tempted to consider its self-understanding and its success as being almost incompatible—then it is unnecessary to pay attention to the programmatic formulation insisted upon by the intermediaries between art and its audiences. Furthermore, the fatal element in the interpretation of art —even the philosophically responsible interpretation—is that it is obliged to explain what is strange in terms of what is already familiar, by bringing the strange to conceptual form, and thereby explaining away that which only needed to be explained. In so far as works of art demand explanation, by precisely so much does each work (even if against its will) commit treason for the sake of conformism. If surrealism were in fact nothing more than a collection of literary and graphic illustrations of Jung, or even of Freud, it would not only duplicate superfluously what the theory itself expresses without disguising it in metaphor, but it would also be so innocent as to leave no room for the scandal which is the meaning and the vital element of surrealism. To bring it down to the level of the psychological theory of dreams already subjects it to the tastes of officialdom. The versified statement: "This is a father-figure," is allied to the complacent statement: "We

Trans. by S. P. Dunn and Ethel Dunn.

know this already," and what is considered to be merely a
dream, as Cocteau recognized, leaves reality itself undam-
aged, however much it may damage the picture of reality.

But this theory misses the point of the thing itself. That
is not the way people dream; no one dreams that way.
Surrealistic images are no more than mere analogies to the
dream, in that they set aside the usual logic and the rules
of the game of empirical existence; however, at the same
time, they respect the single scattered things and their
whole content (including precisely the human part of it),
thereby approximating the actual state of things. This state
is broken into pieces and rearranged, but not dissolved. So
it is with dreams, but in them the world of things appears
incomparably more veiled and less fixed as reality than in
surrealism, where art is battering against its own foundations. The subject, which is at work much more openly
and uninhibitedly in surrealism than in dreams, turns its
energy directly towards its own extinction, for which in
dreams no energy is required; but thereby everything becomes, so to speak, more objective than in dreams, where
the subject, absent in advance, penetrates and gives another color to what it encounters behind the scenes. At the
same time it has occurred to the surrealists that the process of association is not exactly the same in the psychoanalytical situation as it is in their art. Furthermore, the in-
voluntariness of psychoanalytical associations is by no
means involuntary. Every analyst knows how much trouble and exertion, what an effort of will, it requires to command involuntary expression, which the effort itself tends
to shape even in the analytical situation—to say nothing of
the artistic one of the surrealist. In the fragmented world
of surrealism, the essence of the unconscious does not
come to light. The symbols, measured by their relationship
to this essence, show themselves to be far too rationalistic.
Such explications force the luxuriant multiplicity of surrealism into a few patterns; cram it into a few limited categories such as the *Oedipus complex* without attaining to
the power which radiates from the surrealistic ideas, if not
always from surrealistic art itself; thus even Freud seems
to have reacted to Dali.

After the European catastrophe the shocks of surrealism
lost their power. It is as if they had saved Paris by conditioning it to fear: the fall of the city was their target. If

thereafter one wishes to elevate surrealism to a concept, one must go back, not to psychology, but to artistic techniques. The model of these is unquestionably the montage. It can be easily shown that even truly surrealistic painting operates with the motifs of the montage, and that the discontinuous succession of images in the surrealistic lyric has the character of a montage. But as everyone knows, these images derive, partly literally and partly in spirit, from illustrations of the later nineteenth century, with which the parents of Max Ernst's generation were familiar; in the twenties there were already, on this side of the surrealistic domain, collections of pictorial material, such as "Our Fathers" by Allan Bott, which partook—parasitically—of the surrealistic shock, and thereby for the public's sake saved themselves the trouble of making their contents strange through montage. Truly surrealistic practice, however, has replaced these elements with unaccustomed ones. It is precisely these new elements which have lent it the terror of the familiar, the "Where have I seen that before?" One must therefore trace the affinity of surrealistic technique for psychoanalysis, not to a symbolism of the unconscious, but to the attempt to uncover childhood experiences by blasting them out. What surrealism adds to the pictorial rendering of the world of things is what we lost after childhood: when we were children those illustrations, already archaic, must have jumped out at us, just as the surrealistic pictures do now. The action of the montage supplies the subjective momentum, and seeks with unmistakable intention, though perhaps in vain, to produce perceptions as they must have once been. The giant egg out of which the monster of the last judgment can be hatched at any minute is so big because we were so small when we for the first time shuddered before an egg.

But the archaic contributes to this effect. As to modernity, there is a paradox in that, although already under the spell of the uniformity of mass-production, it still has a history. This paradox alienates it and becomes in the "Children's Pictures for Moderns" the expression of a subjectivity which has grown strange to itself. The tension in surrealism which discharges itself in shock is that between schizophrenia and depersonalization, and therefore precisely not a psychological animation. The subject, grown absolute, legislating freely for itself, and liberated from any concern for the empirical world, reveals itself in the face

of complete depersonalization as inanimate and virtually dead, which throws it completely back upon itself and its protest. The dialectical pictures of surrealism are those of a dialectic of subjective freedom in a situation of objective unfreedom. In them, the European *Weltschmerz* confronts that Niobe who lost her children; in them, bourgeois society flings away the hope of its own survival. One would doubt that any of the surrealists knew Hegel's *Phenomenology,* but a sentence from it, which must be thought of together with the more familiar one about history as progress in the awareness of freedom, defines the content of surrealism: "The sole outcome and result of ordinary freedom is death—a death, furthermore, which has no inner scope and fulfillment." Surrealism has made the above critique its own: this explains its political impulses against anarchy which were in contradiction to that content. It has been said of Hegel's sentence that in it the Enlightenment eliminates itself through its own realization: one must think of surrealism paying no less a price, not as a language of the immediate but as a sign of the recoil of abstract freedom in the presence of things and therefore of pure nature. Its montages are the true still lifes. In as much as they arrange the archaic they create *nature morte.* These pictures are not so much those of an inner essence rather they are object-fetishes on which the subjective, the libido, was once fixated. They bring back childhood by fetishism and not by self-submersion. The model of surrealism, in this sense, would be pornographic. What happens in collages—what is convulsively held in suspension in them, like a tense twitch of lasciviousness around the mouth—recalls the changes which a pornographic representation undergoes at the voyeur's moment of gratification. Detached breasts, the legs of mannequins in silk stockings on collages—these are reminiscences of those objects of partial drive to which the libido once awoke. What is forgotten reveals itself in them, impersonal and dead, as what love really desired and what it wishes to make itself resemble—which is what we actually resemble. Surrealism as a paralyzed awakening is akin to photography. To be sure, these images are icons which surrealism takes over—but not the invariable ones of the unconscious subject, which lack a history and into which the conventional conception would like to neutralize them; rather they are historical ones in which the innermost part of the subject is perceived as external, as an imitation of something social and historical. "Go, Joe, and make that old-time music."

Surrealism thereby forms the complement of objectivity which arose at the same time. The terror, which in Alfred Loos' sense of the word, objectivity in front of an icon perceives as a crime, is mobilized by surrealistic shock. A house has a tumor—its balcony. Surrealism paints this: a growth of flesh crops out on the house. For moderns, children's pictures are the substance of what objectivity covers up with a taboo, because this substance reminds it of its depersonalized nature and thereby also reminds it that the matter does not end here, that its rationality remains rational. Surrealism gathers in what objectivity denies men; the misrepresentations show what the effect of inhibiting desire does. Through them surrealism salvages the archaic—an album of idiosyncrasies in which the claim to happiness, which man finds denied in his own technified world, goes up in smoke. If, however, surrealism seems obsolete, it is because man himself refuses the consciousness of renunciation which was fixed in the negative of surrealism. *11/5/86*

The Film Age

BY ARNOLD HAUSER /// /86

Post-impressionist art is the first to renounce all illusion
of reality on principle and to express its outlook on life by
the deliberate deformation of natural objects. Cubism,
constructivism, futurism, expressionism, dadaism, and surrealism turn away with equal determination from nature-
bound and reality-affirming impressionism. But impressionism itself prepared the ground for this development in
so far as it does not aspire to an integrating description of
reality, to a confrontation of the subject with the objective
world as a whole, but marks rather the beginning of that
process which has been called the "annexation" of reality
by art.[1] Post-impressionist art can no longer be called in
any sense a reproduction of nature; its relationship to nature is one of violation. We can speak at most of a kind of
magic naturalism, of the production of objects which exist
alongside reality, but do not wish to take its place. Confronted with the works of Braque, Chagall, Rouault, Picasso, Henri Rousseau, Salvador Dali, we always feel that,
for all their differences, we are in a second world, a su-
per-world which, however many features of ordinary reality it may still display, represents a form of existence sur-
passing and incompatible with this reality.

Modern art is, however, anti-impressionistic in yet
another respect: it is a fundamentally "ugly" art, forgoing
the euphony, the fascinating forms, tones and colours of
impressionism. It destroys pictorial values in painting,
carefully and consistently executed images in poetry and
melody and tonality in music. It implies an anxious escape
from everything pleasant and agreeable, everything purely
decorative and ingratiating. Debussy already plays off a

From Social History of Art, by Arnold Hauser. Published 1951, 1958
by Alfred A. Knopf, Inc. Reprinted by permission.
[1] André Malraux, *Psychologie de l'art,* 1947.

225

coldness of tone and a pure harmonic structure against the sentimentality of German romanticism, and this anti-romanticism is intensified in Stravinsky, Schoenberg, and Hindemith into an anti-*espressivo*, which forswears all connection with the music of the sensitive nineteenth century. The intention is to write, paint and compose from the intellect, not from the emotions; stress is laid sometimes on purity of structure, at others on the ecstasy of a metaphysical vision, but there is a desire to escape at all costs from the complacent sensual aestheticism of the impressionist epoch. Impressionism itself had no doubt already been well aware of the critical situation in which modern aesthetic culture finds itself, but post-impressionist art is the first to stress the grotesqueness and mendacity of this culture. Hence the fight against all voluptuous and hedonistic feelings, hence the gloom, depression and torment in the works of Picasso, Kafka, and Joyce. The aversion to the sensualism of the older art, the desire to destroy its illusions, goes so far that artists now refuse to use even its means of expression and prefer, like Rimbaud, to create an artificial language of their own. Schoenberg invents his twelve-tone system, and it has been rightly said of Picasso that he paints each of his pictures as if he were trying to discover the art of painting all over again.

The systematic fight against the use of the conventional means of expression and the consequent break-up of the artistic tradition of the nineteenth century begins in 1916 with dadaism, a war-time phenomenon, a protest against the civilization that had led to the war and, therefore, a form of defeatism.[2] The purpose of the whole movement consists in its resistance to the allurements of ready-made forms and the convenient but worthless, because worn-out linguistic clichés, which falsify the object to be described and destroy all spontaneity of expression. Dadaism, like surrealism, which is in complete agreement with it in this respect, is a struggle for directness of expression, that is to say, it is an essentially romantic movement. The fight is aimed at that falsification of experience by forms, of which, as we know, Goethe had already been conscious and which was the decisive impulse behind the romantic revolution. Since romanticism the whole development in literature had consisted in a controversy with the tradition-

2 André Breton, *What Is Surrealism?*, 1936, pp. 45ff.

al and conventional forms of language, so that the literary
history of the last century is to some extent the history of
a renewal of language itself. But whereas the nineteenth
century always seeks merely for a balance between the old
and the new, between traditional forms and the spontaneity of the individual, dadaism demands the complete destruction of the current and exhausted means of expression. It demands entirely spontaneous expression, and
thereby bases its theory of art on a contradiction. For how
is one to make oneself understood—which at any rate surrealism intends to do—and at the same time deny and destroy all means of communication? The French critic Jean
Paulhan differentiates between two distinct categories of
writers, according to their relationship to language.[3] He
calls the language-destroyers, that is to say, the romantics,
symbolists, and surrealists, who want to eliminate the commonplace, conventional forms and ready-made clichés
from language completely and who take refuge from the
dangers of language in pure, virginal, original inspiration,
the "terrorists." They fight against all consolidation and
coagulation of the living, fluid, intimate life of the mind,
against all externalization and institutionalization, in other
words, against all "culture." Paulhan links them up with
Bergson and establishes the influence of intuitionism and
the theory of the *"élan vital"* in their attempt to preserve
the directness and orginality of the spiritual experience.
The other camp, that is, the writers who know perfectly
well that commonplaces and clichés are the price of mu-
tual understanding and that literature is communication,
that is to say, language, tradition, "worn-out" and, precisely on that account, unproblematical, immediately intelligible form, he calls the "rhetoricians," the oratorical artists.
He regards their attitude as the only possible one, since
the consistent administration of the "terror" in literature
would mean absolute silence, that is, intellectual suicide,
from which the surrealists can only save themselves by
constant self-deception. For there is actually no more rigid
and narrow-minded convention than the doctrine of surrealism and no more insipid and monotonous art than that
of the sworn surrealists. The "automatic method of writing" is much less elastic than the rationally and aestheti-
cally controlled style, and the unconscious—or at least as

[3] Jean Paulhan, *Les Fleurs de Tarbes*, 1941.

But mine basic

much of it as is brought to light—much poorer and simpler than the conscious mind. The historical importance of dadaism and surrealism does not consist, however, in the works of their official representatives, but in the fact that they draw attention to the blind alley in which literature found itself at the end of the symbolist movement, to the sterility of a literary convention which no longer had any connection with real life.[4] Mallarmé and the symbolists thought that every idea that occurred to them was the expression of their innermost nature; it was a mystical belief in the "magic of the word" which made them poets. The dadaists and the surrealists now doubt whether anything objective, external, formal, rationally organized is capable of expressing man at all, but they also doubt the value of such expression. It is really "inadmissible"—they think—that a man should leave a trace behind him.[5] Dadaism, therefore, replaces the nihilism of aesthetic culture by a new nihilism, which not only questions the value of art but of the whole human situation. For, as it is stated in one of its manifestoes, "measured by the standard of eternity, all human action is futile." [6]

But the Mallarmé tradition by no means comes to an end. The "rhetoricians" André Gide, Paul Valéry, T. S. Eliot, and the later Rilke continue the symbolist trend in spite of their affinity to surrealism. They are the representatives of a difficult and exquisite art, they believe in the "magic of the word," their poetry is based on the spirit of language, of literature and tradition. Joyce's *Ulysses* and T. S. Eliot's *The Waste Land* appear simultaneously, in the year 1922, and strike the two keynotes of the new literature; the one work moves in an expressionistic and surrealistic, the other in a symbolistic and formalistic direction. The intellectualistic approach is common to both, but Eliot's art springs from the "experience of culture," Joyce's from the "experience of pure, prime existence," as defined by Friedrich Gundolf, who introduces these concepts in the preface to his book on Goethe, thereby expressing a typical thought-pattern of the period.[7] In one

[4] Jacques Rivière, *"Reconnaissance à Dada." Nouvelle Revue Française,* 1920, XV, pp 231 fl.—MARCEL RAYMOND: *De Baudelaire au surréalisme,* 1933, p. 390.

[5] André Breton; *Les Pas perdus,* 1924.

[6] Tristan Tzara, *Sept manifestes dada,* 1920.

[7] Friedrich Gundolf, *Goethe,* 1916.

case historical culture, intellectual tradition and the legacy
of ideas and forms is the source of inspiration, in the
other the direct facts of life and the problems of human
existence. With T. S. Eliot and Paul Valéry the primary
foundation is always an idea, a thought, a problem, with
Joyce and Kafka an irrational experience, a vision, a metaphysical or mythological image. Gundolf's conceptual
distinction is the record of a dichotomy which is being
carried through in the whole field of modern art. Cubism
and constructivism, on the one side, and expressionism
and surrealism, on the other, embody strictly formal and
form-destroying tendencies respectively which now appear
for the first time side by side in such sharp contradiction.
The situation is all the more peculiar as the two opposing
styles display the most remarkable hybrid forms and combinations, so that one often acquires more the impression
of a split consciousness than that of two competing trends.
Picasso, who shifts from one of the different stylistic tendencies to the other most abruptly, is at the same time the
most representative artist of the present age. But to call
him an eclectic and a "master of pastiche," [8] to maintain
that he only wants to show to what an extent he has command of the rules of art against which he is in revolt,[9] to
compare him with Stravinsky and to recall how he, too,
changes his models and "makes use of" Bach, then Pergole-
si, then again Tchaikovsky for the purposes of modern
music,[10] is not to tell the whole story. Picasso's eclecticism
signifies the deliberate destruction of the unity of the personality; his imitations are protests against the cult of originality; his deformation of reality, which is always cloth-
ing itself in new forms, in order the more forcibly to demonstrate their arbitrariness, is intended, above all, to con-
firm the thesis that "nature and art are two entirely dissim-
ilar phenomena." Picasso turns himself into a conjurer, a
juggler, a parodist, out of opposition to the romantic with
his "inner voice," his "take it or leave it," his self-esteem
and self-worship. And he disavows not only romanticism,
but even the Renaissance, which, with its concept of genius and its idea of the unity of work and style, anticipates

---

[8] Michael Ayrton, "A Master of Pastiche." *New Writing and Daylight*, 1946, pp. 108 ff.

[9] René Huyghe-Germain Bazin, *Hist. de l'art contemp.*, 1935, p. 223.

[10] Constant Lambert, *Music ho!*, 1934.

romanticism to some extent. He represents a complete break with individualism and subjectivism, the absolute denial of art as the expression of an unmistakable personality. His works are notes and commentaries on reality; they make no claim to be regarded as a picture of a world and a totality, as a synthesis and epitome of existence. Picasso compromises the artistic means of expression by his indiscriminate use of the different artistic styles just as thoroughly and wilfully as do the surrealists by their renunciation of traditional forms.

The new century is full of such deep antagonisms, the unity of its outlook on life is so profoundly menaced, that the combination of the furthest extremes, the unification of the greatest contradictions, becomes the main theme, often the only theme, of its art. Surrealism, which, as André Breton remarks, at first revolved entirely round the problem of language, that is, of poetic expression, and which, as we should say with Paulhan, sought to be understood without the means of understanding, developed into an art which made the paradox of all form and the absurdity of all human existence the basis of its outlook. Dadaism still pleaded, out of despair at the inadequacy of cultural forms, for the destruction of art and for a return to chaos, that is to say, for romantic Rousseauism in the most extreme meaning of the term. Surrealism, which supplements the method of dadaism with the "automatic method of writing," [11] thereby already expresses its belief that a new knowledge, a new truth and a new art will arise from chaos, from the unconscious and the irrational, from dreams and the uncontrolled regions of the mind. The surrealists expect the salvation of art, which they forswear as such just as much as the dadaists and are only prepared to accept it at all as a vehicle of irrational knowledge, from a plunging into the unconscious, into the pre-rational and the chaotic, and they take over the psycho-analytical method of free association, that is, the automatic development of ideas and their reproduction without any rational, moral and aesthetic censorship, [12] because they imagine they have discovered therein a recipe for the restoration of the good old romantic type of inspiration. So, after all,

[11] Edmund Wilson, *Axel's Castle*, 1931, p. 256.
[12] André Breton, (*Premier*) *Manifeste du surréalisme*, 1924.

they still take their refuge in the rationalization of the irrational and the methodical re-production of the spontaneous, the only difference being that their method is incomparably more pedantic, dogmatic and rigid than the
mode of creation in which the irrational and the intuitive
are controlled by aesthetic judgement, taste and criticism,
and which makes reflection and not indiscrimination its
guiding principle. How much more fruitful than the surrealists' recipe was the procedure of Proust, who likewise
put himself into a kind of somnambulistic condition and
abandoned himself to the stream of memories and associations with the passivity of a hypnotic medium,[13] but who
remained at the same time a disciplined thinker and in the
highest degree a consciously creative artist.[14] Freud himself seems to have seen through the trick perpetrated by
surrealism. He is said to have remarked to Salvador Dali,
who visited him in London shortly before his death:
"What interests me in your art is not the unconscious, but
the conscious." [15] Must he not have meant by that: "I am
not interested in your simulated paranoia, but in the method of your simulation."

The basic experience of the surrealists consists in the
discovery of a "second reality," which, although it is insep-
arably fused with ordinary, empirical reality, is nevertheless so different from it that we are only able to make negative statements about it and to point to the gaps and cavi-
ties in our experience as evidence for its existence. Nowhere is this dualism expressed more acutely than in the
works of Kafka and Joyce, who, although they have nothing to do with surrealism as a doctrine, are surrealists in
the wider sense, like most of the progressive artists of the
century. It is also this experience of the double-sidedness
of existence, with its home in two different spheres, which
makes the surrealists aware of the peculiarity of dreams
and induces them to recognize in the mixed reality of
dreams their own stylistic ideal. The dream becomes the
paradigm of the whole world-picture, in which reality and
unreality, logic and fantasy, the banality and sublimation

[13] Louis Reynaud, *La Crise de notre litterature,* 1929, pp. 196-7.
[14] Cf. Charles du Bos, *Approximations,* 1922.—BENJAMIN CRÉ-
MIEUX: XXe *siècle,* 1924—JACQUES RIVIÈRE: *Marcel Proust,* 1924.
[15] J. Th. Soby, *Salvador Dali,* 1946, p. 24.

of existence, form an indissoluble and inexplicable unity. The meticulous naturalism of the details and the arbitrary combination of their relationships which surrealism copies from the dream, not only express the feeling that we live on two different levels, in two different spheres, but also that these regions of being penetrate one another so thoroughly that the one can neither be subordinated to [16] nor set against the other as its antithesis.[17]

The dualism of being is certainly no new conception, and the idea of the *"coincidentia oppositorum"* is quite familiar to us from the philosophy of Nicholas of Cusa and Giordano Bruno, but the double meaning and the duplicity of existence, the snare and the seduction for the human understanding which lie hidden in every single phenomenon of reality, had never been experienced so intensively as now. Only mannerism had seen the contrast between the concrete and the abstract, the sensual and the spiritual, dreaming and waking in a similarly glaring light. The emphasis which modern art lays not so much on the coincidence of the opposites themselves, as on the fancifulness of this coincidence, is also reminiscent of mannerism. The sharp contrast, in the work of Dali, between the photographically faithful reproduction of the details and the wild disorder of their grouping corresponds, on a very humble level, to the fondness for paradox in the Elizabethan drama and the lyric poetry of the "metaphysical poets" of the seventeenth century. But the difference of level between the style of Kafka and Joyce, in which a sober and often trivial prose is combined with the most fragile transparency of ideas, and that of the manneristic poets of the sixteenth and seventeenth centuries is no longer so great. In both cases the real subject of the representation is the absurdity of life, which seems all the more surprising and shocking the more realistic the elements of the fantastic whole are. The sewing machine and the umbrella on the dissecting table, the donkey's corpse on the piano or the naked woman's body which opens like a chest of drawers, in brief, all the forms of juxtaposition and simultaneity into which the non-simultaneous and the incompatible are

[16] André Breton, *What Is Surrealism?*, p. 67.
[17] André Breton, *Second Manifeste du surréalisme*, 1930.—*Maurice Nadeau, Histoire du surréalisme*, 1945, 2nd edit., p. 176.

pressed, are only the expression of a desire to bring unity *No*
and coherence, certainly in a very paradoxical way, into
the atomized world in which we live. Art is seized by a
real mania for totality.[18] It seems possible to bring everything into relationship with everything else, everything
seems to include within itself the law of the whole. The
disparagement of man, the so-called "dehumanization" of
art, is connected above all with this feeling. In a world in
which everything is significant or of equal significance,
man loses his pre-eminence and psychology its authority.

The crisis of the psychological novel is perhaps the most
striking phenomenon in the new literature. The works of
Kafka and Joyce are no longer psychological novels in the
sense that the great novels of the nineteenth century were.
In Kafka, psychology is replaced by a kind of mythology,
and in Joyce, although the psychological analyses are perfectly accurate, just as the details in a surrealistic picture
are absolutely true to nature, there are not only no heroes,
in the sense of a psychological centre, but also no particular psychological sphere in the totality of being. The de-
psychologization of the novel already begins with Proust,[19]
who, as the greatest master of the analysis of feelings and
thoughts, marks the summit of the psychological novel,
but also represents the incipient displacement of the soul
in the balance of reality. For, since the whole of existence
has become merely the content of the consciousness and
things acquire their significance purely and simply through
the spiritual medium by which they are experienced, there
can no longer be any question here of psychology as understood by Stendhal, Balzac, Flaubert, George Eliot, Tolstoy, or Dostoevsky. In the novel of the nineteenth century, the soul and character of man are seen as the opposite pole to the world of physical reality, and psychology as
the conflict between the subject and object, the self and
the non-self, the human spirit and the external world. This
psychology ceases to be predominant in Proust. He is not
concerned so much with the characterization of the individual personality, although he is an ardent portraitist and
caricaturist, as with the analysis of the spiritual mechanism as an ontological phenomenon. His work is a

[18] Julien Benda, *La France byzantine*, 1945, p. 48.
[19] Cf. E. R. Curtius, *Franzoesischer Geist im neuen Europa*,
1925, pp. 75–6.

"Summa" not merely in the familiar sense of containing a total picture of modern society, but also because it describes the whole spiritual apparatus of modern man with all his inclinations, instincts, talents, automatisms, rationalisms and irrationalisms. Joyce's *Ulysses* is therefore the direct continuation of the Proustian novel; we are here confronted literally with an encyclopaedia of modern civilization, as reflected in the tissue of the motifs which make up the content of a day in the life of a great city. This day is the protagonist of the novel. The flight from the plot is followed by the flight from the hero. Instead of a flood of events, Joyce describes a flood of ideas and associations, instead of an individual hero a stream of consciousness and an unending, uninterrupted inner monologue. The emphasis lies everywhere on the uninterruptedness of the movement, the "heterogeneous continuum," the kaleidoscopic picture of a disintegrated world. The Bergsonian concept of time undergoes a new interpretation, an intensification and a deflection. The accent is now on the simultaneity of the contents of consciousness, the immanence of the past in the present, the constant flowing together of the different periods of time, the amorphous fluidity of inner experience, the boundlessness of the stream of time by which the soul is borne along, the relativity of space and time, that is to say, the impossibility of differentiating and defining the media in which the mind moves. In this new conception of time almost all the strands of the texture which form the stuff of modern art converge: the abandonment of the plot, the elimination of the hero, the relinquishing of psychology, the "automatic method of writing" and, above all, the montage technique and the intermingling of temporal and spatial forms of the film. The new concept of time, whose basic element is simultaneity and whose nature consists in the spatialization of the temporal element, is expressed in no other genre so impressively as in this youngest art, which dates from the same period as Bergson's philosophy of time. The agreement between the technical methods of the film and the characteristics of the new concept of time is so complete that one has the feeling that the time categories of modern art altogether must have arisen from the spirit of cinematic form, and one is inclined to consider the film itself as the stylistically most representative, though qualitatively perhaps not the most fertile genre of contemporary art.

Part Four

SOME MAJOR FIGURES

This final section is devoted to a group of essays in which a few of the major literary figures in the modernist period are critically discussed. Most of these essays see the writers under discussion as exemplars or even heroes of literary modernism: figures like Baudelaire, T.S. Eliot, and André Gide. The last of the essays is somewhat different: it discusses the political attitudes of one of the great twentieth-century poets, William Butler Yeats, especially as these were interwoven with his literary approaches and themes.

Baudelaire

BY JEAN-PAUL SARTRE

The perception of our own transcendence and of our unjustifiable gratuitousness must at the same time be a revelation of human freedom. And in fact Baudelaire always felt that he was free. We shall see later what tricks he employed to hide his freedom from himself; but from one end of his work and his correspondence to the other this freedom is affirmed, bursts out in spite of himself. There is no doubt that, for reasons which we have already mentioned, he did not possess the great freedom which is the usual attribute of creative power, but he constantly felt an explosive unpredictability which nothing could hem in. He redoubled his precautions against it, but in vain. He noted down in capital letters in his papers 'the little practical maxims, rules, imperatives, acts of faith and formulas which pre-judge the future.'[1] It was still in vain. He eluded himself; he knew that he could hold on to nothing. If only he could have felt that he was partly a machine, it would have been possible to discover the lever which stopped it, altered its course or accelerated it. Determinism is reassuring. Anyone who knows things by their causes can base his actions on causation; and up to the present the moralists have spent their time trying to persuade us that we are machines which can be regulated by easy means. Baudelaire knew that springs and levers had nothing to do with his case; he was neither cause nor effort. He was free which meant that he could look for no help either inside or outside himself against his own freedom. He bent over it and became giddy at the sight of the gulf:

[1] Blin, *Baudelaire*, Paris, 1939, p. 49.

239

Morally and physically I have always been haunted by the sensation of the gulf, not merely the gulf of sleep, but the gulf of action, dreams, memories, desires, regrets, remorse, the beautiful, numbers, etc. . . .

In another place he wrote:

Now I always feel giddy.

Baudelaire was the man who felt that he was a gulf. Pride, *ennui*, giddiness—he looked right into the bottom of his heart. He saw that he was incomparable, incommunicable, uncreated, absurd, useless, abandoned in the most complete isolation, bearing his burden alone, condemned to justify his existence all alone, and endlessly eluding himself, slipping through his own fingers, withdrawn in contemplation and, at the same time, dragged out of himself in an unending pursuit, a bottomless gulf without walls and without darkness, a mystery in broad daylight, unpredictable yet perfectly known. It was his misfortune that his image still eluded him. He was looking for the reflection of a certain Charles Baudelaire, the son of Mme. Aupick—the General's wife—a poet who had got into debt and the lover of the negress Duval. His gaze encountered the human condition itself. His freedom, his gratuitousness and his abandonment which frightened him were the lot of humanity; they did not belong particularly to him. Could one ever touch *oneself,* see *oneself?* Perhaps this singular unchanging essence was only visible to others. Perhaps it was absolutely necessary to be outside in order to see its characteristics. Perhaps one didn't *exist* for oneself in the manner of an object. Perhaps one didn't *exist* at all. If one were always a question mark, always in suspense, perhaps one would be perpetually obliged to *form* oneself. The whole of Baudelaire's efforts were devoted to hiding these unpleasant thoughts from himself. And since his 'nature' escaped him, he tried to seize it in other people's eyes. His good faith abandoned him; he had to try unceasingly to convince himself, to seize himself with his own eyes. In our eyes—but not in his own—a fresh trait appears: he was the man who felt most deeply his condition as man, but who tried most passionately to hide it from himself.

Because he chose lucidity, because he discovered in spite of himself the gratuitousness, the abandonment, the redoubtable freedom of consciousness, Baudelaire was faced with an alternative—since there were no readymade principles on which he could rely for support, he either had to stagnate in a state of amoral indifference or himself invent Good and Evil. Because the conscious self [2] derives its laws from itself, it must regard itself in Kant's words as the legislator of the city of ends. It must accept complete responsibility and create its own values, must give meaning to the world and to its own life. Indeed, the man who declared that "what is created by the spirit is more alive than matter" had felt more keenly than most other men the power and mission of the conscious self. He had seen very clearly that with the conscious self something comes into being which did not exist before—meaning. It therefore led to perpetual creation at all levels. Baudelaire attached such price to this creation out of nothing, which for him was characteristic of the *spirit,* that the purely contemplative tonelessness of his life was shot through and through by a creative *élan.* This misanthrope subscribed to a humanism based on creation. He admitted that there were 'three sorts of beings who are respectable: the priest, the warrior and the poet. Knowledge, killing and creation.' It will be seen that in this passage destruction and creation form a pair. In both cases there is the production of absolute events; in both a man is responsible alone for a radical change in the universe. This pair is opposed by knowledge which takes us back to the contemplative life. It would be impossible to demonstrate more clearly the complementary nature of the link which for Baudelaire always united the magic powers of the spirit to his own passive lucidity. He defined the human by its power of creation, not by its power of action. Action implies determinism; its efficacity forms part of the chain of cause and effect; it obeys nature in order to obtain command of nature; it submits to principles which it has taken over blindly without questioning their validity. The man of action is the person who interrogates himself about means, but never about ends. No one was farther from action than Baudelaire. At the end of the passage we have just quoted he

[2] In French, *conscience.* The French word is notoriously ambiguous. It normally means either 'conscience' or 'consciousness' according to the context. In spite of the reference to Kant, neither word is a satisfactory translation in this paragraph and I have therefore translated it as 'the conscious self.' *Tr.*

added: "Other men are talliable and liable to forced labor, are made for the stable, that is to say, for carrying on what is known as a *profession*." But creation is pure freedom; before it there is nothing; it begins by creating its own principles. First and foremost it invents its own end and in that way it partakes of the gratuitousness of consciousness. It is a gratuitousness which is willed, thought out and erected into a goal. This explains in part Baudelaire's love of artifice. In his eyes cosmetics, finery and clothes were a sign of the true greatness of man—his creative power. We know that after Rétif, Balzac and Sue, he contributed very largely to the spread of what Roger Caillois calls "the myth of the great city." A city is a perpetual creation: its buildings, smells, sounds and traffic belong to the human kingdom. Everything in it is *poetry* in the strict sense of the term. It is in this sense that the electrically operated advertisements, neon lights and cars which about the year 1920 roused the wonder of young people were profoundly Baudelairean. The great city is a reflection of the gulf which is human freedom. And Baudelaire, who hated man and "the tyranny of the human face," discovered that he was after all a humanist because of his cult of the works of man.

Since this is so a lucid consciousness, which above everything else is in love with its demonic powers, owes it to itself to create first the meaning which will illuminate the whole world for it. Absolute creation—the creation of which all other forms are simply a consequence—is the creation of a scale of values. We should therefore have expected Baudelaire to display the boldness of a Nietzsche in the pursuit of Good and Evil—of *his* Good and *his* Evil. Now anyone who examines the life and works of the poet at all closely is struck by the fact that all his ideas of morality were derived from other people and that he never questioned them. This would be understandable if Baudelaire had assumed an attitude of indifference, an easy-going Epicureanism. But the moral principles which he retained and which were inculcated by a middle-class Catholic education were not in his case mere survivals, mere useless withered organs. Baudelaire possessed an intense moral life; he twisted and turned in his remorse; every day he exhorted himself to do better; he struggled and succumbed; he was overwhelmed by a horrible sense of guilt, so much so that people have wondered whether he was not weighed down by the burden of some secret crime. In his biographical introduction to the *Fleurs du mal,* M. Crépet remarks very justly:

> Was there some crime in his life which time does not obliterate? It is difficult to believe after all the inquests to which it has been subjected. Yet he treats himself as a criminal and declares that he is guilty "on all counts." He denounces himself on the ground that though he possesses a sense of duty and all the moral obligations, he always betrays them (p. xxxviii).

No, Baudelaire was not burdened with some secret crime. The crimes which can be imputed to him are not capital ones: a dryness of heart which was real enough but not total, a certain laziness, abuse of narcotics, probably some sexual peculiarities and a certain lack of scruple which sometimes bordered on fraud. If he had only once made up his mind to challenge the principles in the name of which he was condemned by General Aupick and Ancelle he would have been free. But he took good care not to: he adopted the moral code of his stepfather without questioning it. The famous resolutions which he made about 1862 and wrote down under the heading of *Hygiene, Conduct, Morality* are painfully puerile:

> Epitome of wisdom.
> Dress, prayer, work.
> Work necessarily induces sound morals, sobriety and chastity, and as a result good health, wealth, sustained and progressive genius and charity. *Age quod agis.*

The words sobriety, chastity and work occur again and again in his writings, but they have no positive content. They did not provide him with a line of conduct and they did not enable him to solve the great problems of his relations with other people and with himself. They were simply a system of rigid and strictly negative defenses. Sobriety meant not taking intoxicants; chastity—not going back to those young women who gave him too kindly a welcome and whose names are preserved in his notebook; work—not putting off until tomorrow what could be done today; charity—not being irritable or bitter and not being indifferent to other people. Besides, he recognized that he possessed "a sense of duty," that is to say, he regarded the moral life as a constraint, as a bit which hurt the restive mouth, never as an agonizing quest or a genuine *élan* from the heart:

> *Un ange furieux fond du ciel comme un aigle,*
> *Du mécréant saisit à plein poing les cheveux*
> *Et dit, le secouant: 'Tu connaîtras la règle!*
> *(Car je suis ton bon Ange, entends-tu?) Je le veux.'*

A few crabbed, torturing imperatives whose content was disarming in its poverty—such were the values and rules which served as a basis for the whole of his moral life. When, after being harried by his mother and Ancelle, he suddenly bridled, it was never in order to tell them to their faces that their bourgeois virtues were horrible and stupid; it was to flaunt his vices, to bellow that he was very wicked indeed and might have been even worse:

> Do you imagine then that if I wanted I couldn't ruin you and bring you down to misery in your old age? Don't you know that I am cunning enough and eloquent enough to do it? But I restrain myself . . .[3]

It is impossible that he didn't feel that, in meeting them like this on their own ground and behaving like a sulky child who stamps and exaggerates his faults, he was providing them with hostages and aggravating his own case. But he was pig-headed. It was in the name of those values that he wanted absolution and he preferred to be condemned by them rather than to be whitewashed in the name of a wider and more fruitful ethic which he should have invented himself. His attitude during the trial was still stranger. Not once did he attempt to defend the content of his book; not once did he try to explain to the judges that he did not accept the moral code of "cops" and pimps. On the contrary, he invoked it himself. That was the basis on which he was prepared to argue; and, rather than question whether their interdict was well founded, he accepted the secret shame of lying about the meaning of his work. Sometimes, indeed, he presented it simply as a distraction and he demanded in the name of Art for Art's sake the right to imitate passions from outside without experiencing them. At other times, he claimed that it was a work of edification which was intend-

[3] Letter of March 17th, 1862. (*Lettres inédites à sa mère*, Paris, 1918, p. 261. Not part of the Conard edition of the complete works.)

ed to inspire a horror of vice. It was not until nine years later that he dared to admit the truth to Ancelle:

> Must I tell you—you who haven't guessed any more than the rest—that into this *atrocious* book I put the whole of my *heart,* the whole of my *tenderness,* the whole of my *religion* (travestied), the whole of my *hatred?* It's true that I shall say the opposite, that I shall swear by all the gods that it's a work of *pure art,* monkey tricks, *juggling,* and shall lie like the fellow who tears out your teeth.[4]

He allowed himself to be condemned; he accepted his judges. He even wrote a letter to the Empress saying that he had been treated by Justice with an admirable courtesy. [5] Better still, he postulated a social rehabilitation: first a decoration, then the Academy. He took sides with his executioners, with Ancelle, Aupick and the Imperial police force against all those who like George Sand and Hugo wanted to set men free. He asked for the whip; he wanted them to make him practise the virtues which they preached:

> If, when a man developed habits of laziness, dreaminess and feebleness to the point of always putting off the important thing till the morrow, another man woke him up in the morning with hard lashes of a whip and whipped him mercilessly until, though unable to work for pleasure, he worked through fear, wouldn't this man—the man with the whip—be a true friend and benefactor?

The least thing, a change of mind, a mere look into the eyes of these idols would have been enough to make his chains fall at once to the ground; he didn't do it. All his life he was content to judge his failings and let them be judged by accepted standards. It was he, the *poète maudit* of the banned poems, who sat down one day and wrote:

> It has been necessary at all times and in all countries to have gods and prophets to instil [virtue] into a brutalized humanity and . . . man *alone* would have been incapable of inventing it.

Can you imagine a more complete abdication? Baudelaire proclaims that he alone would have been incapable of discovering virtue, that there was not a germ of it in him, that left to himself he would not even have been able to

---

[4] Letter of February 18th, 1866. (*Lettres,* 1841–1866, Mercure de France, 1906, p. 522.)
[5] *Corres. gén.,* 2, p. 100.

understand its meaning. The principal characteristic of this virtue, which was revealed by the prophets and inculcated forcibly by the whips of priests and ministers, was to be beyond the power of individual men. They would have been incapable of inventing it and they were unable to doubt its validity: let them be content to receive it like a heavenly manna.

Baudelaire's Christian upbringing will certainly be blamed for this; and there is no doubt that it left a deep impress on him. But look at the distance travelled by another Christian—a Protestant, it is true—by André Gide. In the fundamental conflict between his sexual anomaly and accepted morality, he took sides with the former against the latter, and has gradually eaten away the rigorous principles which impeded him like an acid. In spite of a thousand relapses, he has moved forward towards *his* morality; he has done his utmost to invent a new Table of the Law. Yet the impress of Christianity on him was just as deep as it was on Baudelaire; but he wanted to free himself from other peoples' Good; he refused from the first to allow himself to be treated like a black sheep. In a similar situation he made a different choice; he wanted his conscience to be clear, and he understood that he could only achieve liberation by a radical and gratuitous invention of Good and Evil. Why did Baudelaire, the born creator, the poet of creation, suddenly balk at the last moment? Why did he waste his time and energy in preserving a norm which turned him into a guilty man? Why didn't he rise in wrath against this heteronomy which from the outset condemned his conscience and his will to remain forever a bad conscience and a bad will?

Let us return to his famous "difference." The creative act does not allow us to enjoy it. The man who creates is transported, during the period of creation, beyond singularity into the pure sky of freedom. He *is* no longer anything: he *makes*. No doubt he constructs an objective individuality outside himself; but while he is working on it, it is indistinguishable from himself. And later on he no longer enters into that objective individuality; he remains in front of it like Moses on the threshold of the Promised Land. We shall see in due course that Baudelaire wrote his poems in order to rediscover his own image in them. That,

---

6 *l'Art romantique*, p. 97.

however, could not satisfy him for long. It was in his every-day life that he wanted to enjoy his otherness. The great freedom which creates values emerges in the void, and he was frightened of it. A sense of contingency, unjustifiabil-ity and gratuitousness assails the man who tries to bring a new reality into the world and leaves him no respite. If it is in fact an absolutely new reality, then it is something for which no one asked and which no one expected to see on earth; and it remains superfluous like its author.

Baudelaire asserted his singularity against the back-ground of a stable world. He asserted it first of all against his mother and his stepfather in a mood of rage and re-volt. It was in fact a revolt and not a revolutionary act. The revolutionary wants to change the world; he tran-scends it and moves toward the future, toward an order of values which he himself invents. The rebel is careful to preserve the abuses from which he suffers so that he can go on rebelling against them. He always shows signs of a bad conscience and of something resembling a feeling of guilt. He does not want to destroy or transcend the exist-ing order; he simply wants to rise up against it. The more he attacks it, the more he secretly respects it. In the depths of his heart he preserves the rights which he challenges in public. If they disappeared, his own *raison d'être* would disappear with them. He would suddenly find himself plunged into a gratuitousness which frightens him. It never occurred to Baudelaire to destroy the idea of the family. On the contrary, it could be argued that he never pro-gressed beyond the stage of childhood.

People in Proust

BY MARTIN TURNELL

Proust's scepticism was largely responsible for his peculiar method of presenting "character" which is different not merely from that of the classic novelists, but of his own contemporaries. In the classic novelists character—*l'homme absolu*—is in general one of the *données*. The novelist begins by "creating" characters, but once they have been created they do not undergo any fundamental change. All their adventures or experiences are the outcome of character and of the friction of one character on another. The modern writer has no doubt discarded the theory of fixed unchanging character and instead portrays the psychological development of characters who are completely different at the end of the book from the beginning. It should be emphasized that the change is real; it is not, as it sometimes is with the classic writers, that different facets of the main characters are only revealed as the result of the experiences which are described in the book.

The concept of a fixed unchanging character is common to the writers of classical antiquity, the Middle Ages and the English and French novelists of the eighteenth century. In Fielding and Smollett, in Marivaux and Laclos, there is, properly speaking, no development of character. The novelist starts with a special knowledge of his character and he reveals it to the reader by inventing a series of situations in which they become involved.

A different approach, however, can already be discerned in the dramatists as well as in the principal French novelist of the seventeenth century. Although strictly limited, there is development in Corneille, Molière, Racine and Mme de La Fayette. The Alceste who abandons society in

search of an *endroit écarté* in the fifth act of *Le Misanthrope* is certainly different from the fiery reformer of Act
I, though his "change of heart" is the logical outcome of
the *données*. Corneille's characters undergo a moral
growth and become "integrated"; Racine's and Mme de La
Fayette's suffer complete moral collapse.

Another change occurs at the close of the eighteenth
century. There is a strong autobiographical element in
Constant and Stendhal, but comparatively little development. Their characters are all trying to discover what sort
of people they are and their discoveries are the outcome
not so much of action, situation and their relations with
other people as of solitary analysis in a silent room or in
prison.

Proust's approach differs from all these writers or rather
he combines a number of different approaches and produces a new standpoint and a new method. The classical
novelists were convinced that in spite of his changing
moods, man was essentially *one*. Proust was equally convinced that he was *many*. His characters are composed in
layers or, if one prefers, they are all to some degree multi-
ple personalities. The only way of bringing out this complexity and of dealing with the very real problem of our
knowledge of other people was to apply the method of the
memoir-writer to his characters. They are constructed by
direct observation, by encounters between Marcel and the
other characters at different periods of their lives and in
different situations, but also by gossip and hearsay. This
enables Proust to present them from a large number of different angles and to show that the same person may appear completely different to different people. We remember the incident of Saint-Loup's mistress:

> Suddenly Saint-Loup appeared, accompanied by his mis-
> tress, and then, in this woman who was for him all the
> love, every possible delight in life, whose personality, mys-
> teriously enshrined in a body as in a tabernacle, was the
> object that still occupied incessantly the toiling imagination
> of my friend, whom he felt that he would never really
> know, as to whom he was perpetually asking himself what
> could be her secret self, behind the veil of eyes and flesh,
> in this woman I recognized at once 'Rachel when from the
> lord', her who, but a few years since—women change their
> position so rapidly in that world, when they do change—
> used to say to the procuress: 'To-morrow evening, then, if
> you want me for anyone, you will send round, won't
> you. . . .'

I realized also then all that the human imagination can put behind a little scrap of face, such as this girl's face was, if it is the imagination that was the first to know it; and conversely into what wretched elements, crudely material and utterly without value, might be decomposed what had been the inspiration of countless dreams if, on the contrary, it should be so to speak controverted by the slightest actual acquaintance. I saw that what had appeared to me to be not worth twenty francs in the house of ill fame, where it was then for me simply a woman desirous of earning twenty francs, might be worth more than a million, more than one's family, more than all the most coveted positions in life if one had begun by imagining her to embody a strange creature, interesting to know, difficult to seize and to hold. No doubt it was the same thin and narrow face that we saw, Robert and I. But we had arrived at it by two opposite ways, between which there was no communication, and we should never both see it from the same side.

At the end of his Memoirs Saint-Simon describes his book, with the superb confidence of his century, as a *miroir de vérité* which he could not publish during the lifetime of his victims because of the "universal convulsion" which so strong a dose of truth would cause. Proust was always trying to arrive at "truth," but it would never have occurred to him to make the same claim for his book as Saint-Simon. On the contrary, he is at pains to emphasize that our knowledge of other people is always relative. In one of his letters he compares his presentation of character to a town seen from a train. While the train follows its winding track, the town sometimes appears on our right and sometimes on our left. In the same way, he says, the different aspects of the same character will appear like a succession of different people. Such characters, he adds, will later reveal that they are very different from the people for whom we took them, as often happens in life for that matter.[1] The account of Saint-Loup's mistress shows how closely Proust's practice followed his theories:

> No doubt it was the same thin face that we saw, Robert and I. But we had arrived at it by two opposite ways, between which there was no communication, and we should never both see it from the same side.

This seems to me to be a complete answer to those critics who have claimed that Proust's presentation of character was inconsistent and unconvincing. It is no accident

[1] *Lettres de Marcel Proust à Bibesco*, p. 175.

that we often have the impression that we are in a vast room of distorting mirrors which reflect the same person simultaneously from different and often contradictory angles. All of them give us a glimpse of the truth, but none of them the whole truth. In this way Proust subjects us to a series of shocks. We are introduced to Saint-Loup as the sympathetic representative of the old aristocracy, the hero who at once rejoins his old regiment on the outbreak of war only to discover that he either is or has become a rabid homosexual. The effect of this is not merely to emphasize the complexity of human nature and the elusiveness of "personality", but to introduce a moral relativity. Proust is very careful not to judge his main characters. They simply appear in a series of different guises, some of them creditable, others highly discreditable. The *jeune héros* who eventually dies gloriously on the field of battle is the same man who carries on the nefarious traffic with Morel and visits Charlus' *établissement*.

Proust employs a different method still with Marcel and to a certain extent with Swann. It looks at first like the method of Constant. He is certainly trying to answer the same question as the nineteenth-century novelist: "What sort of a man am *I?*" But he is also trying to answer a number of still more urgent and still more searching questions: "What is love?" "What is jealousy?" "What is personality?" "What is time?" "What is reality?" It is one of the signs of Proust's greatness that his problems are always treated concretely. His analysis of love and jealousy is very profound, but it could never be said of him as it was —mistakenly in my opinion—of Racine and Molière that he dealt with the "abstract emotions" or that he shows us the Lover and the Jealous Man as generalized figures. For in his novel, the correspondence between the lover and the jealous man and the individual who is in love and is jealous is absolute.

It will be apparent from what has already been said that Proust's art is largely subjective. He is constantly telling us of his attempts to reach *la vraie vie* and it is a struggle in which all his characters in a greater or lesser degree are engaged. His work with its arguments, its method of trial and error, sometimes reminds us a little oddly of Descartes' *doute méthodique,* but there is one great difference between the seventeenth-century philosopher and the twentieth-century novelist. Descartes' "doubt" is a means of arriving at a truth which he knows exists; but from the first Proust makes us doubt the very existence of *la vraie vie* or, if we do not actually doubt its existence, we certainly doubt whether it is attainable. For in this world values are necessarily relative to the person who suffers the experience. Our interest lies less in the goal than in the pursuit —the *recherche*—and its vicissitudes. The nature of the struggle is evident from a passage in *Swann:*

> Si mes parents m'avaient permis, quand je lisais un livre, d'aller visiter la région qu'il décrivait, j'aurais cru faire un pas inestimable dans la conquête de la vérité. Car si on a la sensation d'être toujours entouré de son âme, ce n'est pas comme d'une prison immobile; plutôt on est comme emporté avec elle dans un perpétuel élan pour la dépasser, pour atteindre à l'extérieur, avec une sorte de découragement, entendant toujours autour de soi cette sonorité identique qui n'est pas écho du dehors mais retentissement d'une vibration interne.

> [Had my parents allowed me, when I read a book, to pay a visit to the country it described, I should have felt that I was making an enormous advance towards the ultimate conquest of truth. For even if we have the sensation of being always enveloped in, surrounded by our own soul, still it does not seem a fixed and immovable prison; rather do we seem to be borne away with it, and perpetually struggling to pass beyond it, to break out into the world, with a perpetual discouragement as we hear endlessly, all around us, that unvarying sound which is no echo from without, but the resonance of a vibration from within.]

This passage explains the peculiar *angoisse* which is always throbbing just below the surface of Proust's novel. Then, from time to time, it suddenly, unexpectedly produces an eruption. We feel a note of hope behind "la conquête de la vérité" which is at once stifled by "entouré de son âme." It is not a tangible prison from which he can escape; the prison itself is mobile and just at the moment when his *élan* seems about to carry him outside the closed circle, when he is on the point of reaching freedom, he hears "cette sonorité identique" and realizes, with fresh discouragement, that there is no escape. For the "echo" is not even a sound from the outside world, but the "retentissement d'une vibration interne."

We can begin to appreciate now how closely the two sides of Proust's world are connected. We have already seen that when he describes, or appears to describe, society objectively, the principal characters always turn out to be "prisoners"—prisoners of a social class, prisoners of the little "groups" or "bands" into which they have formed themselves or simply prisoners of their own vices.

The great myth of the nineteenth century was the "outsider" myth; the great myth of the twentieth century is the myth of the "prisoner." The real hero of *A la Recherche du temps perdu* is the Prisoner. The Prisoner is not Swann or Charlus or even Albertine, but Marcel himself. The heroes of Stendhal are cut off from society by their own exceptional gifts of intelligence and sensibility; but they are always attacking. Julien Sorel disrupts the precarious balance of French society in 1830 and Fabrice del Dongo disorganizes the eighteenth-century political pattern which in the miniature police state of Parma has become rigid and hard. Proust's hero, too, is endowed with exceptional gifts of intelligence and sensibility. He, too, is in a sense an "outsider," but he is the outsider who failed to make his escape and was trapped in his extraordinary mobile prison. Stendhal's view of life implies a philosophy of action, Proust's a highly personal form of quietism. Marcel does not possess the power of attack which is common to Julien and Fabrice; he is the passive victim who is exposed to almost every conceivable kind of pressure and obsession known to human society. For he is the prisoner not so much of "clans" and "groups" as of emotions, habits, of his own sensibility and, ultimately, of time. I think we can add that the symbolical figure who dominates the novel is not simply the Prisoner, but the Artist-Prisoner who after many false starts and misfortunes comes to see that the only hope of escape lies in his "vocation." That is why Proust's withdrawal from the world to meditate on time and memory stamps him as the twentieth-century artist.

M. Maurice Muller has described the book with felicity as

> This psychological comedy in which the characters are Love, Jealousy, Falsehood, Habit, Forgetting, Memory which are incarnate in a being who is very much alive, the narrator—a comedy which is subject to laws which are subtle, but implacable. . . .[2]

The main drama is of course the Prisoner's attempts to

[2] *De Descartes à Marcel Proust* (Collection "Être et Penser"), (second edition, Neuchâtel, 1947), p. 63.

escape from himself, from a prison which seems to have no exit, to attain a truth which will make him free. Now inside this main drama there is a series of "psychological comedies" which are endlessly repeated. They are played out between M. Muller's six characters who assume the proportions of obsessions. When Proust tells us that what is dangerous in love "is not the woman but the habit," we know that we are witnessing the scene between Love and Habit which merges into the scene between Love and Forgetting or Love and Memory. Then there is a sudden switch:

> L'amour n'est provoqué que par le mensonge et consiste seulement dans le besoin de voir nos souffrances apaisées par l'être qui nous a fait souffrir.

> [Love is provoked only by falsehood, and consists merely in our need to see our sufferings appeased by the person who has made us suffer.]

The tension always rises steeply in the scenes between Love and Falsehood. For Falsehood is one of the principal characters in the novel.

It has been pointed out that Proust displayed a particular interest in doctors, diplomats and servants. His interest is very understandable. They are people who are obliged to adopt a professional attitude, are constantly telling "diplomatic lies." They therefore become for the novelist incarnations of Falsehood. Then we gradually realize that social relations are simply "a tissue of lies." Falsehood exists at different levels, appearing sometimes as a series of concentric circles and at others as the mental obstacle which hinders the search for "truth" and maintains *angoisse*. The doctors, diplomats and servants are minor characters in Proust's comedy. They underline the main theme and give Marcel an opportunity of studying their "technique" so that he will have a better chance of catching his mistress out. Charlus plays many roles, but in this particular context he represents the Lie at a rather higher level than the "professional liars." His whole life has become an elaborate lie in order to conceal his sexual aberrations and he provides Marcel with a still better example of the way in which the liar goes about his business. At the centre of the circle stands Albertine. We suspect that the whole of her life, too, is a lie and that she is trying to conceal the same anomaly as Charlus. The drama now becomes much more complex. Jealousy enters the scene. In his endeavours to discover whether Albertine was or was not a Lesbian, Marcel himself is driven to lying; and we find in the end that he is playing a sort of triple role: *Amour—Jalousie—Mensonge*. This is the point at which the drama reaches its maximum intensity.

When we look back to the sentence on lies—

> L'amour n'est provoqué que par le mensonge et consiste seulement dans le besoin de voir nos souffrances apaisées par l'être qui nous a fait souffrir.

we are aware of the vicious circle. Love is aroused by a falsehood. It can only be assuaged by the person who aroused it, but the person who aroused it is Falsehood. There is no way out. The most that we can hope for is one of those comfortable sayings in which Proust's work abounds. "L'amour est un mal inguérissable." The best moments in love contain "la possibilité insoupçonnée du désastre."

It is not difficult to see the bearing of this on human relations as a whole. It is commonly assumed or believed that when two people "fall in love" they suddenly become aware of one another's personality in a new way, discover something in the personality of the loved one which is not apparent to others and makes him or her particularly sympathetic, becomes the foundation of a lifelong attachment. Now Proust's psychology is a reversal of the traditional view. You do not get to know a person to see whether you love her; you love her in order to get to know her or, to use a term which conveys Proust's double purpose, to "possess" her. We are told, for example, of the relations between Swann and Odette that she was

> Plus désireuse peut-être de connaître ce qu'il était que désireuse d'être sa maîtresse.
>
> [More desirous perhaps to know what sort of man he was than desirous to be his mistress.]

According to this conception, love is one of the ways of trying to break out of "prison," to reach "truth" or to still the *angoisse* which continually afflicts you. It is naturally fraught with every kind of difficulty. It is difficult to know all those different beings who are collectively labelled

"Odette" or "Albertine"; a profound scepticism makes you doubt whether you can ever really get to know another human being at all even if there is goodwill on both sides. Goodwill is naturally extremely rare in a world of "lies." You are almost certain to have a rival. Your mistress is probably a Lesbian or has spent her youth in a brothel or has some other shameful secret to conceal. At this point the comedy of Love and Falsehood turns to tragedy.

11/6/86

Thomas Mann and André Gide

BY KENNETH BURKE *11/6/86*

When Gustav von Aschenbach, the hero of Thomas
Mann's *Death in Venice,* was about thirty-five years of
age, he was taken ill in Vienna. During the course of a
conversation, one keen observer said of him: "You see,
Aschenbach has always lived like this," and the speaker
contracted the fingers of his left hand into a fist; "never
like this," and he let his hand droop comfortably from the
arm of a chair. It is with such opening and closing of the
hand that this essay is to deal.

In the early writings of both Mann and Gide the characters are exceptional, though always in keeping with our
metaphor. Mann's concern is with serious and lonely fellows, deviations from type, who are over-burdened with a
feeling of divergency from their neighbors. In stories like
"Der Bajazzo" the deformations are more mental, but generally the subject is simplified by his imagining characters
who are physically extravagant. There is Tobias Minder-
nickel, whose ill-dressed, gaunt, ungainly figure excites the
persecution of all healthy children. He buys a little puppy,
and names it Esau. They become inseparable, but one day
Esau leaps for food, is accidentally wounded by a knife
which Tobias is holding, whereupon Tobias nurses his
puppy with great tenderness. After some days it is cured,
it no longer lies gazing at him with bewildered, suffering
eyes, it leaps down from its sick-bed, goes racing about
with full delight in its puppyhood, with no thought that it
is showing how it no longer needs Tobias's morbid tenderness. It is a cheerful little mutt—and maddened at his loss,
Tobias plunges his knife into it again, then forlornly gathers its dying body in his arms. Similarly, there is the little
Herr Friedemann, who, humble as he is, can by the course
of his story be still further humiliated and, in the very act

Negativism

of taking his life, grovels. Mann also writes of an abnormally fat man, who worships his adulterous wife abjectly, and falls dead of apoplexy at a particularly comical moment, topples like a collapsing building, when he feels the full weight of the indignities which have been heaped upon him. And Piepsam, Herr Gottlob Piepsam, a decayed alcoholic, a victim of life if there ever was one, is insulted as he goes to visit the grave of his wife. On the path to the cemetery he is passed by a boy on a bicycle, the merest child who is too happy to be anything but well-meaning, yet Piepsam resents him and works himself into a fatal rage—the story being told fancifully, even cheerfully. After Piepsam has been bundled off in an ambulance, one feels how brightly the sun is shining.

These outsiders (Mann later took over the word "outsider" from the English) appear under many guises. They watch, they compare themselves with others to their own detriment, they are earnest to the point of self-disgust, and they are weighted with vague responsibilities. In "Tonio Kröger" the concept has matured. Tonio's divergencies are subtler. As a writer, he observes the unliterary with nostalgia. Vacillating by temperament, one might almost say vacillating by profession, he seeks simple people, who form for him a kind of retrogressive ideal. He does not fraternize with them, he spies upon them. A Bohemian, he distrusts Bohemianism. He watches these others, awed by the healthiness, or the ease, of their satisfaction. It is a kind of inverted praising, since he envies them for qualities which he himself has outgrown. And it is melancholy.

Against this earnestness, this non-conforming mind's constant preoccupation with conformity, we find in the early writings of Gide much the same rotten elegance as characterizes Wilde's *The Picture of Dorian Gray*. Religious thinking is perverted to produce an atmosphere of decay and sinfulness. There is the Baudelairean tendency to invoke Satan as redeemer. Even in a work as late as *Les Nourritures terrestres,* we find a crooked evangelism, calling us to vague and unnatural revelations. These artificial prophecies, with a rhetorical, homiletic accent which Gide has since abandoned, suggest a kind of morbid Whitmanism. In place of expansion across an unpeopled continent, we have a pilgrimage through old, decaying cities, erotic excitations at the thought of anonymity and freedom among the ruins of other cultures. The hero who cries out to Nathaniel is seeking, not the vigor of health, but the intensity of corruption. The mood, if I understand it correctly, has by now lost much of its immediacy, but in his later works Gide has shown it capable of great readaptation; what we find earlier, in an archaistic terminology, is subsequently transformed into something wholly contemporary.

The most thorough contrast between these writers probably arises from the juxtaposition of Mann's *Death in Venice* and Gide's *The Immoralist*. Gustav von Aschenbach is nationally respected as a master of his calling. Parts of his works are even among the prescribed reading of school children. His austerity, his "morality of production," is emphasized. Aschenbach has clearly erected a structure of external dignity in keeping with the sobriety, the earnestness, which he has brought to the business of writing. But he is now undergoing a period of enervation. He finds that he cannot tackle his page with the necessary zest. As a purely therapeutic measure, he permits himself a trip to Venice, and here becomes fascinated by a young Polish boy, Tadzio, who is living at the same hotel. In his shy and troubled contemplation of this boy he finds an absorption which is painful, but imperious. Von Aschenbach remains outwardly the man of dignity honored by his nation—he does not, as I recall, ever exchange a word with this Tadzio, whose freshness, liquidity, immaturity, are the sinister counterpart of the desiccation of Aschenbach's declining years. But inwardly he is *notwendig liederlich und Abenteurer des Gefühls*. Necessarily dissolute—an adventurer of the emotions—the words are Mann's, when discussing this book in his *Betrachtungen eines Unpolitischen* years afterwards. We thus find again the notion that the artist faces *by profession* alternatives which are contrary to society. The theme of Aschenbach's gloomy infatuation coexists with the theme of the plague—and we observe the elderly man's erotic fevers metamorphose gradually into the fevers of incipient cholera. A poignant and inventive passage describing his cosmetic treatment at the hands of a barber is followed by Aschenbach's delirious remembrance of lines from the *Phaedrus,* wherein Socrates is speaking words of courtship and metaphysics indiscriminately, a merging which Aschenbach makes more pronounced by his own diseased reworking of the Platonic dialogue. A few pages later "a respectably shocked world" receives the news of his death.

The same themes, sickness and sexual vagary, underlie Gide's *The Immoralist.* Michel, after being at the verge of death and being nursed by his bride into vigorous health, subtly drives her to her own grave. Throughout the novel he is profuse in his tenderness, he is almost hysterically attentive to her, but at the same time he is steadily destroying her—and during the final march of her illness he takes her on that savage pilgrimage from city to city which inevitably results in her death. There has been a young Arab on the fringes of this plot, an insolent fellow who first charmed Michel by stealing from his wife. The reader places him unmistakably as a motive in this unpunishable murder. Despite the parallelism between *Death in Venice* and *The Immoralist,* the emphasis is very different. Whereas in Mann we feel most the sense of resistance, of resignation to the point of distress, and Aschenbach's dissolution is matched by a constant straining after self-discipline, in Gide we hear a narrator who relates with more than pride, with something akin to positive advocacy, the unclean details of his life. *"Je vais vous parler longuement de mon corps,"* he opens one chapter in a tone which I sometimes regret he has seen fit to drop from his later work; there is no mistaking its connotations; it is the accent of evangelism, of pleading.

Buddenbrooks and *Lafcadio's Adventure* do not fall in corresponding stages of their author's developments. *Buddenbrooks,* a remarkably comprehensive realistic novel of life in North Germany, comes much earlier. But the same contrast in attitude is apparent. We might interpret *Buddenbrooks* as having the theme of "Tonio Kröger" greatly subtilized and ramified. This "fall of a family" through four generations is also the "growth of an artist" through four generations. What is lost in health and moral certitude is gained in questioning and conscientiousness, in social and esthetic sensitiveness, until we arrive at little Hanno the musician, who, like Aschenbach, finally mingles inspiration with disease, as we watch his improvisations become the first symptoms of the typhoid fever that is to result in his death. In *Lafcadio's Adventure,* however, we meet with a brilliant type of villainy, an "esthetic criminal" who commits crimes for pure love of the art. The character of Lafcadio is perhaps Gide's most remarkable discovery. It suggests a merging of Stendhal's Julien Sorel with those criminals of Dostoevsky whose transgressions are inexplicable from the standpoint of utilitarian purpose.

In *Lafcadio's Adventure* Gide makes a notable change in nomenclature, recasting his "corruption" in more characteristically contemporary molds of thought. The transgressions have become "secular," advancing from sin to crime. If theology remains, it is relegated to a more superficial function; it becomes background, the story being built about a swindle whereby certain picturesque crooks fleece Catholic pietists. Lafcadio, who remembers five uncles but no father, has placed villainy on a distinguished and difficult plane. The author endows him with accomplishments somewhat lavishly, perhaps even a bit credulously; he seems eager that our sympathies be with this experimenter in crime, who can look upon kindly and vicious acts as almost interchangeable:

> The old woman with the little white cloud above her head, who pointed to it and said: "It won't rain today!" that poor shrivelled old woman whose sack I carried on my shoulders (he had followed his fancy of travelling on foot for four days across the Apennines, between Bologna and Florence, and had slept a night at Covigliajo) and whom I kissed when we got to the top of the hill . . . one of what the *curé* of Covigliajo would have called my "good actions." I could just as easily have throttled her—my hand would have been as steady—when I felt her dirty wrinkled skin beneath my fingers . . . Ah! how caressingly she stroked and dusted my coat collar and said *"figlio mio! carino!"* . . . I wonder what made my joy so intense when afterwards—I was still in a sweat—I lay down on the moss —not smoking though—in the shade of that big chestnut-tree. I felt as though I could have clasped the whole of mankind to my heart in my single embrace—or strangled it, for that matter.

We shall not reconstruct here that gratuitous murder which recommends the hero particularly to our attention when poor Fleurissoire, attracted by this pleasant-seeming lad, chooses to seat himself in the same compartment with him and unknowingly excites Lafcadio to homicidal criticism. Gide exacts a very complex reception on the part of the reader. He asks us to observe a moral outrage committed by a charming scoundrel to whose well-being we are considerably pledged. Fleurissoire is the butt of much injustice in this book but it is Lafcadio, insolent, despotic, with his mercurial slogan "what would happen if . . ." who earns our suffrage.

The war ends, the mythical post-war period begins, and

Thomas Mann issues *The Magic Mountain,* Gide *The Counterfeiters.* Our contrast is by no means imperiled. Mann shows how for seven years, during his illness in the mountains, Hans Castorp has lain exposed to moral questionings. While each day observing his temperature and eating five enormous meals to combat the wastage of his phthisis, he is privileged to hear the grave problems of our culture aired by sparring critics, themselves diseased, who speak with much rhetorical and dialectic finish. In particular, a humanist and a Jesuit altercate for his benefit, until Mynheer Peeperkorn enters (a much grander version of Herr Klöterjahn in the story "Tristan") and routs them both by his inarticulate vitality. He is life, himself ailing, to be sure, but magnificent and overwhelming while he lasts—and Castorp's melancholy respect for him is, in a matured and complex form, Tonio Kröger's respect for the burghers whom he watched with aloof humility. Castorp has the attitude of a student. Under ordinary circumstances he would probably have been unthinking, but he is made sensitive by his illness and his seven years' elevation above the century. He amasses greater understanding chapter by chapter, or at least learns to play one statement against another—until once more we come to that bewildered fever which marks the close of both *Buddenbrooks* and *Death in Venice.* At the last, as we see him on the battlefield, advancing to the aimless business of slaughter, simplified, regimented, unquestioning, we comprehend his evasion. For years he has been uncertain—he now embraces the arbitrary certainty of war. "Moralism, pessimism, humor"—these three qualities, whose interrelation Mann himself has stressed, are the dominant traits of this momentous novel, a summarization book, a comprehensive and symbolic work to be included in the world's literature of last wills and testaments.

To turn from *The Magic Mountain* to *The Counterfeiters* is to turn from brooding to shrewdness. Cruelty, malice, sensuality, intrigue—such elements are assiduously welded into an entertaining volume, of much subtle literary satisfaction. The reader of *The Magic Mountain* may have to deal with the fruits of complexity on the part of the author, but he receives them simply. The reader of *The Counterfeiters* finds complexity unresolved—he is not even at liberty to differentiate between the absurd and the beautiful. He is left fluctuant, in great tenuousness of moral values. The book contains Gide's development from sin to crime, and reaffirms his sympathy with deviations from the average ethical stock.

Returning to Aschenbach, ill at the age of thirty-five in Vienna, we find ourselves with correspondences for the closed and opened hand. It seems that Mann, who himself has situated the mainspring of his work in conscientiousness, is like his protagonist Aschenbach, with the hand contracted. And Gide, whose works could readily be taken by the immature or the trivial as invitations to the most unscrupulous kinds of living, who masters an air of suave corruption beyond any possible corrupt act, Gide can be the hand relaxed. *Gewissenhaftigkeit, Einsamkeit* —loneliness, the sense of responsibility—are Mann's words; but as the most distinctive device for Gide, I would quote from his Journal the triptych: *"nouveauté, vice, art."*

Our primary purpose, however, in establishing this distinction between the conscientious and the corrupt is to destroy it. One need not read far in the writings of Gide to discover the strong ethical trait which dominates his thinking. Perhaps no other modern writer has quoted the New Testament so frequently, or shown such readiness to settle secular issues by formulas drawn from religion. His critical work on Dostoevsky, with its theological distinction between the psychology of humility and the psychology of humiliation, is throughout an exercise in moral sensitiveness. And his Lafcadio is a mass of categorical imperatives. We learn from entries in his diary how, with the athleticism of an anchorite, he plunges a knife into his side for penance, one thrust "for having beaten Protos at chess," another thrust "for having answered before Protos," four thrusts "for having cried at hearing of Faby's death." Faby was one of his "uncles." Protos was his master in adventure, his accomplished rival, and Lafcadio punished himself, it seems, for not having been disdainful enough to let Protos win. Lafcadio's lamentable conduct might even be derived from an excess of scruples, though these scruples are peculiar to himself.

"I began to feel," Gide has written on this subject in his autobiography, *Si le Grain ne meurt,* "that perhaps all men's obligations were not the same, and that God himself might well abhor the uniformity which nature protests but towards which the Christian ideal seems to lead us in aiming to bring nature under control. I could concede none but an individual morality, its imperatives sometimes in conflict with those of other moralities. I was persuaded that each person, or at least each one of the elect, had to play a rôle on earth, which was wholly his own and did not resemble any other. And every attempt to submit to a general rule became treason in my eyes, yes, treason which I likened to that great unpardonable sin against the Holy Ghost, since the individual lost his precise, irreplaceable significance, his 'savor.' "

We should also consider Gide's *Strait is the Gate,* which constructs a sympathetic idyll out of the perverse rigors of chastity. As Alissa is courted by Jerome, the two progress into a difficult relationship, obscuring their sensual attraction in a state of pietistic exaltation. Jerome seeks her patiently and unerringly—and with the vocabulary of nobility she beckons to him while continually delaying the time of their union. At first she can offer logical pretexts for this delay, but as they are one by one removed she retreats behind the subterfuges of her faith, and with the assistance of Biblical quotations, morbidly chosen, she remains to the end difficult, pure, intact, a treasure, while loving Jerome with hysterical effusiveness. From the standpoint of its genesis the book is doubtless a companion piece to *The Immoralist.* Both are perverse studies in the frustration of heterosexual union, the one with the connotations of corruption, the other with connotations of great conscientiousness. When bringing them together, we see that Alissa's moral sensitiveness was no greater than that of Michel. Similarly we should recall in *The Counterfeiters* the brutal letter which the bastard Bernard Profitendieu writes to his nominal father, a dutifully vicious letter, and the first step, we might say, in the growth of Bernard's affection.

Has not Mann, on the other hand, spoken with fervor of a "sympathy with the abyss," an admitting of the morally chaotic, which he considers not merely the prerogative, but the duty, of the artist? Aschenbach is committed to conflict: whatever policy he decides upon for his conduct, he must continue to entertain disintegrating factors in contemplation. That practical "virtuous" procedure which silences the contrary is not allowed him. He must contain dissolution. In "the repellent, the diseased, the degenerate," Mann situates the ethical. Distinguishing between the moral and the virtuous, he finds that the moralist is "exposed to danger" and "resists no evil." As essential components of art he names "the forbidden, the adventurous, scrutiny, and self-abandonment." Defining sin as doubt, he pleads for sinfulness. His work might be called an epistemology of dignity, for he never relinquishes the love of dignity, and never ceases to make the possession of it difficult.

Mann has defined the problematical as the proper sphere of art ("art is the problematical sphere of the human"). In any event, the problematical is the sphere of his own art. Implicit in his work there is a cult of conflict, a deliberate entertaining of moral vacillation, which could not permit a rigid standard of judgments. He has said that the artist must contain his critic, must recognize the validity of contraries. This attitude could make such simple certainty as moral indignation impossible. It would imply exposure to mutually exclusive codes of conduct, diverse modes of behavior. Esthetically, as he himself has said, he finds the unification of this attitude in irony, which merges the sympathetic and antipathetic aspects of any subject. Unlike the satirist, the standpoint of the ironist is shifting —he cannot maintain a steady attack—by the standards of military morale he is treacherous; he belittles the things he lives for, and with melancholy praises what he abandons. He is equally tentative towards *Leben,* life, nature, and *Geist,* spirit, the intellectual order erected above life. The vigor of the pamphleteer is denied him. To the Rooseveltian mind he is corrosive—wherefore that "sympathy with the abyss" which anyone of rigid criteria, of sure distinctions between the admirable and the reprehensible, must feel as corrupting, and which Mann himself, approaching from the attitude of alien criticism, chose to designate as "dissolute." The ironist is essentially impure, even in the chemical sense of purity, since he is divided. He must deprecate his own enthusiasms, and distrust his own resentments. He will unite waveringly, as the components of his attitude, "dignity, repugnance, the problematical art."

To the slogan-minded, the ralliers about a flag, the marchers who convert a simple idea into a simple action, he is an "outsider." Yet he must observe them with nostalgia, he must feel a kind of awe for their fertile assurance, even while remaining on the alert to stifle it with irony each time he discovers it growing in unsuspected quarters within himself. It will continue to rise anew, for man has a tremendous fund of certainty—and one will find only too little of Mann's best ironic manner in his essays written during the war, or will find it without its counterpart of melancholy. Yet I grant that the slogans of his opponents were enough to infuriate any subtle man in his position; the temporary disorientation which turned him away from the ironist and towards the pamphleteer is readily understandable. In *The Magic Mountain,* however, the author has recovered from his citizenship to become again the artist. Castorp descends, not to a specific European war, but to regimentation, to the relief, even the suicidal relief, of the slogan-minded. He, the hero, represents the ultimate betrayal of his author's own most serious message. After years of vacillation he seeks the evasion of a monastery, though in these secular days, when the power of theology has dwindled, the dogmatic certainties for which people are burned will more often be those of patriotism, and the equivalent of churchly penance becomes the advance in numbers under arms.

What Mann does with irony, Gide parallels with experimentalism, with curiosity. He views any set code of values with distrust, because it implies the exclusion of other codes. He speculates as to "what would happen if. . . ." He is on guard lest the possible be obscured by the real. In his autobiography we find him, characteristically, considering a whole civilization gratuitously different from our own:

"I thought of writing the imaginary history of a people, a nation, with wars, revolutions, changes of administration, typical happenings. . . . I wanted to invent heroes, sovereigns, statesmen, artists, an artistic tradition, an apocryphal literature, explaining and criticising movements, recounting the evolution of forms, quoting fragments of masterpieces. . . . And all to what purpose? To prove that the history of man could have been different—our habits, morals, customs, tastes, judgments, standards of beauty could have all been different—and yet the humanity of mankind would remain the same."

By recalling *Gulliver's Travels,* we see again how far removed we are from satire. Perhaps, in a much simpler and more lyrical form, Gide did write this book. I refer to *La Symphonie pastorale,* where he speculates upon a world foreign to him, an arbitrary world so far as this author is concerned, the world of blindness. He even contrives to forget his own knowledge, as when his blind heroine, trying to meditate her way into the world of sight, surmises that sunlight must be like the humming of a kettle.

Perhaps one may interpret Gide's "corruption" too literally. I do not believe that his work can be evaluated properly unless we go beyond the subject-matter to the underlying principles. His choice of material even implies a certain obscurantism, assuming a sophistication on the part of the reader whereby the reader would not attempt too slavishly to become the acting disciple of his author's speculations. Surely Gide would be the first to admit that we could not build a very convenient society out of Lafcadios, however admirable they are. I should take the specific events in Gide as hardly more than symbols: their parallel in life would not be the enacting of similar events, but the exercising of the complex state of mind which arises from the contemplation of such events with sympathy. To live a life like the life in Gide's books would be to commit under another form the very kind of exclusion which he abhors —Lafcadio is for the pious, he is not for poisoners and forgers. Nor must one, in placing this author's malice, forget his *Travels in the Congo,* with its protests against the systematic injustice meted out to the Negroes at the hands of the concessionaires.*

Irony, novelty, experimentalism, vacillation, the cult of conflict—are not these men trying to make us at home in indecision, are they not trying to humanize the state of doubt? A philosopher has recently written of this new wilderness we now face, a wilderness not of nature, but of social forces. Perhaps there is an evasion, a shirking of responsibility, in becoming certain too quickly, particularly when our certainties involve reversions to an ideology which has the deceptive allurement of tradition. To seek the backing of the past may be as cowardly as to seek the

---

* It is doubtful, I grant, whether Gide arrived at his useful position through wholly untrammelled motives. The Olympian result shows traces of troubled, Orphic beginnings. It seems likely that his concern with homosexuality, and his struggle for its "recognition," early gave him a sense of divergence from the social norms among which he lived, and in time this sense of divergence was trained upon other issues. In seeking, let us say, to defend a practice which society generally considered reprehensible, he came to defend practices which society considered more reprehensible—as a child who resented a cruel father might end by slaying the king.

backing of the many, and as flattering to our more trivial needs of conformity. Need people be in haste to rebel against the state of doubt, when doubt has not yet permeated the organs of our body, the processes of our metabolism, the desire for food and companionship, the gratification with sun and water? There is a large reserve of physical unquestioning, and until we find this reserve itself endangered by the humiliation of tentative living and unauthoritative thinking, are we compelled to reach out impetuously for set criteria? Since the body is dogmatic, a generator of belief, society might well be benefited by the corrective of a disintegrating art, which converts each simplicity into a complexity, which ruins the possibility of ready hierarchies, which concerns itself with the problematical, the experimental, and thus by implication works corrosively upon those expansionistic certainties preparing the way for our social cataclysms. An art may be of value purely through preventing a society from becoming too assertively, too hopelessly, itself.

Rilke and Nietzsche

BY ERICH HELLER

We observed them, each in his own way, working, thinking and feeling towards a radical revision of the frontiers between traditionally articulated concepts of thought and, as it were, units of feeling. There remains the question of how and why they came to undertake such a stupendous labour of thought and feeling—"Herzwerk," "work of heart," as Rilke called it. The answer was given for both of them by Nietzsche: because God is dead. And God was so powerful, efficient and secretive a landlord that to look after His Estate all by ourselves involves us in great difficulties. What under His management used to be clearly defined spheres are now objects of confused and conflicting claims. Much that we were powerfully persuaded to accept as true dissolves into sheer illusion. For all the land appears to have been heavily mortgaged. We have lived in splendour, but the splendour was merely loaned. Payment was due on the death of God, and the unknown trascendental creditor lost little time in claiming it. A tremendous effort has to be exacted to restore the glory.

Both Nietzsche and Rilke have made themselves administrators of the impoverished estate. The enormous complexity of their works must not deceive us; the structure behind it is consistently simple; it has the simplicity of that immense single-mindedness with which they, consciously or intuitively, dedicated their lives to the one task: to reassess and re-define all experience in thought and feeling; to show that the traditional modes of thought and feeling,

Reprinted from *The Disinherited Mind* by Erich Heller, by permission of the publisher, Bowes & Bowes, London (published in the U.S. by Farrar, Straus & Cudahy, Inc.).

Rilke's poetry in the German original reprinted by permission of Insel Verlag, Frankfurt am Main; in translation from Rainier Maria Rilke, *Selected Works,* Volume II, translated by J.B. Leishman. All rights reserved. Reprinted by permission of New Directions Publishing Corporation.

in so far as they were determined, or decisively modified, by Christian transcendental beliefs—and to which of them does this not apply?—had been rendered invalid by the end of religion; to replace them; to overcome the great spiritual depression, caused by the death of God, through new and ever greater powers of glory and praise; to adjust, indeed to revolutionize, thought and feeling in accordance with the reality of a world of absolute immanence; and to achieve this without any loss of spiritual grandeur. "Indeed," writes Nietzsche (to Overbeck, May 21st, 1884), "who can feel with me what it means to feel with every shred of one's being that the weight of all things must be defined anew," and Rilke (to Ilse Jahr, February 22nd, 1923): "God, the no longer sayable, is being stripped of his attributes; they return to his creation"; and in "The Letter from the Young Workman" (reversing the debtor-creditor relationship and presenting the bill to Heaven): "It is high time for the impoverished earth to claim back all those loans which have been raised at the expense of her own bliss for the equipment of some super-future." Nietzsche spoke for himself as well as for Rilke when at the time of writing *Zarathustra* he made the following entry in his notebook: "He who no longer finds what is great in God will find it nowhere—he must either deny or create it." It is the most precise formula for the religiously disinherited religious mind.

Nietzsche and Rilke experienced and explored this situation with the utmost consistency, courageously facing the paradox to which it leads: the paradox of affirming from negation, and creating from denial. For the denial of God involves for both Nietzsche and Rilke the denial of man *as he is*. Even before Zarathustra proclaimed the rule of the Superman, Nietzsche, knowing that man has become "impossible" after doing away with God, "the holiest and mightiest that the world possessed," asked: "Is not the greatness of this deed too great for us? To prove worthy of it, must not we ourselves become gods?" And Rilke said of his *Malte Laurids Brigge* that it almost "proved that this life, suspended in a bottomless pit, is impossible."

How is this impossible life to become possible again? How is the vanished glory issuing from a transcendental god to be recreated by a world gloomily imprisoned in its own immanence? At this point both Nietzsche and Rilke indulge in the same alchemy that we have seen employed in their transmutation of pain and suffering. The idea of even heightening the agony of existence in order to increase the resources from which ultimate bliss will be sustained is familiar to both of them. Nietzsche once quoted Cardanus as having said that one ought to seek out as much suffering as possible in order to intensify the joy springing from its conquest; and Rilke wrote of the "holy cunning of the martyrs," taking "the most concentrated dose of pain" to acquire the immunity of continual bliss. Now again they seek in the greatest possible intensification of immanence salvation from the inglorious prison. They almost invent more and more deprivations of transcendence to heighten the pressure within the hermetic vessel. In that, Nietzsche's Eternal Recurrence and Rilke's *"Einmal und nichtmehr"*, *"Once* and no more", are contrasts merely in verbal expression, but identical in meaning. This identity lies in the emphasis both these symbols place on the *eternity* of the moment here and now, the *irrevocability* of the one and unique opportunity and test of living.

The idea of Eternal Recurrence seeks to bestow the paradox of an eternity of finite time on the transient moment, which Rilke, in his turn, eternalizes in the hermetical flame of inner experience, consuming all that is merely corruptible matter and concreteness in our world and leaving us with an essence as imperishable as it is invisible. Rilke states this theme of his mature work with explicit precision as early as his *Tuscan Diary:* "We need *eternity;* for only eternity can provide space for our gestures. Yet we know that we live in narrow finiteness. Thus it is our task to create infinity within these boundaries, for we no longer believe in the unbounded." And the imaginations of both Nietzsche and Rilke have given birth to symbolic creatures moving with perfect grace and ease in a sphere to which man can attain only in the utmost realization of his spiritual powers. These creatures of immanence, transcending immanence in the achievement of a yet profounder immanence, are Nietzsche's Superman and Rilke's Angel. Both are terrible to man, threatening with annihilation the image that, fondly and lazily, he has built up of himself, an image resting on the illusion of transcendence and now shattered in the great undeceiving: "To create the Superman after we have thought, indeed rendered thinkable, the whole of nature in terms of man himself" and then "to *break all your images of man* with the image

of the Superman—this is Zarathustra's will . . ." says one
of Nietzsche's notebooks from the time of *Zarathustra;* and
Rilke's *Duino Elegies* begin with the invocation of the
angelic terror:

> *Wer, wenn ich schriee, hörte mich denn aus der Engel*
> *Ordnungen? und gesetzt selbst, es nähme*
> *einer mich plötzlich ans Herz: ich verginge von seinem*
> *stärkeren Dasein . . .*
>
> > (First Elegy)

> Who, if I cried, would hear me among the angelic orders?
> And even if one of them suddenly
> pressed me against his heart, I should fade in the strength
>   of his
> stronger existence . . .

and

> *Jeder Engel ist schrecklich. Und dennoch, weh mir,*
> *ansing ich euch, fast tödliche Vögel der Seele,*
> *wissend um euch. . . .*
>
> > (Second Elegy)

> Every angel is terrible. Still, though, alas!
> I invoke you, almost deadly birds of the soul,
> knowing of you. . . .

The supreme realization of immanence and its metamorphosis into everlasting inwardness is man's task in a
world dominated by Rilke's Angel, in the same way in
which Nietzsche conceives Eternal Recurrence as the terri-
fying discipline which must break man and make the Superman. Only he, in the glory of his own strength, joy and
power of praise, can *will* again and again a life which,
even if lived only once, must be all but unendurable to
man, as soon as he is exposed to the full impact of its absolute godlessness and senselessness, and no longer shel-
tered from it by the ruins of Christianity among which he
exists. "I perform the great experiment: who can bear the
idea of Eternal Recurrence? He who cannot endure the
sentence, 'There is no redemption,' ought to die." The Superman is for Nietzsche what Orpheus is for Rilke: the
transfigurer of unredeemable existence, with the "mystery
of its unending repetition issuing from superhuman delight."

> *Und so drängen wir uns und wollen es leisten,*

wollens enthalten in unseren einfachen Händen,
im überfüllteren Blick und im sprachlosen Herzen.
Wollen es werden. . . .

(Ninth Elegy)

And so we press on and try to achieve it,
try to contain it within our simple hands,
in the gaze ever more overcrowded and in the speechless
  heart.
Try to become it. . . .

But what we try to achieve here and what overcrowds our
gaze and heart—with "überzähliges Dasein", "Supernu-
merary existence"—is not the vision of Eternal Recurrence, but, on the contrary, of

Einmal

jedes, nur einmal. Einmal und nichtmehr. Und wir
  auch
einmal. Nie wieder. Aber dieses
einmal gewesen zu sein, wenn auch nur einmal:
irdish gewesen zu sein, scheint nicht widerrufbar.

(Ninth Elegy)

Just once,

everything only for once. Once and no more. And
  we, too,
once. And never again. But this
having been once, though only once,
having been once on earth—can it ever be cancelled?

Nietzsche's Eternal Recurrence and Rilke's eternally reiterated "Once" are both the extreme symbols of the determination to wrest the utmost of spiritual significance from
a life that, in traditional terms, has ceased to be spiritually
significant. How to cast eternity from the new mould of
absolute transience, and how to achieve the mode of transcendence within the consciousness of pure immanence, is
one of the main concerns of Nietzsche as well as of Rilke.
This problem links Rilke (and, of course, Nietzsche) with
the philosophers of Existence; Heidegger, for instance, is
said to have remarked that his philosophy is merely the
unfolding in thought of what Rilke has expressed poetically; but even without this confession the affinity would be
obvious. What, above all, Rilke and the existentialists have
in common is the experience of the utter exposure and de-
fencelessness of the frontiers of human existence against
the neighbouring void, that area which once established as the divine home of souls and is now the unassailable fortress of the *nihil,* defeating for ever every new

and heroic attempt of man to assert himself in that re-
gion: hence Jasper's *Scheitern*, Heidegger's *Geworfensein*
and, long before them, Kierkegaard's—and even Pascal's
—*Angst*. The focal point of all existentialist philosophies
is this "marginal situation" of man in the border-districts
of immanence and the realization of the existence of a
sphere which seems to invite and yet relentlessly beat back
every attempt at transcendence.

It is this impenetrable void against which Zarathustra
hurls his armies of men, knowing that they will not be victorious, but utterly routed; yet a few will return in
triumph, having gained the strength of supermen in the
purifying defeat. For life is a "Wagnis," a perpetual stak-
ing of existence, man a mere "essay in existence" and lov-
able only because he is "ein Übergang and ein Unter-
gang," at once transition and perdition. The same frontier
is the defeat of Malte Laurids Brigge, until the mature
Rilke succeeds in concluding an everlasting truce with the
anonymous powers on the other side—by appropriating
their territory "inwardly." Where man knew merely the
terror of the monstrous emptiness beyond, there is now
the peace of "reiner Bezug," "pure relatedness," which is
so pure because no real "otherness" enters into it. In this
"reiner Bezug" life and death are one. As soon as it is
achieved,

> *entsteht*
> *aus unsern Jahreszeiten erst der Umkreis*
> *des ganzen Wandelns. Über uns hinüber*
> *spielt dann der Engel. . . .*
>
> (Fourth Elegy)

> arises
> from our seasons the cycle
> of the entire motion. Over and above us,
> then, there is the Angel's play. . . .

Or, one is tempted to add, the Superman's dance, the joy
of the creatures who have gained eternity in the resigned
and yet victorious return to themselves. Rilke, in the Su-
per-Narcissus image of his Angels, at the same time expresses the essence of Nietzsche's race of Supermen who
assert their power and beauty in the cycle of Eternal Recurrence:

> *. . . die die entströmte eigene Schönheit*
> *weiderschöpfen zurück in das eigene Antlitz.*
>
> (Second Elegy)

some Idea of the Modern

Ortega y Gasset, 94 Arts pure sci = indicators of an change
: 92 Eclecticist mod-art theory 96 Orig & reaction to previous X

Pg. 85 - 86 Realism : 19 Century

... drawing up their own
outstreamed beauty into their faces again.

It is not correct to say that after the *Duino Elegies*
Rilke returned, as some critics suggest, to a "simpler" and
"purely lyrical" mode of expression. The apparent simplicity and pure lyricism of the final phase are not different in
kind from the simplicity and lyricism of *Sonnets to Orpheus*. There is, indeed, repose; but it is the repose of a
poetry that appears to have settled peacefully on the very
pastures which had for so long been the goal of the struggle. If the *Duino Elegies* were the invocation of the Angel,
some of the poems that come afterwards sound like the
Angel's own poetry; and it is hardly surprising that it could
also be said: like the poetry of the Superman. This, indeed, does not make them easier to understand. It is the
poetry of achievement, and not the poetry of return.
There is little gain in it for those who find the "ideas" of
the preceding period disturbing. The ideas are not abandoned, but realized; for instance, in the poem written in
1924:

> *Da dich das geflügelte Entzücken*
> *über manchen frühen Abgrund trug,*
> *baue jetzt der unerhörten Brücken*
> *kühn berechenbaren Bug.*
>
> *Wunder ist nicht nur im unerklärten*
> *Überstehen der Gefahr;*
> *erst in einer klaren reingewährten*
> *Leistung wird das Wunder wunderbar.*
>
> *Mitzuwirken ist nicht Überhebung*
> *an dem unbeschreiblichen Bezug,*
> *immer inniger wird die Verwebung,*
> *nur Getragensein ist nicht genug.*
>
> *Deing ausgeübten Kräfte spanne,*
> *bis sie reichen, zwischen zwein*
> *Widersprüchen.... Denn im Manne*
> *Will der Gott beraten sein.*

As the winged ecstasy
has borne you over many an early abyss,
now, with mathematical audacity
build the arches of unheard-of bridges.

Wonder is not merely in the inexplicable
surviving of danger;

only in the clear and purely granted
achievement is the miracle miraculous.

To participate in the indescribable
relating, is not presumption,
ever more intense becomes the pattern,
only being borne along will not suffice.

Stretch your practised powers till they span
the distance between two contradictions,
for the god must find
counsel in the man.

Or in Rilke's last known poem in German, which, if it
is simple, has the inexhaustibly complex simplicity of a
sphere so esoteric that it renders it completely untranslatable, defeating even the attempt to give a prose version of
it in English. Yet all that has been said here about Rilke
and Nietzsche could easily be based on this one poem
alone and would need no further support. It is dated August 24th, 1926, four months before Rilke's death, and is
dedicated to Erika Mitterer "for the feast of praise":

Taube, die draussen blieb,   ausser dem Taubenschlag,
wieder in Kreis und Haus,   einig der Nacht, dem Tag,
weiss sie die Heimlichkeit,   wenn sich der Einbezug
fremdester Schrecken schmiegt   in den gefühlten Flug.

Unter den Tauben, die   allergeschonteste,
niemals gefährdetste,   kennt nicht die Zärtlichkeit
wiedererholtes Herz   ist das bewohnteste:
freier durch Widerruf   freut sich die Fähigkeit.

Über dem Nirgendssein   spannt sich das Überall!
Ach der geworfene,   ach der gewagte Ball,
füllt er die Hände nicht   anders mit Wiederkehr:
rein um sein Heimgewicht   ist er mehr.

T. S. Eliot as the International Hero

BY DELMORE SCHWARTZ

A culture hero is one who brings new arts and skills to mankind. Prometheus was a culture hero and the inventors of the radio may also be said to be culture heroes, although this is hardly to be confounded with the culture made available by the radio.

The inventors of the radio made possible a new range of experience. This is true of certain authors; for example, it is true of Wordsworth in regard to nature, and Proust in regard to time. It is not true of Shakespeare, but by contrast it is true of Surrey and the early Elizabethan playwrights who invented blank verse. Thus the most important authors are not always culture heroes, and thus no rank, stature, or scope is of necessity implicit in speaking of the author as a culture hero.

When we speak of nature and of a new range of experience, we may think of a mountain range: some may make the vehicles by means of which a mountain is climbed, some may climb the mountain, and some may apprehend the new view of the surrounding countryside which becomes possible from the heights of the mountain. T. S. Eliot is a culture hero in each of these three ways. This becomes clear when we study the relationship of his work to the possible experiences of modern life. The term, possible, should be kept in mind, for many human beings obviously disregard and turn their backs upon much of modern life, although modern life does not in the least cease to circumscribe and penetrate their existence.

The reader of T. S. Eliot by turning the dials of his radio can hear the capitals of the world, London, Vienna, Athens, Alexandria, Jerusalem. What he hears will be news of the agony of war. Both the agony and the width of this experience are vivid examples of how the poetry of T. S. Eliot has a direct relationship to modern life. The width and the height and the depth of modern life are ex-

From *Partisan Review*, XII, No. 2. Copyright 1945 by Partisan Review.

hibited in his poetry; the agony and the horror of modern life are represented as inevitable to any human being who does not wish to deceive himself with systematic lies. Thus it is truly significant that E. M. Forster, in writing of Eliot, should recall August 1914 and the beginning of the First World War; it is just as significant that he should speak of first reading Eliot's poems in Alexandria, Egypt, during that war, and that he should conclude by saying that Eliot was one who had looked into the abyss and re-fused henceforward to deny or forget the fact.

We are given an early view of the international hero in the quasi-autobiographical poem which Eliot entitles: "Mélange Adultère Du Tout." The title, borrowed from a poem by Corbière, is ironic, but the adulterous mixture of practically everything, every time and every place, is not ironic in the least: a teacher in America, the poem goes, a journalist in England, a lecturer in Yorkshire, a literary ni-hilist in Paris, overexcited by philosophy in Germany, a wanderer from Omaha to Damascus, he has celebrated, he says, his birthday at an African oasis, dressed in a giraffe's skin. Let us place next to this array another list of names and events as heterogeneous as a circus or America itself: St. Louis, New England, Boston, Harvard, England, Paris, the First World War, Oxford, London, the Russian Revo-lution, the Church of England, the post-war period, the world crisis and depression, the Munich Pact, and the Sec-ond World War. If this list seems far-fetched or forced, if it seems that such a list might be made for any author, the answer is that these names and events are *presences* in Eliot's work in a way which is not true of many authors, good and bad, who have lived through the same years.

Philip Rahv has shown how the heroine of Henry James is best understood as the heiress of all the ages. So, in a further sense, the true protagonist of Eliot's poems is the heir of all the ages. He is the descendant of the essential characters of James in that he is the American who visits Europe with a Baedeker in his hand, just like Isabel Ar-cher. But the further sense in which he is the heir of all the ages is illustrated when Eliot describes the seduction of a typist in a London flat from the point of view of Tiresias, a character in a play by Sophocles. To suppose that this is the mere exhibition of learning or reading is a banal mis-understanding. The important point is that the presence of Tiresias illuminates the seduction of the typist just as much as a description of her room. Hence Eliot writes in his notes to *The Waste Land* that "what Tiresias *sees* is the substance of the poem." The illumination of the ages is available at any moment, and when the typist's indifference and boredom in the act of love must be represented, it is possible for Eliot to invoke and paraphrase a lyric from a play by Oliver Goldsmith. Literary allusion has become not merely a Miltonic reference to Greek gods and Old Testament geography, not merely the citation of parallels, but a powerful and inevitable habit of mind, a habit which issues in judgment and the representation of different levels of experience, past and present.

James supposed that his theme was the international theme: would it not be more precise to speak of it as the transatlantic theme? This effort at a greater exactness defines what is involved in Eliot's work. Henry James was concerned with the American in Europe. Eliot cannot help but be concerned with the whole world and all history. Tiresias sees the nature of love in all times and all places and when Sweeney outwits a scheming whore, the fate of Agamemnon becomes relevant. So too, in the same way exactly, Eliot must recognize and use a correspondence between St. Augustine and Buddha in speaking of sensuality. And thus, as he writes again in his notes to *The Waste Land*, "The collocation of these two representatives of eastern and western asceticism as the culmination of this part of the poem is not an accident." And it is not an accident that the international hero should have come from St. Louis, Missouri, or at any rate from America. Only an American with a mind and sensibility which is cosmopolitan and expatriated could have seen Europe as it is seen in *The Waste Land*.

A literary work may be important in many ways, but surely one of the ways in which it is important is in its relationship to some important human interest or need, or in its relationship to some new aspect of human existence. Eliot's work is important in relationship to the fact that experience has become international. We have become an international people, and hence an international hero is possible. Just as the war is international, so the true causes of many of the things in our lives are world-wide, and we are able to understand the character of our lives only when we are aware of all history, of the philosophy of history, of primitive peoples and the Russian Revolution, of

ancient Egypt and the unconscious mind. Thus again it is
no accident that in *The Waste Land* use is made of *The
Golden Bough,* and a book on the quest of the Grail;
and the way in which images and associations appear in the
poem illustrates a new view of consciousness, the depths of
consciousness and the unconscious mind.

The protagonist of *The Waste Land* stands on the banks
of the Thames and quotes the Upanishads, and this very
quotation, the command to "give, sympathize, and control," makes possible a comprehensive insight into the difficulty of his life in the present. But this emphasis upon
one poem of Eliot's may be misleading. What is true of
much of his poetry is also true of his criticism. When the
critic writes of tradition and the individual talent, when he
declares the necessity for the author of a consciousness of
the past as far back as Homer, when he brings the reader
back to Dante, the Elizabethans and Andrew Marvell, he
is also speaking as the heir of all the ages.

The emphasis on a consciousness of literature may also
be misleading, for nowhere better than in Eliot can we see
the difference between being merely literary and making
the knowledge of literature an element in vision, that is to
say, an essential part of the process of seeing anything and
everything. Thus, to cite the advent of Tiresias again, the
literary character of his appearance is matched by the unliterary actuality by means of which he refers to himself
as being "like a taxi throbbing waiting." In one way, the
subject of *The Waste Land* is the sensibility of the protagonist, a sensibility which is literary, philosophical, cosmopolitan and expatriated. But this sensibility is concerned
not with itself as such, but with the common things of
modern life, with two such important aspects of existence
as religious belief and making love. To summon to mind
such profound witnesses as Freud and D. H. Lawrence is
to remember how often, in modern life, love has been the
worst sickness of human beings.

The extent to which Eliot's poetry is directly concerned
with love is matched only by the extent to which it is concerned with religious belief and the crisis of moral values.
J. Alfred Prufrock is unable to make love to women of his
own class and kind because of shyness, self-consciousness,
and fear of rejection. The protagonists of other poems in
Eliot's first book are men or women laughed at or rejected

in love, and a girl deserted by her lover seems like a body deserted by the soul.

In Eliot's second volume of poems, an old man's despair issues in part from his inability to make love, while Sweeney, an antithetical character, is able to make love, but is unable to satisfy the woman with whom he copulates. In *The Waste Land,* the theme of love as a failure is again uppermost. Two lovers return from a garden after a moment of love, and the woman is overcome by despair or pathological despondency. A lady, perhaps the same woman who has returned from the garden in despair, becomes hysterical in her boudoir because her lover or her husband has nothing to say to her and cannot give her life any meaning or interest: "What shall I do now?" she says, "what shall I ever do?" The neurasthenic lady is succeeded in the poem by cockney women who gossip about another cockney woman who has been made ill by contraceptive pills taken to avoid the consequences of love; which is to say that the sickness of love has struck down every class in society: "What you get married for, if you don't want children?" And then we witness the seduction of the typist; and then other aspects of the sickness of love appear when, on the Thames bank, three girls ruined by love rehearse the sins of the young men with whom they have been having affairs. In the last part of the poem, the impossibility of love, the gulf between one human being and another, is the answer to the command to give, that is to say, to give oneself or surrender oneself to another human being in the act of making love.

Elsewhere love either results in impotence, or it is merely copulation. In "The Hollow Men," the hollow men are incapable of making love because there is a shadow which falls between the desire and the spasm. The kinship of love and belief is affirmed when the difficulty of love and of religious belief are expressed in the same way and as parallels, by means of a paraphrase and parody of the Lord's Prayer. In "Sweeney Agonistes," Sweeney returns to say that there is nothing in love but copulation, which, like birth and death, is boring. Sweeney's boredom should be placed in contrast with the experience of Burbank, who encountered the Princess Volupine in Venice, and found himself impotent with her. A comparison ought also to be made between Sweeney and the protagonist of one of Eliot's poems in French who harks back to a childhood experience of love: "I tickled her to make her laugh. I experienced a moment of power and delirium." Eliot's characters when they make love either suffer from what the psychoanalysts term "psychic impotence," or they make love so inadequately that the lady is left either hysterical or indifferent when the episode is over. The characters who are potent and insensitive are placed in contrast with the characters who are impotent and sensitive. Grishkin has a bust which promises pneumatic bliss, while Burbank's kind, the kind of a man who goes to Europe with a Baedeker, has to crawl between the dry ribs of metaphysics because no contact possible to flesh is satisfactory. The potent and the insensitive, such as Sweeney, are not taken in by the ladies, the nightingales and the whores; but Burbank, like Agamemnon, is betrayed and undone.

This synoptic recitation might be increased by many more examples. Its essence is expressed perfectly in "Little Gidding": "Love is the unfamiliar name." But we ought to remember that the difficulty of making love, that is to say, of entering into the most intimate of relationships, is not the beginning but the consequence of the whole character of modern life. That is why the apparatus of reference which the poet brings to bear upon failure in love involves all history ("And I Tiresias have foresuffered all") and is international. So too the old man who is the protagonist of "Gerontion" must refer to human beings of many nationalities, to Mr. Silvero at Limoges, Hakagawa, Madame de Tornquist, Fräulein von Kulp and Christ [the tiger] and he finds it necessary to speak of all history as well as his failure in love. History is made to illuminate love and love is made to illuminate history. In modern life, human beings are whirled beyond the circuit of the constellations: their intimate plight is seen in connection or relation with the anguish of the Apostles after Calvary, the murder of Agamemnon, the insanity of Ophelia and children who chant that London bridge is falling down. In the same way, the plight of Prufrock is illuminated by means of a rich, passing reference to Michelangelo, the sculptor of the strong and heroic man. Only when the poet is the heir of all the ages can he make significant use of so many different and distant kinds of experience. But conversely, only when experience becomes international, only when many different and distant kinds of experience are encountered by the

poet, does he find it necessary to become the heir of all
the ages.

Difficulty in love is inseparable from the deracination
and the alienation from which the international man
suffers. When the traditional beliefs, sanctions and bonds
of the community and of the family decay or disappear in
the distance like a receding harbor, then love ceases to be
an act which is in relation to the life of the community,
and in immediate relation to the family and other human
beings. Love becomes purely personal. It is isolated from
the past and the future, and since it is isolated from all
other relationships, since it is no longer celebrated, evaluated and given a status by the community, love does become merely copulation. The protagonist of "Gerontion"
uses one of the most significant phrases in Eliot's work
when he speaks of himself as living in a *rented* house;
which is to say, not in the house where his forbears lived.
He lives in a rented house, he is unable to make love, and
he knows that history has many cunning, deceptive, and
empty corridors. The nature of the house, of love and of
history are interdependent aspects of modern life.

When we compare Eliot's poetry to the poetry of
Valèry, Yeats and Rilke, Eliot's direct and comprehensive
concern with the essential nature of modern life gains an
external definition. Yeats writes of Leda and he writes of
the nature of history; Valèry writes of Narcissus and the
serpent in the Garden of Eden; Rilke is inspired by great
works of art, by Christ's mother and by Orpheus. Yet in
each of these authors the subject is transformed into a
timeless essence. The heritage of Western culture is available to these authors and they use it many beautiful ways;
but the fate of Western culture and the historical sense as
such does not become an important part of their poetry.
And then if we compare Eliot with Auden and with
Pound, a further definition becomes clear. In his early
work, Auden is inspired by an international crisis in a social and political sense; in his new work, he writes as a
teacher and preacher and secular theologian. In neither
period is all history and all culture a necessary part of the
subject or the sensibility which is dealing with the subject.
With Pound, we come closer to Eliot and the closeness
sharpens the difference. Pound is an American in Europe
too, and Pound, not Eliot, was the first to grasp the histor-

ical and international dimension of experience, as we can see in an early effort of his to explain the method of the *Cantos* and the internal structure of each *Canto:* "All times are contemporaneous," he wrote, and in the *Cantos,* he attempts to deal with all history as if it were part of the present. But he fails; he remains for the most part an American in Europe, and the *Cantos* are never more than a book of souvenirs of a tour of the world and a tour of culture.

To be international is to be a citizen of the world and thus a citizen of no particular city. The world as such is not a community and it has no constitution or government: it is the turning world in which the human being, surrounded by the consequences of all times and all places, must live his life as a human being and not as the citizen of any nation. Hence, to be the heir of all the ages is to inherit nothing but a consciousness of how all heirlooms are rooted in the past. Dominated by the historical consciousness, the international hero finds that all beliefs affect the holding of any belief (he cannot think of Christianity without remembering Adonis); he finds that many languages affect each use of speech (*The Waste Land* concludes with a passage in four languages).

When nationalism attempts to renew itself. it can do so only through the throes of war. And when nationalism in America attempts to become articulate, when a poet like Carl Sandburg writes that "The past is a bucket of ashes," or when Henry Ford makes the purely American remark that "History is the bunk," we have only to remember such a pilgrimage as that of Ford in the Peace Ship in which he attempted to bring the First World War to an end in order to see that anyone can say whatever he likes: no matter what anyone says, existence has become international for everyone.

Eliot's political and religious affirmations are at another extreme, and they do not resemble Ford's quixotic pilgrimage except as illustrating the starting-point of the modern American, and his inevitable journey to Europe. What should be made explicit here is that only one who has known fully the deracination and alienation inherent in modern life can be moved to make so extreme an effort at returning to the traditional community as Eliot makes in attaching himself to Anglo-Catholicism and Royalism. Coming back may well be the same thing as going away;

or at any rate, the effort to return home may exhibit the same predicament and the same topography as the fact of departure. Only by going to Europe, by crossing the Atlantic and living thousands of miles from home, does the international hero conceive of the complex nature of going home.

Modern life may be compared to a foreign country in which a foreign language is spoken. Eliot is the international hero because he has made the journey to the foreign country and described the nature of the new life in the foreign country. Since the future is bound to be international, if it is anything at all, we are all the bankrupt heirs of the ages, and the moments of the crisis expressed in Eliot's work are a prophecy of the crises of our own future in regard to love, religious belief, good and evil, the good life and the nature of the just society. *The Waste Land* will soon be as good as new.

Tradition and Modernity: Wallace Stevens

BY J. V. CUNNINGHAM

I have defined tradition in such a way that every poem necessarily has a tradition, but this is not the common meaning of the term. For we distinguish between what is traditional and what is not, and in the latter case the principle is a negative one. This is a concern for tradition that is a modern concern, and provoked by something so simple as a sense of alienation from the past, a feeling for history as distinct. It is motivated by the persuasion that tradition has been lost and is only recoverable in novelty. From this arises a corollary concern with modernity in poetry, for which the poetry of Wallace Stevens will serve as an illustration. He himself writes in the poem entitled "Of Modern Poetry":

> The poem of the mind in the act of finding
> What will suffice. It has not always had
> To find: the scene was set; it repeated what
> Was in the script.
>   Then the theatre was changed
> To something else.   Its past was a souvenir.[1]

To be modern in this sense is not the same thing as to be contemporary, to be living and writing in our time, or to have lived and written within our normal life span. There are many contemporary poets who are not modern. The modern poet writes the new poetry, as it was called some years ago. His poetry is modern in that it is different from the old, the traditional, the expected; it is new. This is the sense in which *modern* has always been used in these contexts: the modern poets in Roman antiquity were Calvus and Catullus who wrote in new and untraditional poetic forms, in forms borrowed from another language and regarded by the traditionalists of the times as effete and decadent; whose subjects were novel and daring; and

Reprinted from *Tradition and Poetic Structure* by J. V. Cunningham. By permission of the Estate of Alan Swallow, Publisher.
[1] *Collected Poems* (New York, 1954), p. 239.

whose attitudes were in conscious distinction from those of the old morality. Again, the *moderni*, the modern thinkers in the late Middle Ages, were those who advocated and embraced the new logic of that time and whose attitudes were thought to be dangerous to the established order; it was later said that they caused the Reformation.

The modern poet, then, is modern only in the light of tradition, only as distinguished from the old. His forms, his models, his subjects, and his attitudes are different from and in opposition to the customary and expected forms, models, subjects, and attitudes of his own youth and of his readers. Consequently to be modern depends on a tradition to be different from, upon the firm existence of customary expectations to be disappointed. The new is parasitic upon the old. But when the new has itself become the old, it has lost its quality of newness and modernity and must shift for itself.

This is the situation with respect to what is still called modern poetry; it is rapidly becoming the old and the traditional. There appeared some years ago a number of articles in the leading conventional journals of this country in defense of modern poetry. Had the poetry still needed defense, the articles would never have been accepted by the editors of those journals. But modern poetry is, in fact, in secure possession of the field, and its heroes are aged men with a long public career behind them. Wallace Stevens, in fact, died recently at the age of seventy-six after a public career of forty years. Yet the attitude of modernity still persists. These poets still represent to the young writer of today the new, the adventurous, the advance-guard, the untried. Their names are still sacred to the initiate.

For it is the condition of modernity in art that it appeal to the initiate, that it provoke the opposition of the ordinary reader who has the customary and old expectations which it is the purpose of modern art to foil. Hence it lives in an attitude of defense; is close and secret, not open and hearty; has its private ritual and its air of priesthood —*odi profanum vulgus et arceo,* "I despise the uninitiated crowd, and I keep them at a distance." It is obscure, and its obscurities are largely calculated; it is intended to be impenetrable to the vulgar. More than this, it is intended to exasperate them.

There is something of this in all art that is genuine. For the genuine in art is that which attains distinction, and the distinguished is uncommon and not accessible to the many. It is different, it must be different, and as such provokes the hostility of the many, and provokes it the more in that its difference is a claim to distinction, to prestige, and to exclusion. This claim is diminished by time. Wordsworth is now regarded as quite traditional, quite stuffy and conventional. For the particular qualities of difference in an older body of poetry that has been absorbed into the tradition become part of that tradition, and so something that the reader actually need not see since he does not know it is different. He may then in his early years and through his school days develop a set of social responses to the received body of poetry; he may enjoy that poetry without effort, be pleased by his conditioned responses, and think of himself as a lover and judge of poetry. When the audience for poetry becomes satisfied with a customary response to a customary poem, when they demand of the poet that he write to their expectations, when distinction is lost in commonness, there is need for the modern in art, for a poetry that is consciously different, even if it often mistakes difference for distinction. The poet must exasperate his reader, or succumb to him.

Such was the situation out of which Stevens wrote, at least as it seemed to him and to those of his contemporaries who have become the aged fathers of modern poetry. They sought to appear different, and hence distinguished, and they succeeded perhaps too well. The first thing that strikes the reader of Wallace Stevens, and the quality for which he was for a long time best known, is the piquant, brilliant, and odd surface of his poems. They are full of nonsense cries, full of virtuoso lines, such as

> Chieftain Iffucan of Azcan in caftan
> Of tan with henna hackles, halt! [2]

which unexpectedly make grammar and sense if you read them slowly with closed ears. They are thronged with exotic place-names, but not the customary ones of late romantic poetry; instead of "Quinquereme of Nineveh from distant Ophir" there is "a woman of Lhassa," there is Yucatan. Rare birds fly, "the green toucan," and tropical fruits abound, especially the pineapple. Odd characters appear —Crispin, Redwood Roamer, Babroulbadour, black Sly,

---

[2] "Bantams in Pine-Woods," p. 75.

Nanzia Nunzio—and are addressed in various languages —my semblables, Nino, ephebi, o iuventes, o filii. And they wear strange hats.

A good deal of this, of course, is simply the unexpected in place of the expected; a new and different collection of proper names, for example, instead of the old collection, but used largely for the same purpose while seeming to deny this by being designedly different.

> Canaries in the morning, orchestras
> In the afternoon, balloons at night. That is
> A difference, at least, from nightingales,
> Jehovah, and the great sea-worm.[3]

The process is common in Stevens, and can be seen neatly in one of his most engaging stanzas. The theme of the stanza is the traditional one of Tom Nashe's

> Brightness falls from the hair,
> Queens have died young and fair.

But instead of Helen and Iseult there are references to the beauties in Utamaro's drawings and to the eighteenth century belles of Bath:

> Is it for nothing, then, that old Chinese
> Sat titivating by their mountain pools
> Or in the Yangtse studied out their beards?
> I shall not play the flat historic scale.
> You know how Utamaro's beauties sought
> The end of love in their all-speaking braids.
> You know the mountainous coiffures of Bath.
> Alas! Have all the barbers lived in vain
> That not one curl in nature has survived?[4]

A woman's hair is here used as a synecdoche for her beauty. Have all those who have cared for and cherished her hair, have all the barbers, lived in vain, that though much has survived in art, none has survived in nature? The poet concludes then, expressing the sense of the couplet of a Shakespearean sonnet:

> This thought is as a death, which cannot choose
> But weep to have that which it fears to lose.

[3] "Academic Discourse at Havana," p. 142.
[4] "Le Monocle de Mon Oncle," p. 14.

in the more specialized terms of his synecdoche, but almost as movingly:

> Why, without pity on these studious ghosts
> Do you come dripping in your hair from sleep?

Much of this is rather amusing, and even, as we say
now, intriguing. Sometimes, indeed, it is much more than
that, as in the stanza just quoted which is poetry of a rare
though too precious kind. But Wallace Stevens had a
public career in poetry for forty years, and forty years is a
little too long for this sort of pepper to retain its sharpness
and piquancy. We have to ask, then, what is the motive
and purpose in this?

It is usually said that these aspects of Stevens' work derive from a study of the French poets of the latter nineteenth century, the Symbolists and Parnassians, and this
explanation no doubt is true enough. But it is not a sufficient explanation. The prestige of that poetry was not so
high in Stevens' youth as to serve as a motive, though it
might be sufficient now. The motive is rather a more
human one. It is disdain—disdain of the society and of the
literary tradition in which he grew up, of himself as a part
of that society, and of his readers so far as they belonged
to it. He sought, he tells us:

> when all is said, to drive away
> The shadow of his fellows from the skies,
> And, from their stale intelligence released,
> To make a new intelligence prevail.

How did he go about it? He celebrated the rankest trivia
in the choicest diction. He was a master of the traditional
splendors of poetry and refused to exercise his mastery in
the traditional way; he displayed it in the perverse, the
odd:

> he humbly served
> Grotesque apprenticeship to chance event . . .

He became "a clown" though "an aspiring clown." In his
own summary, in the passage that immediately follows the
lines quoted above, he explains:

> Hence the reverberations in the words
> Of his first central hymns, the celebrants

Of rankest trivia, tests of the strength
Of his aesthetic, his philosophy,
The more invidious, the more desired.
The florist asking aid from cabbages,
The rich man going bare, the paladin
Afraid, the blind man as astronomer,
The appointed power unwielded from disdain.[5]

He possessed "the appointed power"—the Miltonic and
Scriptural phrasing is blasphemous in this context, and
deliberately so—but would not wield it from disdain. The
question then is: Why should he have felt such disdain?
The answer can be collected from various of his poems
but is given full and detailed exposition in the one from
which I have just quoted. This is "The Comedian as the
Letter C," the show-piece and longest poem in his first
book. The poem is sufficiently complex to have several
centers of concern. I shall intepret it, however, in terms
of our question, and we shall find that this will turn out to
be a primary concern of the poem.

The poem consists of six sections, each of a little under
a hundred lines of blank verse. It is in form and subject a
poem that depicts the growth of a poet's mind, and though
the main character is given the fictitious name of Crispin,
he may be taken as an aspect of the author, a mask for
Wallace Stevens the poet, so that the poem in effect is autobiographical. It belongs, then, to that literary form of
which the model and prototype is Wordsworth's *Prelude*.
It is not a wholly easy poem to read, partly because much
of it is written in Stevens' fastidious and disdainful manner, partly because its structure is not adequately adjusted
to its theme. The hero of the poem makes a sea voyage to
a strange and exotic country, in this case Yucatan, and
back to his own land. The motive for the voyage is explicitly given late in the poem in the passage already quoted:

What was the purpose of his pilgrimage,
Whatever shape it took in Crispin's mind,
If not, when all is said, to drive away
The shadow of his fellows from the skies,
And, from their stale intelligence released,
To make a new intelligence prevail?

His voyage is a rejection of his society as banal and trite,
of its intelligence as stale, and his quest is the quest of a

5 "The Comedian as the Letter C," IV, pp. 37, 39, 37.

new intelligence. His problem was the problem that every teacher of freshman composition sets his better students, the problem of striking through routine phrasing and syntax to the genuine, the honest, the possibly distinguished.

The hero is portrayed as having been before this trip a man who was master of his environment, but he was a little man, "the Socrates of snails," "this nincompated pedagogue," and the environment itself was trivial; it was a land "of simple saladbeds, of honest quilts." It was, in fact, to quote Stevens' own summary of his early environment in an essay of later date, "the comfortable American state of life of the 'eighties, the 'nineties, and the first ten years of the present century." [6] It was the time and place when the sun

> shone
> with bland complaisance on pale parasols,
> Beetled, in chapels, on the chaste bouquets.

It was that middle class culture of business, public chastity, and official Christianity which we often call, with some historical injustice, Victorianism. In this world Crispin wrote the conventional poetry of the times. He was one

> that saw
> The stride of vanishing autumn in a park
> By way of decorous melancholy . . .
> That wrote his couplet yearly to the spring,
> As dissertation of profound delight . . .

However, he found that

> He could not be content with counterfeit . . .

It was this dissatisfaction with the conventional—in society and in poetry—"That first drove Crispin to his wandering." He alludes to it as "The drenching of stale lives," a life of "ruses" that was shattered by the experience of his voyage.

He found the sea overwhelming; he "was washed away by magnitude." "Here was no help before reality." It was not so much that he was cut off from the snug land; he was cut off from his old self:

---

[6] *The Necessary Angel* (New York, 1951), p. 26.

> What counted was mythology of self,
> Blotched out beyond unblotching.

and hence from his environment. He was destitute and bare:

> The salt hung on his spirit like a frost,
> The dead brine melted in him like a dew
> Of winter, until nothing of himself
> Remained, except some starker, barer self
> In a starker, barer world . . .

From this experience he came to Yucatan. The poetasters of that land, like the poetasters at home, in spite of the vividness of experience around them

> In spite of hawk and falcon, green toucan
> And jay . . .

still wrote conventional verses about the nightingale, as if their environment were uncivilized. But Crispin's conversion at sea—for it was obviously a conversion—had enlarged him, made him complicated

> and difficult and strange
> In all desires . . .

until he could reduce his tension only by writing an original and personal poetry, different and unconventional.

The experience at sea is now reinforced by another experience in Yucatan, of the same elemental, overwhelming sort:

> one
> Of many proclamations of the kind,
> Proclaiming something harsher than he learned

from the commonplace realism of home:

> From hearing signboards whimper in cold nights.

It was rather "the span / Of force, the quintessential fact,"

> The thing that makes him envious in a phrase.

It was the experience that altered and reinvigorated his poetry, the source from which he drew that distinction of

style that marks off his published work from the sentimental verses he had printed in the college magazine some
twenty years before. The experience was of the type of a
religious experience:

> His mind was free
> And more than free, elate, intent, profound
> And studious of a self possessing him,
> That was not in him in the crusty town
> From which he sailed.

The poetry he now wrote issued from this context. It
was conditioned by the kind of dissatisfaction that drove
Crispin to his wandering, by such an experience as Crispin's on the voyage and in Yucatan, and by its results.
This dissatisfaction lies behind a good many of Stevens'
poems, which deal, if one looks beneath the distracting
surface, simply with the opposition between the aridities of
middle-class convention and the vivid alertness of the unconventional, as in "Disillusionment at Ten O'clock."
Some repeat in smaller compass and with other properties
the subject of "The Comedian", as "The Doctor of Ge-
neva." In others he attempts to deal directly with the experience of the sea, but this was a religious experience
without the content of traditional religion. In fact, it had
no content at all beyond the intuition of a bare reality behind conventional appearance, and hence was an unfertile
subject for poetry since it was unproductive of detail. He
treated it in one of his best short poems "The Snow Man,"
but when he had stated it, there was nothing more to be
done with it, except to say it over again in another place.
This he has repeatedly done, though with a prodigality of
invention in phrasing that is astounding.

Most of what is interesting in Stevens issues from this
problem. It can be put in various terms. It is the problem
of traditional religion and modern life, of imagination and
reality, but it can be best put for Stevens in the terms in
which it is explicitly put in "The Comedian." The problem
is the relationship of a man and his environment, and the
reconciliation of these two in poetry and thus in life. The
two terms of this relationship are really Wordsworth's two
terms: the one, what the eye and ear half create; the
other, what they perceive. The reconciliation in Wordsworth is in a religious type of experience:

With what strange utterance did the loud dry wind
Blow through my ear! the sky seemed not a sky
Of earth—and with what motion moves the clouds!

Dust as we are, the immortal spirit grows
Like harmony in music; there is a dark
Inscrutable workmanship that reconciles
Discordant elements, makes them cling together
In one society.[7]

The reconciliation in Stevens is sought in poetry, in

> those
> True reconcilings, dark, pacific words,
> And the adroiter harmonies of their fall.

For poetry is the supreme fiction of which religion is a manifestation:

> Poetry
>
> Exceeding music must take the place
> Of empty heaven and its hymns,
>
> Ourselves in poetry must take their place . . .

What Crispin is seeking is such a reconciliation, a oneness between himself and his environment. He began in the illusion that he was the intelligence of his soil, but the experience of reality overwhelmed him, and he came to believe that his soil was his intelligence. At this extreme he wrote poems in which a person is described by his surroundings. But he perceived that this too was sentimental, and so he settled for the ordinary reality of daily life, married, had four daughters, and prospered. However, he did not give up poetry entirely; he recorded his adventures in the poem, and hoped that the reader would take it as he willed: as a summary

> strident in itself
> But muted, mused, and perfectly revolved
> In those portentous accents, syllables,

---

[7] *Prelude,* 1.337-44.
[8] "Academic Discourse at Havana," IV, p. 144; "The Man with the Blue Guitar," V, p. 167.

> And sounds of music coming to accord
> Upon his law, like their inherent sphere,
> Seraphic proclamations of the pure
> Delivered with a deluging onwardness.

Such is Stevens' account of the source of his distinctive style and distinctive subjects. But he owed more than he acknowledged to the old and the traditional. He owed "the appointed power" which was "unwielded from disdain."

That he once had the appointed power is clear in his greatest poem, and one of his earliest, "Sunday Morning." [9] The poem is traditional in meter—it is in eight equal stanzas of blank verse—and has as its subject a deep emotional attachment to traditional Christianity and a rejection of Christianity in favor of the clear and felt apprehension of sensory detail in this life, together with an attempt to preserve in the new setting the emotional aspects of the old values.

The poem depicts a woman having late breakfast on a Sunday morning, when of course she should have been at church. She is for the moment at one with her surroundings, which are vivid, sensory, familiar, and peaceful. All this serves to dissipate the traditional awe of Christian feeling, but the old feeling breaks through:

> She dreams a little, and she feels the dark
> Encroachment of that old catastrophe,
> As a calm darkens among water-lights.

Her mood "is like wide water, without sound," and in that mood she passes over the seas to the contemplation of the Resurrection. The remainder of the poem consists of the poet's comment and argument on her situation, on two short utterances she delivers out of her musing, and finally on the revelation that comes to her in a voice.

The poet asserts that Christianity is a religion of the dead and the unreal. In this living world of the sun, in these vivid and sensory surroundings, there is that which can assume the values of heaven:

> Divinity must live within herself:
> Passions of rain, or moods in falling snow;
> Grievings in loneliness, or unsubdued
> Elations when the forest blooms; gusty
> Emotions on wet roads on autumn nights;
> All pleasures and all pains, remembering
> The bough of summer and the winter branch,
> These are the measures destined for her soul.

9 pp. 66-70.

The truly divine is the human and personal in this world: it consists in the association of feeling with the perception of natural landscape, in human pleasure and pain, in change, as in the change of seasons.

He then argues that the absolute God of religion was originally inhuman, but that the Incarnation by mingling our blood with His, by mingling the relative and human with the Absolute, satisfied man's innate desires for a human and unabsolute Absolute. Certainly, if "the earth" should "Seem all of paradise that we shall know," we would be much more at home in our environment:

> The sky will be much friendlier then than now . . .
> Not this dividing and indifferent blue.

At this point the woman speaks in her musing, and says that she could acquiesce in this world, that she could find an earthly paradise, a contentment, in the perception of Nature, in the feel of reality, except that the objects of her perception change and disappear. Nature is an impermanent paradise. The poet, however, answers that no myth of a religious afterworld has been or ever will be as permanent as the stable recurrences of Nature:

> There is not any haunt of prophesy,
> Nor any old chimera of the grave,
> Neither the golden underground, nor isle
> Melodious, where spirits gat them home,
> Nor visionary south, nor cloudy palm
> Remote on heaven's hill, that has endured
> As April's green endures; or will endure
> Like her remembrance of awakened birds,
> Or her desire for June and evening, tipped
> By the consummation of the swallow's wings.

The woman speaks again, and says:

> "But in contentment I still feel
> The need of some imperishable bliss."

There remains the desire for the eternal happiness of tradition. The lines that comment on this present some difficulties to interpretation until it is seen that the poet in his answer proceeds by developing the woman's position. Yes, he says, we feel that only in death is there fulfillment of our illusions and our desires. Even though death be in fact the obliteration of all human experience, yet it is attractive to us; it has the fatal attractiveness of the willow in old poetry for the love-lorn maiden. Though she has lovers who bring her gifts—that is, the earth and its beauty—she disregards the lovers and, tasting of the gifts, strays impassioned toward death.

Yet the paradise she would achieve in death is nothing but an eternal duplicate of this world, and lacking even the principle of change, leads only to ennui. Therefore, the poet creates a secular myth, a religion of his irreligion. The central ceremony is a chant, a poem to the sun,

> Not as a god, but as a god might be . . .

It is an undivine fiction that preserves the emotions of the old religion but attaches them to a poetry in which the sensory objects of a natural landscape enter into a union in celebration of the mortality of men:

> And whence they came and whither they shall go
> The dew upon their feet shall manifest.

The biblical phrasing creates a blasphemous religion of mortality.

The poem now concludes with a revelation. Out of the woman's mood a voice cries to her, saying that the place of the Resurrection is merely the place where a man died and not a persisting way of entry into a spiritual world. The poet continues:

> We live in an old chaos of the sun,
> Or old dependency of day and night,
> Or island solitude, unsponsored, free,
> Of that wide water, inescapable.
> Deer walk upon our mountains, and the quail
> Whistle about us their spontaneous cries;
> Sweet berries ripen in the wilderness;
> And, in the isolation of the sky,
> At evening, casual flocks of pigeons make
> Ambiguous undulations as they sink,
> Downward to darkness, on extended wings.

We live, in fact, in a universe suggested by natural science, whose principle is change, an island without religious sponsor, free of the specific Christian experience. It is a sensory world, it has its delights, its disorder, and it is mortal.

The poem is an argument against the traditional Chris-

tianity of Stevens' youth, and especially against the doctrine and expectation of immortality, in favor of an
earthly and mortal existence that in the felt apprehension
of sensory detail can attain a vivid oneness with its surroundings and a religious sense of union comparable to
the traditional feeling. The former is undeniably traditional, and much of the deep feeling of the poem is derived
from the exposition in sustained and traditional rhetoric of
the position which is being denied. In this sense it is parasitic on what it rejects. But the positive argument is almost
as traditional in the history of English poetry and in the
literary situation of Stevens' youth: it is, with the important difference of a hundred years and the denial of immortality, Wordsworthian in idea, in detail, in feeling, and
in rhetoric. Passages comparable to the appositive enumer-
ation of details of natural landscape associated with human
feeling, as in

> Passions of rain, and moods in falling snow;
> Grievings in loneliness, or unsubdued elations
> When the forest blooms . . .

are scattered throughout Wordsworth's poetry, especially
through the blank verse. I have already quoted a short
passage; let me quote another:

> What want we? have we not perpetual streams,
> Warm woods, and sunny hills, and fresh green fields,
> And mountains not less green, and flocks and herds,
> And thickets full of songsters, and the voice
> Of lordly birds, an unexpected sound
> Heard now and then from morn to latest eve,
> Admonishing the man who walks below
> Of solitude and silence in the sky?

The movement of the verse is Stevens', the syntax, and
the relation of syntax to the line-ends. The kind of detail
is the same. And the idea, if one reads it out of the specific context of Wordsworth's system, is Stevens' idea; for the
passage in isolation says, What does man need, what need
he desire, more than a live appreciation of the detail of
natural landscape, for the world beyond, the birds admon-
ish us—or, Nature tells us—is a world of solitude and silence. This is not precisely what Wordsworth would have
endorsed, but certainly what a young man who was
drenched in Wordsworth could make of it. And as he read
on in the poem—it is "The Recluse"—he would come to

the rhetoric of one of his greatest stanzas and the theme
of his greatest poem: he would read in Wordsworth:

> Paradise, and groves
> Elysian, Fortunate fields,—like those of old
> Sought on the Atlantic Main—why should they be
> A history only of departed things,
> Or a mere fiction of what never was?
> For the discerning intellect of Man,
> When wedded to this goodly universe
> In love and holy passion, shall find these
> The simple produce of the common day.[10]

and he would write:

> There is not any haunt of prophesy,
> Nor any old chimera of the grave . . .

The central concern of Stevens' poetry, the concern that
underlay Crispin's voyage and the poet's meditative argument with the woman in "Sunday Morning," as well as
most of the more or less curious divergencies of his career,
is a concern to be at peace with his surroundings, with this
world, and with himself. He requires for this an experience of the togetherness of himself and Nature, an inter-
penetration of himself and his environment, along with
some intuition of permanence in the experience of absoluteness, though this be illusory and transitory, something
to satisfy the deeply engrained longings of his religious
feeling. Now, there is an experience depicted from time to
time in the romantic tradition—it is common in Wordsworth—and one that has perhaps occurred to each of us
in his day, a human experience of absoluteness, when we
and our surroundings are not merely related but one,
when "joy is its own security." It is a fortuitous experience; it cannot be willed into being, or contrived at need.
It is a transitory experience; it cannot be stayed in its
going or found when it is gone. Yet though fortuitous and
transitory, it has in its moment of being all the persuasion
of permanence; it seems—and perhaps in its way it is—a
fulfillment of the Absolute:

> It is and it
> Is not and, therefore, is. In the instant of speech,
> The breadth of an accelerando moves,
> Captives the being, widens—and was there. [11]

[10] Lines 126-33 and 800-8.
[11] "A Primitive Like an Orb," II, p. 440.

Stevens attempted to will it into being. He constructed a series of secular myths, like the one in "Sunday Morning," that affirm the traditional religious feeling of the nobility and unity of experience, but the myths remain unconvincing and arbitrary, and conclude in grotesqueries that betray the poet's own lack of belief in his invention, as in "A Primitive Like an Orb," in which he evokes:

> A giant, on the horizon, glistening,
>
> And in bright excellence adorned, crested
> With every prodigal, familiar fire,
> And unfamiliar escapades: whiroos
> And scintillent sizzlings such as children like,
> Vested in the serious folds of majesty . . .

For, as he asks in an earlier poem:

> But if
> It is the absolute why must it be
> This immemorial grandoise, why not
> A cockle-shell, a trivial emblem great
> With its final force, a thing invincible
> In more than phrase? [12]

He has attempted to contrive it by a doctrine of metaphor and resemblances, which is precisely Wordsworth's doctrine of affinities. He has sought to present in a poem any set of objects and to affirm a resemblance and togetherness between them, but all the reader can see is the objects and the affirmation, as in "Three Academic Pieces," where a pineapple on a table becomes:

> 1. The hut stands by itself beneath the palms.
> 2. Out of their bottle the green genii come.
> 3. A vine has climbed the other side of the wall . . .
>
> These casual exfoliations are
> Of the tropic of resemblance . . .[13]

But there is a poem in "Transport to Summer," one of the perfect poems, as far as my judgment goes, in his later work, that achieves and communicates this experience. It is a short poem in couplets entitled "The House Was Quiet and the World Was Calm." There is no fiddle-dee-dee

[12] "Life on a Battleship," *Opus Posthumus,* ed. Samuel French Morse (New York, 1957), p. 79.
[13] *The Necessary Angel,* p. 86.

here. The setting is ordinary, not exotic. It is about a man reading alone, late at night. The phrasing is exact and almost unnoticeable. The style is bare, less rich than "Sunday Morning," but with this advantage over that poem, that none of its effect is drawn from forbidden sources, from what is rejected. The meter is a loosened iambic pentameter, but loosened firmly and as a matter of course, almost as if it were speech becoming meter rather than meter violated. It has in fact the stability of a new metrical form attained out of the inveterate violation of the old. It is both modern and traditional:

> The house was quiet and the world was calm.
> The reader became the book; and summer night
>
> Was like the conscious being of the book.
> The house was quiet and the world was calm.
>
> The words were spoken as if there was no book,
> Except that the reader leaned above the page,
>
> Wanted to lean, wanted much most to be
> The scholar to whom his book is true, to whom
>
> The summer night is like the perfection of thought.
> The house was quiet because it had to be.
>
> The quiet was part of the meaning, part of the mind:
> The access of perfection to the page.
>
> And the world was calm. The truth in a calm world,
> In which there is no other meaning, itself
>
> Is calm, itself is summer and night, itself
> Is the reader leaning late and reading there.[14]

14 pp. 358-9.

Yeats and Irish Politics

BY CONOR CRUISE O'BRIEN

It must be agreed that whatever one might demonstrate about Yeats the political man would not and could not detract in any way from the greatness of his poetry. Supposing we were to demonstrate, for example, that Yeats was in politics a Fascist; this would not diminish his stature as a poet. Therefore, I think it is not necessary to say or imply, as so many critics and admirers of Yeats have, that he took a passing, fleeting interest in Fascism. He took an interest in Fascism which began with the march on Rome and ended with his death and I don't think it could be less fleeting than that. In biographies as in literary histories, we too often find, instead of the complexities of actual political conjunctures, a generalized "political background" lacking the texture and the weight of real politics. It is often assumed, I think, that this does not matter much in the case of a writer like Yeats because his politics, if they existed, were probably rather vague and generalized themselves. In what follows I shall present some reasons for believing that Yeats's politics were less vague than is commonly supposed.

At the bottom of it all was the Anglo-Irish predicament. It's not ever quite enough to speak of Yeats as an Irish poet; I think the Anglo-Irish has to be made clear. The Irish Protestant stock from which Yeats came was no longer in his youth a ruling class but it was still a superior caste and thought of itself in this way. When he wrote towards the end of his life of "the caste system that had saved the intellect of India," [1] he was almost certainly thinking not so much of India as of Ireland. His people, as

---

Reprinted by permission of the author. A fuller treatment of the same theme by the same author appears in the Macmillan Centenary Volume, *In Excited Reverie* (1965), under the title "Passion and Cunning: An essay on the politics of W.B. Yeats."

[1] On The Boiler

is universal with the descendants of conquerors, were in the habit of looking down on their Catholic neighbors— the majority of those among whom they lived. This habit was imparted to Yeats early and I don't think he ever did quite lose it. But when he went to school in England Yeats was to find, as Parnell and others had found before him, that this distinction had lost much of its validity. Unsophisticated Englishmen made no more distinction between Protestant Irish and Catholic Irish than they did between Bramin and Untouchable. The Irish were known by their brogue—which in Yeats's case must have been quite marked at this stage—and the Irish were all comic, inferior and mad (among the sophisticated classes these same categories found gentler nuances: witty, impractical, imaginative). The Irish Protestant thus acquired two basic bits of information: the important thing about him in relation to Ireland was that he was a Protestant; in relation to England, that he was an Irishman.

For proud and sensitive natures, exposed at this period to the English view of the Irish, a political reaction was predictable, starting from the premises: "I, an Irishman, am as good as any Englishman. Ireland is therefore as good as England. Yet England governs herself; Ireland is governed by England. Can this be right?" Parnell thought not; Yeats's father thought not; Yeats thought not.

It used to be widely assumed, especially in Ireland, that Yeats became entangled in politics by Maude Gonne. This is of course wrong; Yeats had been drawn into politics before he ever heard of Maude Gonne, and the most active phases of his political life were to come after he had quarreled with Maude Gonne. Yeats entered politics under the influence of John O'Leary, the Fenian convict and exile who returned to Ireland in 1884. Yeats now became what he was to remain all his life—as he was to repeat towards the end—"a nationalist of the school of John O'Leary." The school of John O'Leary was one of radical and uncompromising Irish republicanism. But at this time the circle was somewhat inactive because of O'Leary's concept that the thing to do was to prepare for a rising which was necessarily remote. And of course this was what the Irish Republican Brotherhood to which Yeats adhered—though he never seems to have taken the oath—was doing during these years. His involvement no doubt became intensified after his meeting with Maude Gonne but I doubt if one could trace much specific political influence there. Maude

Gonne, for example, became drawn into the Agrarian Movement which was one of the most active groups at that time. But Yeats, with his aristocratic concept and his sense of belonging to a superior caste, never joined in that. His active political involvement, as distinct from his rather passive association with John O'Leary, came not as a result of his association with Maude Gonne; it came a little later at the time of the death of Parnell in 1891.

The fall and death of Parnell had a powerful impact on him. "The modern literature of Ireland," Yeats told the Swedish Academy in 1925, "and indeed all that stir of thought which prepared for the Anglo-Irish War began when Parnell fell from power in 1891. A disillusioned and embittered Ireland turned from parliamentary politics; an event was conceived and the race began, as I think, to be troubled by that event's long gestation." [2] Elsewhere he speaks of four bells, four deep, tragic notes in Irish history, the first being the war that ended with the flight of the earls in 1603, the fourth being the death of Parnell in 1891. "I heard the first note of the fourth bell forty years ago on a stormy October morning. I had gone to Kingston Pier to meet the Mail Boat that arrived about 6 a.m. I was expecting a friend, but met what I thought much less of at the time, the body of Parnell." [3] On Parnell's death Yeats entered immediately into an active form of propaganda and politics. On the day of the funeral he published, in what had been Parnell's paper, an Elegy on Parnell. It is a rather bad poem which he never reprinted, called "Mourn and Then Onward!" but it certainly brought him to the attention of the Irish Nationalist public and he retained that attention during the next decade or so and even more. In fact he never wholly lost it.

At a later time, when the fighting started, a phrase used to be used with ironic overtones. It used to be said of somebody who was verbally very revolutionary, "X, you know, is on the literary side of the movement." But during the 1890s, and the early 1900s the literary side of the movement was the only side that was moving and Yeats was doing most of the leading and the moving of it. This

[2] Lecture on accepting the Nobel Prize. Text in *Autobiographies*, p. 559.
[3] Commentary on the poem "Parnell's Funeral." Text in Allt and Alspach, *The Variorum Edition of W. B. Yeats*, p. 834.

phase of his career, of course, culminated in 1902 with the production of *Cathleen Ni Houlihan* with Maude Gonne as Cathleen. This was the play which so moved people that P. S. O'Hagerty spoke of it as "A sort of sacrament" [4] to the men of his generation and Stephen Gwynn said of it, "I went home asking myself if such plays should be produced unless one was prepared for people to go out to shoot and be shot." [5] And this, of course, came back to Yeats towards the end of his days when he examined his mind on the question:

> "Did that play of mine send out
> Certain men the English shot?" [6]

In 1903 there occurred an important event, Maude Gonne's marriage; and it was at this time Yeats broke with active Nationalist politics. After the curtain fell on *Cathleen Ni Houlihan* in 1902 it could fairly be said that Yeat's work for the Irish revolution had been accomplished. The poet—having acquired in his political years an audience and the dramatic society that was about to become the Abbey Theatre—now turned aside from Irish politics. He did not cease—he never ceased—to be an Irish Nationalist but his nationalism now became aristocratic and archaizing, instead of being popular and active. Aristocratic nationalism was not, in Ireland, practical politics because the aristocracy was almost entirely Unionist, that is to say anti-national. This did not matter to Yeats who had enough, for the moment, of practical politics. In his new aristocratism he was releasing a part of his personality which he had been forced to try to suppress during the years of political activity. In these years the Irish Protestant had necessarily emphasized his Irishness, minimizing or denying the separate and distinct tradition which the word Protestant implies. The Protestant now re-emerged with an audible sigh of relief. It had been stuffy in there, and getting stuffier. During this period, from 1903 to about 1906, there is in his work an increasing note of impatience and distaste for the rising Catholic middle class. He disliked this class doubly. He disliked

---

[4] "W. B. Yeats and the Revolutionary Ireland of his Time" in *The Dublin Magazine*, July-Sept. 1939
[5] Quoted in A. N. Jeffares, *W. B. Yeats*, p. 138
[6] "The Man and The Echo" 11. 11-12.

them as a member of his own class, the Irish Protestant middle class, and he also disliked them for their Philistinism and for many other disagreeable qualities. Concerning them he wrote in the culminating poem on that particular subject, "September 1913."

> "What need you, being come to sense,
> But fumble in a greasy till
> And add the halfpence to the pence
> And prayer to shivering prayer, until
> You have dried the marrow from the bone?
> For men were born to pray and save:
> Romantic Ireland's dead and gone,
> It's with O'Leary in the grave." [7]

The alliance of savings and prayers is a good symbolic definition of the rising Catholic middle class.

Most of the leaders who planned the rising which proved—three years later—that romantic Ireland was not yet dead and gone, belonged to the general class which Yeats distrusted; not to the most climbing and aggressive of it but to the "clerks and shopkeepers" whom he often thought of as "the base"; they included the basest of the base—from Yeats's point of view—Major McBride himself who had married Maude Gonne. They had all been engaged for years in the kind of politics on which he had turned his back. But in 1916 they were shot by the English:

> "All changed, changed utterly
> A terrible beauty is born."

The poems, "Easter 1916," "Sixteen Dead Men," "The Rose Tree," and "On a Political Prisoner" drew strength from the complexity as well as the intensity of the emotions involved—the sense—which became explicit years after—of his own share in the "gestation" of the event; the presence in the event of the strongest love and the strongest personal hatred of his life; an old hate, and even a kind of disgust, for much of what the insurrection meant,

> "Blind and leader of the blind
> Drinking the foul ditch where they lie" [8]

an even older and deeper hate for those who crushed the

[7] "September 1913" 11. 1-8.
[8] "On a Political Prisoner" 11. 11-12

insurrection; and finally, a prophetic sense of the still more bitter struggle yet to come:

> "But who can talk of give and take
> What should be and what not
> While those dead men are loitering there
> To stir the boiling pot?" [9]

By the time these poems were published in the Autumn of 1920 the pot had boiled over and the Black and Tan war was in full swing. It was a bold act to publish them. It was known in 1920 that Ireland was going to get some form of self-government. If the Rebels were beaten it would be the home rule (with partition) of the British Act of 1920. If the Rebels won, it would be the Republic proclaimed in 1916. The two poems that Yeats chose to publish covered, as it happened, both eventualities neatly. The spirit of the Proclamation of the Republic was in them:

> " 'But where can we draw water'
> Said Pearse to Connolly
> 'When all the wells are parched away
> As plain as plain can be
> There's nothing but our own red blood
> Can make a right rose tree' "[10]

But there are also in them the doubts and reservations which most Irishmen had felt about the Proclamation of 1916: the doubts and reservations of those for whom home rule and the Act of 1920 represented an acceptable settlement:

> "Was it needless death, after all?
> For England may keep faith
> For all that is done and said.
> We know their dream; enough
> To know they dreamed and are dead;
> And what if excess of love
> Bewildered them until they died" [11]

In the event, the Anglo-Irish Treaty brought to Ireland the realities of the Act of 1920 with some of the trappings of 1916. This treaty set up, not the Republic proclaimed in

[9] "Sixteen Dead Men" 11. 3-6
[10] "The Rose Tree" 11.13-18
[11] "Easter 1916" 11. 67-72

1916, but a Free State within the Empire and without the six counties of the northeast. Many of those who had been fighting felt that this was a betrayal, as Yeats's Pearce and Connolly might have felt:

> "Maybe a breath of politic words
> Has withered our rose tree."

Those who felt in this way tried to reject the treaty and carry on the struggle. The majority of the people, tired of war, had voted, in effect, for the acceptance of the treaty and the Free State Government began liquidating the people who did not accept the treaty. At this time Yeats accepted a seat in the Senate from the Cosgrave government which had just put down the other side in the Civil War using the means which were probably necessary for that purpose and were certainly ruthless and harsh. Yeats was now an established public figure and he was soberly pleased about his political position and prospects. "We," he wrote of himself and his fellow Senators, "are a fairly distinguished body and should get much government into our hands." [12] His political options were now explicitly reactionary: "Out of all this murder and rapine," he wrote in 1922, "will come not a demagogic but an authoritarian government." [13] and again: "Everywhere one notices a drift towards Conservatism, perhaps towards Autocracy." [14] His ideas for Ireland were explicitly linked with the rise of fascism in Europe. "We are preparing here, behind our screens of bombs and smoke, a return to conservative politics as elsewhere in Europe, or at least to a substitution of the historical sense for logic. The return will be painful and perhaps violent but many educated men talk of it and must soon work for it and perhaps riot for it. . . . The Ireland that reacts from the present disorder is turning its eyes towards individualist Italy." [15] "Individualist Italy" is a curious synonym for Fascist Italy but that is what he was referring to.

One of the major limitations in Yeats's right wing politics in Ireland now came into play. Any right wing govern-

---

[12] To Edmund Dulac, 1 December 1922, in Wade, *The Letters of W. B. Yeats,* p. 694
[13] To Olivia Shakespear, May 1922, *Letters,* p. 682
[14] To the same. October 1922, *Letters,* p. 690
[15] To H. J. C. Grierson, 6 November 1922, *Letters,* p. 693

ment in Ireland that was going to work and any pro-Fascist government that might conceivably have emerged would have needed one thing and that was the support of the Church. And, in fact, the government which Yeats had worked for now became increasingly dependent on clerical support. They no longer needed British artillery which they had used before but they did need their flanks covered by the Canons of the Church. And they were. The clergy, for the degree of support which they supplied, exacted their price, in the form of specifically Catholic legislation from the Parliament of the day. This included legislation on divorce. Most Protestants swallowed this because in most cases their options had now become bourgeois options rather than specifically theological ones. But Yeats was outraged; he denounced the divorce legislation and of course it became clear that his nomination to the Senate would not be renewed. He became at this period a rather isolated figure in politics and remained so until 1932.

The year 1932 was a turning point in Irish political history. In that year the party, led by Mr. Cosgrave, which had won the Civil War and ruled the country since the foundation of the State, fell from power. The party, led by De Valera, which represented the losers in the Civil War, now won a General Election and took over the Government. The respect for democratic process shown by Mr. Cosgrave's Government was, in the circumstances, rather remarkable. It was indeed too remarkable to please many of the members of the fallen party, and some of these now set about organizing a para-military movement, on the Fascist model, for the intimidation of their opponents and the recovery of power. "They have the Blackshirts in Italy," said one of the politicians concerned, "they have the Brownshirts in Germany and now in Ireland we have the Blueshirts."

The picture presented of Yeats's association with this movement—by him, retrospectively, and by other commentators on it—is, I think, in some ways a little misleading. His association is probably best covered, for anyone who wishes to follow it, in the letters which he wrote to Olivia Shakespear, who sympathized with his views at this time. Afterwards, I think, he was rather inclined to minimize the degree of enthusiasm which he did feel for this movement at a given moment. He says in one letter to her, "I find myself constantly urging the despotic rule of the educated classes. . . . I know half a dozen men any one of whom may be Caesar—or Catiline. It is amusing to live in a country where men will always act. Where nobody is satisfied with thought. There is so little in our stocking that we are ready at any moment to turn it inside out and how can we not feel emulous when we see Hitler juggling with his sausage of stocking. Our chosen color is blue and blue shirts are marching about all over the country." [16] And then: "When I wrote to you, the Fascist organizer of the blue-shirts had told me that he was about to bring to see me the man he had selected for leader that I might talk my anti-democratic philosophy. I was ready, for I had just rewritten for the seventh time the part of *A Vision* that deals with the future. The leader turned out to be a Gen[eral] O'Duffy, head of the Irish police for twelve years and a famous organizer. . . . Italy, Poland, Germany then perhaps Ireland. Doubtless I shall hate it (though not so much as I hate Irish democracy) but it is September and we must not behave like the gay young sparks of May or June." [17] He took apparently the view that it was inevitable that this should happen.

And this goes on. The excitement goes on until about September, at which time the government took firm action against the Blue Shirts and the movement began to collapse and Yeats dissociated himself from it. The poem "Church and State" was written at this time and expresses his disillusion with it. It is customary to say that, at this point, Yeats had become disillusioned with Fascism. One may accept this judgment, but must also remark that a principal illusion which had been dissipated was the illusion that Fascism in Ireland stood a good chance of winning. In the spring and summer of 1933 the fascism of the Irish Blueshirts looked to many people like a possible winner and in this phase Yeats was with the Blueshirts. By the autumn and winter of 1933/4, the Government's energetic measures—described by Yeats as "panic measures"—made it clear that De Valera was no von Papen. O'Duffy, failing to devise anything effective in reply, revealed that he was no Hitler. The blue began to fade, and Yeats's interest in it faded proportionally.

Comment on the question of Yeats's attitude to Fascism has been be-deviled I think by the assumption that a great

[16] To Olivia Shakespear, 13 July 1933, *Letters*, pp. 811-812
[17] To The Same, 23 July 1933, *Letters*, pp. 812-813

poet must be, even in politics, "a nice guy." If this be assumed then it follows that, as Yeats obviously was a great poet he cannot really have favored Fascism, which was obviously not a nice cause. Thus the critic or biographer is led to postulate a "true Yeats," so that Yeats's recorded words and actions of Fascist character must have been perpetrated by some bogus person with the same name and outward appearance. If one drops the assumption, about poets having always to be nice in politics, then the puzzle disappears and we see, I believe, that Yeats the man was as near to being a Fascist as the conditions of his own country and class permitted. His unstinted admiration had gone to Kevin O'Higgins, the most ruthless "strong man" of his time in Ireland, and he linked his admiration explicitly to his rejoicing at the rise of Fascism in Europe —and this at the very beginning, within a few days of the March on Rome. Ten years later, after Hitler had moved to the center of the political stage in Europe, Yeats was trying to create a movement in Ireland which would be overtly Fascist in language, costume, behavior and intent. He turned his back on this movement when it began to fail, not before.

Post-war writers, touching with some embarrassment on Yeats's pro-Fascist opinions, have tended to treat these as a curious aberration of an idealistic but ill-informed poet. In fact such opinions were quite usual in his class and in his time and were shared by very many respectable people like Mr. Eliot. Of course, it is said that Yeats was not a Fascist but he was an aristocratic authoritarian; he certainly would have preferred something more strictly aristocratic than Fascism but since he was living in the 20th century he was attracted to Fascism as the best available form of anti-democratic theory and practise. It has been said that Yeats was really closer to Swift or Jefferson than he was to Mussolini but unfortunately Yeats was interested in contemporary politics and he was a contemporary not of Swift's or Jefferson's but of Mussolini's. George Orwell, though critical and up to a point percipient, about Yeats's tendencies, thought that Yeats misunderstood what an authoritarian society would be like. Such a society, Orwell pointed out, "will not be ruled by noblemen with Van Dyke faces, but by anonymous millionaires, shiny-bottomed bureaucrats and murderous gangsters." This implies a degree of innocence in Yeats which cannot reasonably be postulated. Yeats was a man with quite a lot of political avatars. O'Higgins and O'Duffy were not "noblemen with Van Dyke faces," and Yeats had considerable experience of practical politics, both in the " 'nineties" and in the early " 'twenties." When he thought of rule by an elite, it seems to have been a possible elite, resembling in many ways the nominated members of the Senate in which he sat. The membership of that Senate—bankers, organizers, ex-officers—would correspond roughly to what Orwell, in more emotive language, describes.

Yet in challenging the assumption that Yeats's pro-Fascism was either not "truly Yeats" or not "truly pro-Fascist," one must not overlook the intermittent character of his pro-Fascism and of all his political activity. If his pro-Fascism was real, his irony and caution were real too and his phases of detachment were not less real than his phases of political commitment. The long phase of nationalist commitment (1887-1903) was followed by a long phase (1903-1916) of detachment from almost all practical politics, by a critique of Irish nationalist politics, and by the formation of an aristocratic attitude which did not find practical political expression until after 1916 when—after a new flare-up of nationalist feeling—he re-entered Irish politics on the right, in the Free State Senate. After clerical pressures had made the Senate uncongenial to him and had extruded him from it, he withdrew again from active politics (1928-33) only returning when a situation propitious to Fascism seemed to present itself. When O'Duffy's Irish Fascists failed ignominiously he turned away from politics again. And always, in these long phases of withdrawal he tended to write of all politics with a kind of contempt, a plague-on-both-your-houses air. He wrote to Ethel Mannin, "If I did what you want I would seem to hold one form of government more responsible than any other and that would betray my convictions. Communist, Fascist nationalist, clerical, anti-clerical, are all responsible according to the number of their victims."

This was "the true Yeats"—the true Yeats of a period of political inactivity when he watched, bitterly or sardonically, a game he had no chance of playing. But when he had a chance, when he saw political opportunities, as in 1891 or 1920, or thought he saw them as in 1933, he wrote differently, and with excitement. These "manic" phases of political activity were no less real or important than the "depressive" phases which followed them. And the options of the "manic" phases were not haphazard or middle-of-the-road. They were either anti-English or—in Irish politics—aristocratic and, from the time Fascism had appeared, distinctly and exultantly pro-Fascist.

It was Yeats's misfortune as a politician, and his great good fortune as a poet, that his political opportunities or temptations were few and far between. Irish politics in their normal run have not, since the introduction of universal suffrage, been receptive to poets, aristocrats or Protestants—there have been distinguished exceptions, but that has been the general rule for many years. It is only in rare conjunctures, times of great national stress and division, that an Irish party is likely to find room for such exotics for, in such times, men welcome an ally with a name and a voice. Such moments of excitement and emotion, which offered opportunities, were also the moments which most stirred the poet. Such times were the Parnell split of 1891 and the Sinn Fein split of 1920/22. The abortive Fascist movement of 1933 seemed to be, but was not, the opening of another profound fissure in Irish life. In the first two cases, the world of Irish politics proved, when "normalcy" had returned, no place for the poet. In the third case, the poet retired from a political movement which had lost momentum. It is fairly safe to say that, if it had succeeded, it would have dropped him or forced him out, not through any great aversion on his part from thugs in colored shirts but because an Irish Fascism, to have any chance of staying in power would necessarily have to become an intensely clerical Fascism. In fact, the successor movement to the Blueshirts—the Christian Front—was a noisily Catholic clerical-Fascist movement. This was a kind of Fascism—perhaps the only kind—which Yeats would not accept or tolerate, since his authoritarian view of life derived ultimately from his concept of the caste to which he belonged, and the distinguishing mark of that class was its Protestantism.

In the political writings of his last years the two elements in his politics—the "Irish" and the "Protestant" elements—entered into a new set of relations. The "Irish" element became more vocal than it had been since 1916 and the "Protestant" element was obliged to break finally with the traditional right wing in Irish politics. Anti-English feeling, long dormant in Yeats, became increasingly pronounced in the period 1937/9. A series of poems, "Roger Casement," "The Ghost of Roger Casement," "The O'Rahilly," "Come Gather round Me Parnellites," both expressed and did much to rekindle the old pride in Irish nationalism which the cynicism which followed the Civil War had dulled. The Casement poems especially had a powerful anti-English charge.

> "O what has made that sudden noise
> What on the threshold stands?
> It never crossed the sea because
> John Bull and the sea are friends;
> But this is not the old sea
> Nor this the old sea shore
> What gave that roar of mockery
> That roar in the sea's roar?
> The ghost of Roger Casement
> Is beating on the door."

No Irishman, reading those lines on the eve of the Second World War, had forgotten that Casement had been hanged as well as "morally assassinated" for trying, in 1916, to bring help to Ireland from Germany. And some Irishmen, at least, must have reflected that if the sea was no longer the whole sea, which had been friends with John Bull, the reason for this might be that the nation from which Casement had tried to bring help now possessed a powerful airforce. Potentially, "The Ghost of Roger Casement" was as explosive as *Cathleen Ni Houlihan*.

Just at this time Yeats was writing to Ethel Mannin that, while he liked neither side in Spain, and did not want to see his old leader O'Duffy—now fighting for Franco—return to Ireland with enhanced prestige to "the Catholic Front," he was attracted by the thought that a Fascist victory would weaken England. "I am an old Fenian and I think the Fenian in me would rejoice if a Fascist nation or government controlled Spain because that would weaken the British Empire, force England to be civil to India and loosen the hand of English finance in the Far East of which I hear occasionally. But this is mere instinct, a thing I would never act on." [19]

At this period also he became reconciled to some extent with the de Valera Government and his anti-British language and attitude are recorded by, among others, Doro-

[18] To Ethel Mannin, 8 April, 1936, *Letters*, p. 851
[19] To Ethel Mannin, 11 February, 1937, *Letters* p. 881

thy Wellesley, who wondered why he hated the English so much at a time when they were so weak and when they had ceased to oppress Ireland. She said that there was something in him which rather liked the "ranting, roaring oppressors" and was contemptuous of the "stuffed lion."

During Yeats's life, the English Government gave him a Civil List pension, and the Athenaeum Club gave him the signal honor of a special election. Since his death, the British Council has presented him to the world as one of England's glories. There is therefore some irony in the thought that there was something in him that would have taken considerable pleasure—though not without a respectful backward glance at Shakespeare—in seeing England occupied by the Nazis, the royal family exiled and the mother of Parliaments torn down. Meanwhile in Ireland one would have expected to see him at least a cautious participant, or ornament in a collaborationist regime.

It is probably fortunate for his future reputation, and especially his standing with the British Council, that he died in January 1939 before the political momentum of his last years could carry him any further than *On the Boiler*.

What all this has to do with his poetry is a question that one would need a good deal of time to answer. I would like to suggest in relation to it that Yeats had a greater feeling than most other poets, most other writers, for what was happening in Europe, an understanding of the telepathic waves of violence coming from Europe which touched something in his own heart and character. He understood what was happening with the calculating, managing, diplomatic side of his mind, he entered into those sorts of relation that we have just touched on here. The sort of "premonitory" intuition present in *The Second Coming* and in other poems necessarily affected Yeats in his ordinary life as well as in his poetry. Yeats the manager, the Senator, the politician, stands in a diplomatic relation to these intimations of power. In the poetry, however, the raw intimations of what is impending—the "telepathic waves of violence and fear"—make themselves known not in the form of calculated practical deductions, but in the attempt to reveal through metaphoric insight what is actually happening. The poet, like the lady, is

". . . so caught up
So mastered by the brute blood of the air"

that he does indeed take on the knowledge of what is happening with the power to make it known. The political man had his cautious understanding with Fascism, the diplomatic relation to a great force. The poet conveyed the nature of the force, the dimension of the tragedy.